English-
Russian-English

Word to Word®
Bilingual Dictionary

Compiled by:
C. Sesma, M.A.

Translated by:
Ekaterina Strieby

BilingualDictionaries.com
WordtoWord.com

Russian Word to Word® Bilingual Dictionary
2nd Edition © Copyright 2011

Published in the USA by:

Bilingual Dictionaries, Inc.
PO Box 1154
Murrieta, CA 92564
T: (951) 296-2445 • F: (951) 296-9911
E: support@bilingualdictionaries.com

BilingualDictionaries.com
WordtoWord.com

ISBN13: 978-0-933146-92-1

Print 110819

Printed In India

Publisher

Bilingual Dictionaries, Inc. was established in 1994. We are committed to providing schools, libraries and educators with a great selection of bilingual materials for students. Along with bilingual dictionaries we also publish ESL workbooks and children's bilingual picture dictionaries.

The first Word to Word® bilingual dictionary was published in 2008. The Word to Word® series now has over 40 editions with languages from around the world. For more information regarding any of our publications please visit us online.

Our series provides ELL students from different native language backgrounds a standardized selection of bilingual dictionaries. The Word to Word® series is designed to create an approved resource that adheres to the guidelines set by school districts and states.

Sesma's Russian Word to Word® Bilingual Dictionary was created specifically with students in mind to be used for reference and testing. This dictionary contains approximately 17,500 entries targeting common words used in the English language.

List of Irregular Verbs

present - past - past participle

arise - arose - arisen
awake - awoke - awoken, awaked
be - was - been
bear - bore - borne
beat - beat - beaten
become - became - become
begin - began - begun
behold - beheld - beheld
bend - bent - bent
beseech - besought - besought
bet - bet - betted
bid - bade (bid) - bidden (bid)
bind - bound - bound
bite - bit - bitten
bleed - bled - bled
blow - blew - blown
break - broke - broken
breed - bred - bred
bring - brought - brought
build - built - built
burn - burnt - burnt *
burst - burst - burst
buy - bought - bought
cast - cast - cast
catch - caught - caught
choose - chose - chosen
cling - clung - clung
come - came - come
cost - cost - cost
creep - crept - crept
cut - cut - cut
deal - dealt - dealt

dig - dug - dug
do - did - done
draw - drew - drawn
dream - dreamt - dreamed
drink - drank - drunk
drive - drove - driven
dwell - dwelt - dwelt
eat - ate - eaten
fall - fell - fallen
feed - fed - fed
feel - felt - felt
fight - fought - fought
find - found - found
flee - fled - fled
fling - flung - flung
fly - flew - flown
forebear - forbore - forborne
forbid - forbade - forbidden
forecast - forecast - forecast
forget - forgot - forgotten
forgive - forgave - forgiven
forego - forewent - foregone
foresee - foresaw - foreseen
foretell - foretold - foretold
forget - forgot - forgotten
forsake - forsook - forsaken
freeze - froze - frozen
get - got - gotten
give - gave - given
go - went - gone
grind - ground - ground
grow - grew - grown
hang - hung * - hung *
have - had - had

hear - heard - heard
hide - hid - hidden
hit - hit - hit
hold - held - held
hurt - hurt - hurt
hit - hit - hit
hold - held - held
keep - kept - kept
kneel - knelt * - knelt *
know - knew - known
lay - laid - laid
lead - led - led
lean - leant * - leant *
leap - lept * - lept *
learn - learnt * - learnt *
leave - left - left
lend - lent - lent
let - let - let
lie - lay - lain
light - lit * - lit *
lose - lost - lost
make - made - made
mean - meant - meant
meet - met - met
mistake - mistook - mistaken
must - had to - had to
pay - paid - paid
plead - pleaded - pled
prove - proved - proven
put - put - put
quit - quit * - quit *
read - read - read
rid - rid - rid
ride - rode - ridden

ring - rang - rung
rise - rose - risen
run - ran - run
saw - sawed - sawn
say - said - said
see - saw - seen
seek - sought - sought
sell - sold - sold
send - sent - sent
set - set - set
sew - sewed - sewn
shake - shook - shaken
shear - sheared - shorn
shed - shed - shed
shine - shone - shone
shoot - shot - shot
show - showed - shown
shrink - shrank - shrunk
shut - shut - shut
sing - sang - sung
sink - sank - sunk
sit - sat - sat
slay - slew - slain
sleep - sleep - slept
slide - slid - slid
sling - slung - slung
smell - smelt * - smelt *
sow - sowed - sown *
speak - spoke - spoken
speed - sped * - sped *
spell - spelt * - spelt *
spend - spent - spent
spill - spilt * - spilt *
spin - spun - spun

spit - spat - spat
split - split - split
spread - spread - spread
spring - sprang - sprung
stand - stood - stood
steal - stole - stolen
stick - stuck - stuck
sting - stung - stung
stink - stank - stunk
stride - strode - stridden
strike - struck - struck (stricken)
strive - strove - striven
swear - swore - sworn
sweep - swept - swept
swell - swelled - swollen *
swim - swam - swum
take - took - taken
teach - taught - taught
tear - tore - torn

tell - told - told
think - thought - thought
throw - threw - thrown
thrust - thrust - thrust
tread - trod - trodden
wake - woke - woken
wear - wore - worn
weave - wove * - woven *
wed - wed * - wed *
weep - wept - wept
win - won - won
wind - wound - wound
wring - wrung - wrung
write - wrote - written

**Those tenses with an * also have
regular forms.**

English-Russian

Abbreviations

a - article
n - noun
e - exclamation
pro - pronoun
adj - adjective
adv - adverb
v - verb
iv - irregular verb
pre - preposition
c - conjunction

abandon *v* оставлять
abandonment *n* оставление
abbey *n* аббатство
abbot *n* аббат
abbreviate *v* сокращать
abbreviation *n* сокращение
abdicate *v* отрекаться
abdication *n* отречение
abdomen *n* живот
abduct *v* похищать
abduction *n* похищение
aberration *n* заблуждение
abide by *v* соблюдать
ability *n* способность
ablaze *adj* пылающий
able *adj* способный
aboard *adv* на борту
abolish *v* отменять
abort *v* прекращать
abortion *n* выкидыш
abound *v* изобиловать
about *pre* около, о
about *adv* вокруг
above *pre* наверху
abreast *adv* на одной линии
abridge *v* сокращать
abroad *adv* за границей
abrogate *v* отменять
abruptly *adv* внезапно

absence *n* отсутствие
absent *adj* отсутствующий
absolute *adj* абсолютный
absolution *n* освобождение
absolve *v* освобождать
absorb *v* впитывать
absorbent *adj* поглощающий
abstinence *n* воздержание
abstract *adj* абстрактный
absurd *adj* абсурдный
abundance *n* изобилие
abundant *adj* изобилующий
abuse *n* оскорбление
abysmal *adj* бездонный
abyss *n* бездна
academy *n* академия
accelerate *v* ускорять
accelerator *n* ускоритель
accent *n* ударение
accept *v* принимать
acceptable *adj* приемлемый
acceptance *n* принятие
access *n* доступ
accessible *adj* доступный
accident *n* авария
accidental *adj* случайный
acclaim *v* приветствовать
accommodate *v* обеспечивать
accompany *v* сопровождать
accomplice *n* сообщник
accomplish *v* совершать
accomplishment *n* достижение

accord *n* согласие
according to *pre* согласно
accordion *n* аккордеон
account *n* счет; отчет
accountable *adj* ответственный
accountant *n* бухгалтер
accumulate *v* накапливать
accuracy *n* правильность
accurate *adj* правильный
accusation *n* обвинение
accuse *v* обвинять
accustom *v* приучать
ace *n* знаток
ache *n* боль
achieve *v* достигать
achievement *n* достижение
acid *n* кислота
acidity *n* кислотность
acknowledge *v* признавать
acorn *n* желудь
acoustic *adj* акустический
acquaint *v* знакомить
acquaintance *n* знакомство
acquire *v* приобретать
acquisition *n* приобретение
acquit *v* оправдывать
acquittal *n* оправдание
acre *n* акр
acrobat *n* акробат
across *pre* через
act *v* действовать
action *n* действие

activate *v* активизировать
activation *n* активация
active *adj* активный
activity *n* активность
actor *n* актер
actress *n* актрисса
actually *adv* действительно
acute *adj* острый
adamant *adj* непреклонный
adaptation *n* адаптация
adapter *n* адаптер
add *v* прибавлять
addiction *v* объяснять
addiction *n* пристрастие
addition *n* добавление
additional *adj* добавочный
address *n* адрес
address *v* обращаться
addressee *n* получатель
adequate *adj* адекватный
adhere *v* прилипать
adhesive *adj* липкий
adjacent *adj* смежный
adjoin *v* граничить
adjoining *adj* граничащий
adjourn *v* откладывать
adjustable *adj* регулируемый
adjustment *n* регулирование
administer *v* руководить
admiral *n* адмирал
admiration *n* восхищение
admire *v* восхищаться

admirer *n* поклонник
admissible *adj* приемлемый
admission *n* прием
admit *v* допускать
admittance *n* доступ
admonish *v* предостерегать
adolescence *n* юность
adolescent *n* юноша
adopt *v* усыновлять
adoption *n* усыновление
adoptive *adj* приемный
adorable *adj* обожаемый
adoration *n* обожание
adore *v* обожать
adorn *v* украшать
adulation *n* лесть
adult *n* взрослый
adulterate *v* разбавлять
adultery *n* прелюбодеяние
advance *n* продвижение
advantage *n* преимущество
Advent *n* Адвент
adventure *n* приключение
adverb *n* наречие
adversary *n* враг
adverse *adj* враждебный
adversity *n* бедствия
advertising *n* реклама
advice *n* совет
advisable *adj* разумный
advise *v* советовать
adviser *n* консультант

advocate *v* защищать
aeroplane *n* самолет
aesthetic *adj* эстетический
afar *adv* вдалеке
affable *adj* приветливый
affair *n* дело
affect *v* любить
affection *n* любовь
affectionate *adj* любящий
affiliate *v* присоединять
affiliation *n* присоединение
affinity *n* близость
affirm *v* подтверждать
affix *v* прикреплять
afflict *v* беспокоить
affliction *n* несчастье
affluence *n* достаток
affluent *adj* изобильный
afford *v* позволить себе
affordable *adj* возможный
affront *v* унижать
affront *n* унижение
afloat *adv* на плаву
afraid *adj* испуганный
afresh *adv* опять
after *pre* за, после
afternoon *n* дневное время
afterwards *adv* впоследствии
again *adv* вновь
against *pre* против
age *n* возраст
agency *n* агентство

agenda *n* план
agent *n* агент
agglomerate *v* собирать
aggravate *v* ухудшать
aggravation *n* ухудшение
aggregate *v* объединять
aggression *n* агрессия
aggressive *adj* агрессивный
aggressor *n* агрессор
agile *adj* проворный
agitator *n* агитатор
agnostic *n* агностик
agonize *v* страдать
agonizing *adj* мучительный
agony *n* мучение
agree *v* соглашаться
agreeable *adj* приятный
agreement *n* согласие
ahead *pre* впереди
aid *n* помощь
aid *v* помогать
aide *n* помощник
ailing *adj* больной
ailment *n* нездоровье
aim *v* стремиться
aimless *adj* бесцельный
air *n* воздух
air *v* проветривать
aircraft *n* самолет
airfield *n* аэродром
airmail *n* авиапочта
airplane *n* самолет

airport *n* аэропорт
airspace *n* щель
airtight *adj* герметичный
aisle *n* проход
ajar *adj* приоткрытый
akin *adj* родственный
alarm *n* тревога
alarm clock *n* будильник
alarming *adj* тревожный
alcoholic *adj* алкогольный
alcoholism *n* алкоголизм
alert *adj* бдительный
algebra *n* алгебра
alien *n* иностранец
alight *adv* зажженный
align *v* равняться
alignment *n* выравнивание
alike *adj* похожий
alive *adj* живой
all *adj* весь
allegation *n* заявление
allege *v* заявлять
allegedly *adv* будто бы
allegiance *n* преданность
allegory *n* аллегория
allergic *adj* аллергический
allergy *n* аллергия
alleviate *v* облегчать
alley *n* аллея
alliance *n* альянс
allied *adj* родственный
alligator *n* аллигатор

allocate *v* назначать

allot *v* распределять

allow *v* позволять

alloy *n* сплав

allusion *n* упоминание

ally *n* союзник

ally *v* объединяться

almanac *n* альманах

almighty *adj* всемогущий

almond *n* миндаль

almost *adv* почти

alms *n* милостыня

alone *adj* единственный

along *pre* вдоль, по

alongside *pre* около

aloof *adj* сторонящийся

aloud *adv* вслух

alphabet *n* алфавит

already *adv* уже

alright *adv* хорошо

also *adv* тоже

altar *n* алтарь

alter *v* менять

alteration *n* изменение

altercation *n* ссора

alternate *v* чередоваться

alternate *adj* чередующийся

alternative *n* альтернатива

although *c* хотя

altitude *n* высота

altogether *adj* совершенно

aluminum *n* алюминий

always *adv* всегда

amass *v* копить

amateur *adj* любительский

amaze *v* изумлять

amazement *n* изумление

amazing *adj* изумительный

ambassador *n* посол

ambition *n* честолюбие

ambitious *adj* честолюбивый

ambivalent *adj* двойственный

ambulance *n* скорая помощь

amenable *adj* ответственный

amend *v* исправлять

amendment *n* поправка

amenities *n* красоты

American *adj* американский

amiable *adj* дружелюбный

amicable *adj* дружеский

amid *pre* между

ammonia *n* аммиак

ammunition *n* боеприпасы

amnesia *n* амнезия

amnesty *n* амнистия

among *pre* среди

amoral *adj* аморальный

amorphous *adj* аморфный

amount *n* величина

amount to *v* равняться

amphibious *adj* земноводный

amphitheater *n* амфитеатр

ample *adj* изобильный

amplifier *n* усилитель

amplify *v* усиливать
amputate *v* ампутировать
amputation *n* ампутация
amuse *v* развлекать
amusement *n* развлечения
amusing *adj* забавный
analogy *n* аналогия
analysis *n* анализ
analyze *v* анализировать
anarchist *n* анархист
anarchy *n* анархия
anatomy *n* анатомия
ancestor *n* прародитель
ancestry *n* предки
anchor *n* якорь
anchovy *n* анчоус
ancient *adj* древний
and *c* и
anecdote *n* анекдот
anemia *n* анемия
anemic *adj* анемичный
anesthesia *n* анестезия
anew *adv* ещё раз
angel *n* ангел
angelic *adj* ангельский
anger *v* сердить
anger *n* гнев
angina *n* ангина
angle *n* угол
Anglican *adj* англиканский
angry *adj* сердитый
anguish *n* страдание

animal *n* животное
animate *v* оживить
animation *n* анимация
animosity *n* враждебность
ankle *n* лодыжка
annex *n* приложение
annexation *n* присоединение
annihilate *v* истреблять
annihilation *n* истребление
anniversary *n* годовщина
annotate *v* комментировать
annotation *n* комментарий
announce *v* объявлять
announcer *n* диктор
annoy *v* раздражать
annual *adj* ежегодный
annul *v* аннулировать
annulment *n* аннулирование
anonymity *n* анонимность
anonymous *adj* анонимный
another *adj* другой
answer *v* отвечать
answer *n* ответ
ant *n* муравей
antecedent *n* прошлое
antecedents *n* предки
antelope *n* антилопа
antenna *n* антенна
anthem *n* гимн
antibiotic *n* антибиотик
anticipate *v* предвкушать
anticipation *n* предвкушение

antidote *n* антидот
antipathy *n* антипатия
antiquity *n* старина
anvil *n* наковальня
anxiety *n* беспокойство
any *adj* какой-нибудь
anybody *pro* кто-нибудь
anyhow *pro* как-нибудь
anyone *pro* кто-нибудь
anything *pro* что-нибудь
apart *adv* отдельно
apartment *n* комната
apathy *n* апатия
ape *n* обезьяна
aperitif *n* аперитив
apex *n* вершина
aphrodisiac *adj* чувственный
apiece *adv* поштучно
apocalypse *n* откровение
apologize *v* извиняться
apology *n* извинение
apostle *n* апостол
apostolic *adj* апостольский
apostrophe *n* апостроф
appall *v* ужасать
appalling *adj* ужасающий
apparel *n* одеяние
apparent *adj* видимый
apparently *adv* очевидно
apparition *n* появление
appeal *n* призыв
appeal *v* апеллировать

appealing *adj* трогательный
appear *v* появляться
appearance *n* появление
appease *v* успокаивать
appeasement *n* умиротворение
appendicitis *n* аппендицит
appendix *n* добавление
appetite *n* аппетит
appetizer *n* закуска
applaud *v* аплодировать
applause *n* аплодисменты
apple *n* яблоко
appliance *n* устройство
applicable *adj* применимый
applicant *n* кандидат
application *n* просьба
apply *v* применять
apply for *v* просить о
appoint *v* назначать
appointment *n* назначение
appraisal *n* оценка
appraise *v* оценивать
appreciate *v* ценить
appreciation *n* оценка
apprehend *v* понимать
apprentice *n* ученик
approach *v* подходить
approach *n* подход
approachable *adj* достижимый
approbation *n* одобрение
appropriate *adj* подходящий
approval *n* одобрение

approve *v* одобрять
approximate *adj* близкий
apricot *n* абрикос
April *n* апрель
apron *n* фартук
aptitude *n* пригодность
aquarium *n* аквариум
aquatic *adj* водный
aqueduct *n* акведук
Arabic *adj* арабский
arable *adj* пахотный
arbiter *n* арбитр
arbitrary *adj* произвольный
arbitration *n* арбитраж
arc *n* дуга
arch *n* арка
archaeology *n* археология
archaic *adj* архаичный
archbishop *n* архиепископ
architect *n* архитектор
architecture *n* архитектура
archive *n* архив
arctic *adj* арктический
ardent *adj* страстный
ardor *n* страсть
arduous *adj* трудный
area *n* площадь
arena *n* арена
argue *v* спорить
argument *n* аргумент
arid *adj* засушливый
arise *iv* возникать

aristocracy *n* аристократия
aristocrat *n* аристократ
arithmetic *n* арифметика
ark *n* ковчег
arm *n* рука
arm *v* вооружать
armchair *n* кресло
armed *adj* вооружённый
armistice *n* перемирие
armor *n* броня
armpit *n* подмышка
army *n* армия
aromatic *adj* ароматный
around *pre* вокруг
arouse *v* будить
arrange *v* расставлять
arrangement *n* договорённость
array *n* боевой порядок
arrest *v* арестовывать
arrest *n* арест
arrival *n* прибытие
arrive *v* прибывать
arrogance *n* надменность
arrogant *adj* надменный
arrow *n* стрела
arsenal *n* арсенал
arsenic *n* мышьяк
arson *n* поджог
arsonist *n* поджигатель
art *n* искусство
artery *n* артерия
arthritis *n* артрит

artichoke *n* артишок
article *n* статья
articulation *n* артикуляция
artificial *adj* искусственный
artillery *n* артиллерия
artisan *n* мастеровой
artist *n* художник
artistic *adj* артистический
as *c* как
as *adv* как
ascend *v* подниматься
ascendancy *n* господство
ascertain *v* выяснять
ascetic *adj* аскетический
ash *n* зола; ясень
ashamed *adj* пристыженный
ashore *adv* к берегу
ashtray *n* пепельница
aside *adv* в сторону
aside from *adv* помимо
ask *v* спрашивать
asleep *adj* спящий
asparagus *n* спаржа
aspect *n* аспект
asphalt *n* асфальт
asphyxiate *v* задыхаться
asphyxiation *n* удушение
aspiration *n* стремление
aspire *v* стремиться к
aspirin *n* аспирин
assail *v* нападать
assailant *n* противник

assassin *n* убийца
assassinate *v* убивать
assassination *n* убийство
assault *n* нападение
assault *v* атаковать
assemble *v* собирать
assembly *n* ассамблея
assent *v* соглашаться
assert *v* утверждать
assertion *n* утверждение
assess *v* оценивать
assessment *n* оценка
asset *n* ценное качество
assets *n* актив
assign *v* назначать
assignment *n* назначение
assimilate *v* усваивать
assimilation *n* ассимиляция
assist *v* помогать
assistance *n* помощь
associate *v* объединять
association *n* объединение
assortment *n* ассортимент
assume *v* предполагать
assumption *n* предположение
assurance *n* гарантия
assure *v* уверять
asterisk *n* звёздочка
asteroid *n* астероид
asthma *n* астма
asthmatic *adj* астматический
astonish *v* изумлять

astonishing *adj* изумительный
astound *v* поражать
astounding *adj* поразительный
astray *v* заблудившись
astrologer *n* астролог
astrology *n* астрология
astronaut *n* космонавт
astronomer *n* астроном
astronomy *n* астрономия
astute *adj* хитроумный
asunder *adv* на части
asylum *n* пристанище
at *pre* у, в, за, на
atheism *n* атеизм
atheist *n* атеист
athlete *n* спортсмен
athletic *adj* атлетический
atmosphere *n* атмосфера
atmospheric *adj* атмосферный
atom *n* атом
atomic *adj* атомный
atone *v* искупать
atonement *n* искупление
atrocious *adj* свирепый
atrocity *n* жестокость
atrophy *v* атрофия
attach *v* прикреплять
attachment *n* привязанность
attack *n* атака
attack *v* атаковать
attacker *n* атакующий
attain *v* достигать

attainable *adj* достижимый
attainment *n* достижение
attempt *v* пытаться
attempt *n* попытка
attend *v* посещать
attendance *n* посещение
attention *n* внимание
attentive *adj* внимательный
attenuate *v* истощать
attenuating *adj* исхудавший
attest *v* удостоверять
attic *n* чердак
attitude *n* отношение
attorney *n* адвокат
attract *v* привлекать
attribute *v* объяснять
auction *n* аукцион
auctioneer *n* аукционист
audacious *adj* отважный
audacity *n* отвага
audible *adj* слышимый
audience *n* публика
auditorium *n* аудитория
augment *v* усиливать
August *n* август
aunt *n* тётя
auspicious *adj* благоприятный
austere *adj* строгий
austerity *n* строгость
authentic *adj* подлинный
authenticate *v* заверять
authenticity *n* подлинность

author *n* автор
authoritarian *adj* авторитарный
authority *n* власть
authorization *n* разрешение
authorize *v* уполномочивать
autograph *n* автограф
automatic *adj* автоматический
automobile *n* автомашина
autonomous *adj* независимый
autonomy *n* независимость
autopsy *n* аутопсия
autumn *n* осень
availability *n* наличие
available *adj* наличный
avalanche *n* лавина
avarice *n* алчность
avaricious *adj* алчный
avenge *v* отомстить
avenue *n* аллея
average *n* средний
aversion *n* отвращение
avert *v* отворачиваться
aviation *n* авиация
aviator *n* лётчик
avid *adj* жадный
avoid *v* избегать
avoidance *n* уклонение
await *v* дожидаться
awake *iv* будить
awake *adj* проснувшийся
awakening *n* пробуждение
award *v* присуждать

award *n* присуждение
aware *adj* осведомлённый
away *adv* далеко
awe *n* трепет
awesome *adj* потрясающий
awful *adj* ужасный
awkward *adj* неловкий
awning *n* навес
ax *n* топор
axiom *n* аксиома
axis *n* ось
axle *n* полуось

babble *v* лепетать
baby *n* младенец
babysitter *n* няня
bachelor *n* холостяк
back *n* спина
back *adv* назад
back *v* двигаться назад
back down *v* отступать
back up *v* поддерживать
backbone *n* позвоночник
backdoor *n* чёрный ход
background *n* фон
backing *n* поддержка

B

backlog *n* задолженность
backpack *n* рюкзак
backup *n* резерв
backward *adj* обратный
backwards *adv* назад
backyard *n* задний двор
bacon *n* бекон
bacteria *n* бактерия
bad *adj* плохой
badge *n* значок
badly *adv* плохо; крайне
baffle *v* сбивать с толку
bag *n* сумка
baggage *n* багаж
baguette *n* багет
bail *n* залог
bait *n* наживка
bake *v* выпекать
baker *n* пекарь
bakery *n* булочная
balance *n* весы
balcony *n* балкон
bald *adj* лысый
bale *n* кипа
ball *n* шар; бал
balloon *n* воздушный шар
ballot *n* голосование
ballroom *n* танцевальный зал
balm *n* бальзам
balmy *adj* благоухающий
bamboo *n* бамбук
ban *n* запрещение

ban *v* запрещать
banality *n* банальность
banana *n* банан
band *n* тесьма
bandage *n* бинт
bandage *v* бинтовать
bandit *n* разбойник
bang *v* ударять
banish *v* изгонять
banishment *n* изгнание
bank *n* банк
bankrupt *v* обанкротить
bankruptcy *n* банкротство
banner *n* знамя
banquet *n* банкет
baptism *n* крещение
baptize *v* крестить
bar *n* брусок; бар
bar *v* запираться
barbarian *n* варвар
barbaric *adj* варварский
barbarism *n* варварство
barbecue *n* барбекю
barber *n* парикмахер
bare *adj* голый
barefoot *adj* босой
barely *adv* едва
bargain *n* сделка
bargain *v* торговаться
bargaining *n* торг
barge *n* баржа
bark *v* лаять

B

bark *n* кора; кожа
barley *n* ячмень
barmaid *n* барменша
barman *n* бармен
barn *n* амбар
barometer *n* барометр
barracks *n* казармы
barrage *n* заграждение
barrel *n* бочка; баррель
barren *adj* бесплодный
barricade *n* баррикада
barrier *n* барьер
barring *pre* исключая
bartender *n* бармен
barter *v* обменивать
base *n* основа
base *v* базировать
baseball *n* бейсбол
basement *n* подвал
bashful *adj* застенчивый
basic *adj* основной
basics *n* основы
basin *n* миска; бассейн
basis *n* базис
bask *v* греться
basket *n* корзина
basketball *n* баскетбол
bat *n* летучая мышь; бита
batch *n* порция
bath *n* ванна
bathe *v* купаться
bathrobe *n* купальный халат

bathroom *n* ванная комната
bathtub *n* ванна
baton *n* жезл
battalion *n* батальон
batter *v* избивать
battery *n* батарея
battle *n* сражение
battle *v* сражаться
battleship *n* линкор
bay *n* бухта
bayonet *n* штык
bazaar *n* базар
be *iv* быть; жить
be born *v* родиться
beach *n* берег
beacon *n* бакен
beak *n* клюв
beam *n* балка
bean *n* фасоль
bear *n* медведь
bear *iv* нести; выносить
bearable *adj* сносный
beard *n* борода
bearded *adj* бородатый
bearer *n* носильщик
beast *n* зверь
beat *iv* бить; побеждать
beat *n* удар; дозор
beaten *adj* битый
beating *n* избиение
beautiful *adj* красивый
beautify *v* украшать

B

beauty *n* красота
beaver *n* бобр
because *c* потому что
because of *pre* из-за
beckon *v* манить
become *iv* становиться
bed *n* кровать; клумба
bedroom *n* спальня
bee *n* пчела
beef *n* говядина
beef up *v* подкреплять
beehive *n* улей
beer *n* пиво
beet *n* свёкла
beetle *n* жук
before *adv* впереди
before *pre* до
beforehand *adv* заранее
befriend *v* содействовать
beg *v* просить
beggar *n* попрошайка
begin *iv* начинать
beginner *n* новичок
beginning *n* начало
beguile *v* развлекать
behalf (on) *adv* в интересах
behave *v* держаться
behavior *n* поведение
behead *v* обезглавливать
behind *pre* позади
behold *iv* смотри
being *n* существование

belated *adj* запоздалый
belch *v* рыгать
belch *n* отрыжка
belfry *n* колокольня
Belgian *adj* бельгийский
Belgium *n* Бельгия
belief *n* убеждение
believe *v* верить
believer *n* верующий
belittle *v* принижать
bell *n* колокол; раструб
bell pepper *n* перец
belligerent *adj* воюющий
belly *n* живот
belly button *n* пуп
belong *v* принадлежать
belongings *n* имущество
beloved *adj* возлюбленный
below *adv* ниже
below *pre* под; хуже
belt *n* ремень
bench *n* скамья
bend *iv* сгибать
bend down *v* загибать
beneath *pre* под
benediction *n* благословение
benefactor *n* благодетель
beneficial *adj* благотворный
beneficiary *n* бенефициарий
benefit *n* выгода
benefit *v* приносить пользу
benevolent *adj* благожелательный

benign *adj* добрый
bequeath *v* завещать
bereaved *adj* скорбящий
bereavement *n* тяжёлая утрата
beret *n* берет
berserk *adv* яростный
berth *n* спальное место
beseech *iv* упрашивать
beset *iv* осаждать
beside *pre* рядом с
besides *pre* кроме того
besiege *iv* осаждать
best *adj* лучший
best man *n* шафер
bestial *adj* скотский
bestiality *n* скотство
bestow *v* даровать
bet *iv* держать пари
bet *n* пари
betray *v* предавать
betrayal *n* предательство
better *adj* лучший
between *pre* между
beverage *n* напиток
beware *v* остерегаться
bewilder *v* смущать
bewitch *v* заколдовывать
beyond *adv* далеко
bias *n* наклон
bible *n* Библия
biblical *adj* библейский
bibliography *n* библиография

bicycle *n* велосипед
bid *n* заявка
big *adj* большой
bigamy *n* бигамия
bigot *n* поборник
bigotry *n* фанатизм
bike *n* велосипед
bile *n* желчь
bilingual *adj* двуязычный
bill *n* счёт; законопроект
billiards *n* бильярд
billion *n* миллиард
billionaire *n* миллиардер
bin *n* бункер
bind *iv* связывать
binding *adj* связующий
binoculars *n* бинокль
biography *n* биография
biological *adj* биологический
biology *n* биология
bird *n* птица
birth *n* рождение
birthday *n* день рождения
biscuit *n* печенье
bishop *n* епископ
bison *n* бизон
bit *n* кусочек; удила
bite *iv* кусать; колоть
bite *n* укус
bitter *adj* горький
bitterly *adv* горько
bitterness *n* горечь

bizarre *adj* странный
black *adj* чёрный
blackberry *n* ежевика
blackboard *n* классная доска
blackmail *n* шантаж
blackmail *v* шантажировать
blackness *n* чернота
blackout *n* затемнение
blacksmith *n* кузнец
bladder *n* мочевой пузырь
blade *n* лезвие
blame *n* осуждение
blame *v* осуждать
bland *adj* вежливый
blank *adj* пустой
blanket *n* одеяло
blaspheme *v* богохульствовать
blasphemy *n* богохульство
blast *n* взрыв
blaze *v* пылать
bleach *v* отбеливать
bleach *n* отбеливание
bleak *adj* промозглый
bleed *iv* кровоточить
bleeding *n* кровотечение
blemish *n* недостаток
blemish *v* повреждать
blend *n* смесь
blend *v* смешивать
blender *n* блендер
bless *v* благословлять
blessing *n* благословение

blind *v* ослеплять
blind *adj* слепой
blindfold *n* повязка на глаза
blindfold *v* завязывать глаза
blindly *adv* вслепую
blindness *n* слепота
blink *v* моргать
bliss *n* блаженство
blissful *adj* блаженный
blister *n* волдырь
blizzard *n* буран
bloat *v* раздуваться
bloated *adj* раздутый
block *n* препятствие
block *v* блокировать
blockade *v* блокировать
blockade *n* блокада
blockage *n* блокировка
blond *adj* белокурый
blood *n* кровь
bloodthirsty *adj* кровожадный
bloody *adj* кровавый
bloom *v* цвести
blossom *v* расцветать
blot *n* пятно
blot *v* загрязнять
blouse *n* блузка
blow *n* дуновение
blow *iv* дуть
blow out *iv* задувать
blow up *iv* раздувать
blowout *n* разрыв

bludgeon v бить дубинкой	**bondage** n рабство
blue adj синий	**bone** n кость
blueprint n проект	**bone marrow** n костный мозг
bluff v обманывать	**bonfire** n костёр
blunder n промах	**bonus** n премия
blunt adj тупой	**book** n книга
bluntness n затупление	**bookcase** n книжный шкаф
blur v марать	**bookkeeper** n бухгалтер
blurred adj запачканный	**bookkeeping** n бухгалтерия
blush v краснеть	**booklet** n брошюра
blush n румянец	**bookseller** n продавец книг
boar n хряк	**bookstore** n книжный магазин
board n доска; совет	**boom** n гудение; стрела
boast v хвастать	**boom** v громыхать
boat n лодка	**boost** v поднимать
bodily adj телесный	**boost** n повышение
body n тело; ствол	**boot** n ботинок
bog n болото	**booth** n киоск
bog down v увязнуть	**booty** n трофеи
boil v кипятить	**booze** n выпивка
boil down to v сводиться	**border** n граница; край
boil over v перекипать	**border on** v граничить с
boiler n котёл	**borderline** adj пограничный
bold adj отважный	**bore** v носить
boldness n смелость	**bored** adj скучающий
bolt n засов; болт	**boredom** n скука
bolt v выпалить	**boring** adj скучный
bomb n бомба	**born** adj родившийся
bomb v бомбить	**borough** n городок
bombing n бомбёжка	**borrow** v занимать
bombshell n бомба	**bosom** n пазуха
bond n связь	**boss** n босс

B

bossy *adj* повелительный
botany *n* ботаника
botch *v* неумело латать
both *adj* оба
bother *v* надоедать
bothersome *adj* надоедливый
bottle *n* бутылка
bottle *v* хранить в бутылках
bottom *n* дно
bottomless *adj* бездонный
bough *n* сук
boulder *n* галька
boulevard *n* бульвар
bounce *v* отскакивать
bounce *n* отскок
bound *adj* связанный
boundary *n* граница
boundless *adj* безграничный
bounty *n* щедрость
bourgeois *adj* буржуазный
bow *n* дуга; поклон
bow *v* кланяться
bowels *n* сочувствие
bowl *n* чаша; застолье
box *n* коробка
boxer *n* боксёр
boxing *n* бокс; упаковка
boy *n* мальчик
boycott *v* бойкотировать
boyfriend *n* друг
boyhood *n* отрочество
bra *n* бюстгальтер

brace for *v* приготовится к
bracelet *n* браслет
bracket *n* скобка
brag *v* хвастаться
braid *n* шнурок
brain *n* мозг
brake *n* тормоз
brake *v* тормозить
branch *n* ветвь
branch office *n* филиал
branch out *v* разветвляться
brand *n* бренд
brand-new *adj* совершенно новый
brandy *n* бренди
brave *adj* смелый
bravely *adv* смело
bravery *n* смелость
brawl *n* скандал
breach *n* пролом
bread *n* хлеб
breadth *n* ширина
break *n* разлом
break *iv* ломать
break away *v* сбежать от
break down *v* сломить
break free *v* освобождаться
break in *v* вламываться
break off *v* прекращать
break open *v* взламывать
break out *v* вырываться
break up *v* заканчивать
breakable *adj* ломкий

breakdown *n* поломка
breakfast *n* завтрак
breakthrough *n* продвижение
breast *n* грудь
breath *n* дыхание
breathe *v* дышать
breathing *n* дыхание
breathtaking *adj* захватывающий
breed *iv* вынашивать
breed *n* порода
breeze *n* бриз
brethren *n* братия
brevity *n* краткость
brew *v* варить
bribe *v* подкупать
bribe *n* подкуп
bribery *n* взяточничество
brick *n* кирпич
bricklayer *n* каменщик
bridal *adj* свадебный
bride *n* невеста
bridegroom *n* жених
bridge *n* мост
bridle *n* узда
brief *adj* короткий
brief *v* резюмировать
briefcase *n* портфель
briefing *n* брифинг
briefly *adv* коротко
briefs *n* шорты
brigade *n* бригада
bright *adj* яркий

brighten *v* полировать
brightness *n* яркость
brilliant *adj* бриллиант
brim *n* край
bring *iv* приносить
bring back *v* напоминать
bring down *v* сломить, снижать
bring up *v* воспитывать
brink *n* край
brisk *adj* оживленный
Britain *n* Британия
British *adj* британский
brittle *adj* ломкий
broad *adj* широкий
broadcast *n* радиовещание
broadcaster *n* диктор
broaden *v* расширять
broadly *adv* широко
broadminded *adj* терпимый
brochure *n* брошюра
broil *v* жарить на огне
broiler *n* бройлер
broke *adj* безнадежный
broken *adj* разбитый
bronchitis *n* бронхит
bronze *n* бронза
broom *n* метла
broth *n* отвар
brothel *n* публичный дом
brother *n* брат
brotherhood *n* братство
brother-in-law *n* зять

B

brotherly *adj* братский

brow *n* бровь

brown *adj* коричневый

browse *v* объедать

browser *n* браузер

bruise *n* синяк

bruise *v* ушибать

brunch *n* поздний завтрак

brunette *adj* темноволосый

brush *n* щётка

brush *v* чистить щеткой

brush aside *v* игнорировать

brusque *adj* бестактный

brutal *adj* бесчеловечный

brutality *n* жестокость

brutalize *v* звереть

brute *adj* животный

bubble *n* пузырёк

buck *n* самец животного

bucket *n* ведро

buckle *n* пряжка

buckle up *v* прикреплять

bud *n* почка

buddy *n* дружище

budge *v* шевелиться

budget *n* бюджет

buffalo *n* буйвол

bug *n* клоп

build *iv* строить

builder *n* строитель

building *n* здание

buildup *n* накопление

built-in *adj* встроенный

bulb *n* луковица

bulge *n* выпуклость

bulk *n* груда

bulky *adj* громоздкий

bull *n* бык

bull fight *n* бой быков

bullet *n* пуля

bulletin *n* бюллетень

bully *adj* превосходный

bulwark *n* бастион

bum *n* бездельник

bump *n* выпуклость

bump into *v* встретиться

bumper *n* бампер

bumpy *adj* ухабистый

bun *n* булочка

bunch *n* связка

bundle *n* узел

bundle *v* связывать в узел

bunker *n* бункер

buoy *n* буй

burden *n* ноша

burden *v* нагружать

bureau *n* бюро

bureaucracy *n* бюрократия

bureaucrat *n* бюрократ

burger *n* гамбургер

burglar *n* взломщик

burglarize *v* грабить

burglary *n* грабеж

burial *n* похороны

burly *adj* плотный

burn *iv* гореть

burn *n* ожог

burp *v* рыгать

burp *n* отрыжка

burrow *n* нора

burst *iv* разрываться

burst into *v* вспыхнуть

bury *v* хоронить

bus *n* автобус

bush *n* куст

busily *adv* деловито

business *n* дело

businessman *n* бизнесмен

bust *n* бюст

bustling *adj* суетливый

busy *adj* деятельный

but *c* но

butcher *n* мясник

butchery *n* скотобойня

butler *n* дворецкий

butt *n* большая бочка

butter *n* масло

butterfly *n* бабочка

button *n* пуговица

buttonhole *n* петля

buy *iv* покупать

buy off *v* откупаться от

buyer *n* покупатель

buzz *n* гул

buzz *v* гудеть

buzzard *n* гриф

buzzer *n* сирена

by *pre* у, при, около

bye *e* пока

bypass *n* обход

bypass *v* обходить

bystander *n* свидетель

C

C

cab *n* такси

cabbage *n* капуста

cabin *n* убогое жилище

cabinet *n* правительство

cable *n* кабель

cafeteria *n* кафетерий

caffeine *n* кофеин

cage *n* клетка

cake *n* торт

calamity *n* бедствие

calculate *v* вычислять

calculation *n* вычисление

calculator *n* калькулятор

calendar *n* календарь

calf *n* телёнок

caliber *n* калибр

calibrate *v* калибровать

call *n* крик; звонок

call *v* кричать; звонить

C

call off *v* отменять
call on *v* призывать
call out *v* выявлять
calling *n* призвание
callous *adj* загрубелый
calm *adj* спокойный
calm *n* спокойствие
calm down *v* успокаиваться
calorie *n* калория
calumny *n* клевета
camel *n* верблюд
camera *n* фотоаппарат
camouflage *n* камуфляж
camp *n* лагерь
campaign *n* кампания
campfire *n* костёр
can *iv* консервировать
can *v* мочь
can *n* жестянка
canal *n* канал
canary *n* канарейка
cancel *v* отменять
cancellation *n* отмена
cancer *n* рак
cancerous *adj* раковый
candid *adj* откровенный
candidacy *n* кандидатура
candidate *n* кандидат
candle *n* свеча
candlestick *n* подсвечник
candor *n* блеск
candy *n* конфета

cane *n* тростник; палка
canister *n* контейнер
cannibal *n* каннибал
canoe *n* каноэ
canonize *v* канонизировать
cantaloupe *n* канталупа
canteen *n* столовая
canvas *n* холст
canvas *v* накрыть холстом
canyon *n* каньон
cap *n* кепка
capability *n* способность
capable *adj* способный
capacity *n* вместимость
cape *n* накидка; мыс
capital *n* капитал
capitalism *n* капитализм
capitulate *v* капитулировать
capsize *v* опрокидывать
capsule *n* капсула
captain *n* капитан
captivate *v* очаровывать
captive *n* пленник
captivity *n* плен
capture *v* захватывать
capture *n* захват
car *n* автомобиль
carat *n* карат
caravan *n* караван
carburetor *n* карбюратор
carcass *n* туша
card *n* карта; карда

cardboard *n* картон
cardiac *adj* сердечный
cardiology *n* кардиология
care *n* забота
care *v* заботиться
care about *v* заботиться
care for *v* ухаживать за
career *n* карьера
carefree *adj* беззаботный
careful *adj* заботливый
careless *adj* небрежный
carelessness *n* небрежность
caress *n* ласка
caress *v* ласкать
caretaker *n* смотритель
cargo *n* груз
caricature *n* карикатура
caring *adj* заботливый
carnage *n* резня
carnal *adj* плотский
carnation *n* гвоздика
carol *n* хорал
carpenter *n* плотник
carpet *n* ковер
carriage *n* экипаж
carrot *n* морковь
carry *v* нести
carry on *v* продолжать
carry out *v* осуществлять
cart *n* тележка
cart *v* перевозить
cartoon *n* карикатура

cartridge *n* патрон
carve *v* резать
cascade *n* каскад
case *n* случай; ящик
cash *n* деньги
cashier *n* кассир
casino *n* казино
casket *n* шкатулка
casserole *n* запеканка
cassock *n* сутана
cast *iv* бросать
castaway *n* изгнанник
caste *n* каста
castle *n* замок
casual *adj* повседневный
casualty *n* авария
cat *n* кот
cataclysm *n* катаклизм
catacomb *n* катакомба
catalog *n* каталог
catalog *v* заносить в каталог
cataract *n* ливень; катаракта
catastrophe *n* катастрофа
catch *iv* ловить
catch up *v* наверстать
catching *adj* заразный
catchword *n* ключевое слово
catechism *n* катехизис
category *n* категория
cater to *v* стараться угодить
caterpillar *n* гусеница
catholic *adj* католический

Catholicism *n* католичество
cauliflower *n* цветная капуста
cause *n* причина
cause *v* заставлять
caution *n* осторожность
cautious *adj* осторожный
cavalry *n* кавалерия
cave *n* пещера
cave in *v* сдаваться
cavern *n* пещера
cavity *n* впадина
cease *v* прекращать
ceiling *n* потолок
celebrate *v* праздновать
celebration *n* празднование
celebrity *n* популярность
celery *n* сельдерей
celestial *adj* небесный
celibacy *n* целибат
cellar *n* подвал
cellphone *n* сотовый телефон
cement *n* цемент
cemetery *n* кладбище
censorship *n* цензура
censure *v* порицать
census *n* перепись
cent *n* цент
centenary *n* столетие
center *n* центр
centimeter *n* сантиметр
central *adj* центральный
centralize *v* централизовать

century *n* век
ceramic *n* керамический
cereal *n* крупа
cerebral *adj* церебральный
ceremony *n* церемония
certain *adj* определённый
certainty *n* достоверность
certificate *n* свидетельство
certify *v* удостоверять
chagrin *n* досада
chain *n* цепь
chain *v* заковывать в цепи
chainsaw *n* бензопила
chair *n* стул
chairman *n* председатель
chalet *n* шале
chalice *n* чаша
chalk *n* мел
chalkboard *n* доска
challenge *v* бросать вызов
challenge *n* вызов
challenging *adj* побуждающий
chamber *n* комната
champion *n* чемпион
champion *v* бороться
chance *n* шанс
chancellor *n* канцлер
chandelier *n* люстра
change *v* изменять
change *n* изменение
channel *n* канал
chant *n* песнь

chaos *n* хаос
chaotic *adj* беспорядочный
chapel *n* часовня
chaplain *n* капеллан
chapter *n* глава
char *v* чистить
character *n* характер
characteristic *adj* характерный
charade *n* шарада
charbroil *adj* жареный на углях
charcoal *n* древесный уголь
charge *v* заряжать
charisma *n* харизма
charm *v* очаровывать
charm *n* очарование
chart *n* карта; график
charter *n* льгота; устав
chase *n* погоня
chase *v* догонять
chase away *v* развеять
chasm *n* расщелина
chaste *adj* целомудренный
chastise *v* наказывать
chastisement *n* наказание
chastity *n* целомудрие
chat *v* болтать
chauffeur *n* шофёр
cheap *adj* дешёвый
cheat *v* жульничать
cheater *n* жулик
check *n* проверка
check *v* проверять

check in *v* регистрироваться
check up *n* выяснять
checkbook *n* чековая книжка
cheek *n* щека
cheekbone *n* скула
cheeky *adj* нахальный
cheer *v* ободрять
cheer up *v* не унывать
cheerful *adj* весёлый
cheers *n* будьте здоровы
cheese *n* сыр
chef *n* шеф-повар
chemical *adj* химический
chemist *n* химик
chemistry *n* химия
cherish *v* ухаживать
cherry *n* вишня
chess *n* шахматы
chest *n* ящик; грудь
chestnut *n* каштан
chew *v* жевать
chick *n* цыплёнок
chicken *n* курица
chicken out *v* струсить
chicken pox *n* ветряная оспа
chide *v* ругать
chief *n* руководитель
chiefly *adv* в основном
child *n* ребенок
childhood *n* детство
childish *adj* детский
childless *adj* бездетный

children *n* дети
chill *n* простуда
chill *v* охлаждать
chill out *v* успокаиваться
chilly *adj* прохладный
chimney *n* труба
chimpanzee *n* шимпанзе
chin *n* подбородок
chip *n* тонкий ломтик
chisel *n* долото
chocolate *n* шоколад
choice *n* выбор
choir *n* церковный хор
choke *v* душить
cholera *n* холера
cholesterol *n* холестерин
choose *iv* выбирать
choosy *adj* разборчивый
chop *v* рубить
chop *n* сильный удар
chopper *n* резак
chore *n* рутинная работа
chorus *n* хор
christen *v* крестить
christening *n* крещение
christian *adj* христианский
Christianity *n* христианство
Christmas *n* Рождество
chronic *adj* хронический
chronicle *n* хроника
chronology *n* хронология
chubby *adj* круглолицый

chuckle *v* посмеиваться
chunk *n* ломоть
church *n* церковь
chute *n* стремнина
cider *n* сидр
cigar *n* сигара
cigarette *n* сигарета
cinder *n* угольный мусор
cinema *n* кинематография
cinnamon *n* корица
circle *n* круг
circle *v* окружать
circuit *n* окружность
circular *adj* круглый
circulate *v* циркулировать
circulation *n* круговорот
circumcision *n* обрезание
circumstance *n* обстоятельство
circus *n* цирк
cistern *n* цистерна
citizen *n* гражданин
citizenship *n* гражданство
city *n* город
city hall *n* городские власти
civic *adj* городской
civil *adj* гражданский
civilization *n* цивилизация
civilize *v* цивилизовать
claim *v* требовать
claim *n* требование
clam *n* моллюск
clamor *v* шуметь

clamp *n* зажим
clan *n* клан
clandestine *adj* тайный
clap *v* хлопать
clarification *n* ректификация
clarify *v* очищать
clarinet *n* кларнет
clarity *n* ясность
clash *v* сталкиваться
clash *n* грохотанье
class *n* класс; урок
classic *adj* классический
classmate *n* одноклассник
classy *adj* отличный
clause *n* пункт
claw *n* коготь
claw *v* царапать
clay *n* глина
clean *adj* чистый
clean *v* чистить
cleanliness *n* чистота
cleanse *v* очищать
cleanser *n* очиститель
clear *adj* ясный
clear *v* осветлять
clearance *n* расчистка
clear-cut *adj* отчётливый
clearly *adv* ясно
clearness *n* ясность
cleft *n* расселина
clemency *n* мягкость
clench *v* зажимать

clergy *n* духовенство
clergyman *n* священник
clerical *adj* духовный
clerk *n* клерк
clever *adj* умный
click *v* щёлкать
client *n* клиент
clientele *n* клиентура
climate *n* климат
climatic *adj* климатический
climax *n* кульминация
climb *v* взбираться
climbing *n* скалолазание
clinch *v* забивать гвоздь
cling *iv* цепляться
clinic *n* поликлиника
clip *v* зажимать; стричь
clipping *n* обрезок; стрижка
cloak *n* плащ
clock *n* часы
clog *v* задерживать
cloister *n* монастырь
clone *v* клонировать
cloning *n* клонирование
close *v* закрывать
close *adj* близкий
close to *pre* близко от
closed *adj* закрытый
closely *adv* близко
closet *n* шкаф
closure *n* закрытие
clot *n* комок

C

cloth *n* ткань
clothe *v* одевать
clothes *n* одежда
clothing *n* одежда
cloud *n* облако
cloudless *adj* безоблачный
cloudy *adj* облачный
clown *n* клоун
club *n* клуб; дубинка
clue *n* клубок
clumsy *adj* неповоротливый
cluster *n* гроздь
cluster *v* толпиться
clutch *n* захват
coach *v* тренировать
coach *n* репетитор
coaching *n* тренировка
coagulate *v* сгущать
coagulation *n* свёртывание
coal *n* уголь
coalition *n* объединение
coarse *adj* грубый
coast *n* побережье
coastal *adj* прибрежный
coastline *n* береговая линия
coat *n* куртка; покров
coax *v* убеждать
cob *n* ком
cobblestone *n* булыжник
cobweb *n* паутина
cocaine *n* кокаин
cock *n* петух

cockpit *n* арена борьбы
cockroach *n* таракан
cocktail *n* коктейль
cocky *adj* самоуверенный
cocoa *n* какао
coconut *n* кокос
cod *n* треска
code *n* свод законов; код
codify *v* зашифровывать
coefficient *n* коэффициент
coerce *v* сдерживать
coercion *n* принуждение
coexist *v* сосуществовать
coffee *n* кофе
coffin *n* гроб
coherent *adj* связанный
cohesion *n* сплочённость
coin *n* монета
coincide *v* совпадать
coincidence *n* совпадение
coincidental *adj* совпадающий
cold *adj* холодный
coldness *n* холод
colic *n* колика
collaborate *v* сотрудничать
collaboration *n* сотрудничество
collaborator *n* соавтор
collapse *v* обваливаться
collapse *n* обрушение
collar *n* воротничок
collarbone *n* ключица
collateral *adj* сопутствующий

colleague n коллега
collect v собирать
collection n коллекция
collector n коллекционер
college n колледж
collide v сталкиваться
collision n столкновение
colon n двоеточие
colonel n полковник
colonial adj колониальный
colonization n колонизация
colonize v колонизировать
colony n колония
color n цвет
color v красить; влиять
colorful adj красочный
colossal adj колоссальный
colt n жеребёнок
column n колонна
coma n кома
comb n гребень
comb v расчесывать
combat n бой
combat v сражаться
combatant n боец
combination n сочетание
combine v сочетать
combustible n горючий
combustion n возгорание
come iv приходить
come about v появляться
come across v быть понятным

come apart v разваливаться
come back v возвращаться
come down v уменьшаться
come forward v выделяться
come from v происходить
come in v входить
come out v выходить
come over v заходить
come up v подниматься
comeback n возвращение
comedian n комик
comedy n комедия
comet n комета
comfort n утешение
comfortable adj удобный
comforter n утешитель
comical adj забавный
coming n прибытие
coming adj ожидаемый
comma n запятая
command v приказывать
commander n командир
commandment n заповедь
commemorate v помнить
commence v начинать
commend v одобрять
commendation n
  благодарность
comment n комментарий
commerce n коммерция
commercial adj коммерческий
commission n доверенность

C

commit v совершать
commitment n обязательство
committed adj преданный
committee n комитет
common adj общий
commotion n беспорядки
communicate v сообщать
communication n коммуникация
communion n причастие
community n общность
commute v заменять
compact adj компактный
compact v компоновать
companion n товарищ
companionship n товарищество
company n компания
comparable adj сопоставимый
comparative adj сравнительный
compare v сравнивать
comparison n сравнение
compartment n отделение
compass n граница
compassion n сострадание
compassionate adj сострадательный
compatibility n совместимость
compatible adj совместимый
compatriot n соотечественник
compel v заставлять
compelling adj непреодолимый
compendium n сборник
compensate v компенсировать
compensation n компенсация

compete v состязаться
competence n компетентность
competent adj компетентный
competition n соревнование
competitive adj соперничающий
competitor n конкурент
compile v составлять
complain v жаловаться
complaint n жалоба
complement n дополнение
complete adj завершённый
complete v завершать
completely adv полностью
completion n завершение
complex adj комплексный
complexion n цвет лица
complexity n сложность
compliance n согласие
compliant adj покладистый
complicate v затруднять
complication n сложность
complicity n соучастие
compliment n комплимент
complimentary adj бесплатный
comply v исполнять
component n компонент
compose v сочинять
composed adj невозмутимый
composer n композитор
composition n сочинение
compost n удобрение
compound n смесь

compound v смешивать
comprehend v понимать
comprehensive adj всесторонний
compress v сжимать
compression n сжатие
comprise v включать
compromise n компромисс
compulsion n принуждение
compulsory adj обязательный
compute v подсчитывать
computer n компьютер
comrade n приятель
con man n мошенник
conceal v скрывать
concede v уступать
conceited adj самоуверенный
conceive v постигать
concentrate v концентрат
concentration n концентрация
concentric adj концентрический
concept n понятие
conception n понимание
concern v касаться
concern n отношение
concerning pre относительно
concert n концерт
concession n уступка
conciliate v умиротворять
conciliatory adj примирительный
concise adj краткий
conclude v завершать
conclusion n вывод; закрытие

conclusive adj завершающий
concoct v состряпать
concoction n приготовление
concrete n бетон
concrete adj бетонный
concur v совпадать
concurrent adj совпадающий
concussion n сотрясение
condemn v осуждать
condemnation n осуждение
condensation n конденсация
condense v уплотнять
condescend v снизойти
condiment n приправа
condition n состояние
conditional adj условный
conditioner n кондиционер
condo n кондоминиум
condone v потворствовать
conducive adj благоприятный
conduct n руководство
conduct v сопутствовать
conductor n кондуктор
cone n конус
confer v жаловать
conference n конференция
confess v исповедовать
confession n исповедание
confessional n исповедальня
confessor n исповедник
confidant n наперсник
confide v доверять

confidence *n* уверенность
confident *adj* уверенный
confine *v* ограничивать
confinement *n* ограничение
confirm *v* подтверждать
confirmation *n* подтверждение
confiscate *v* конфисковать
confiscation *n* конфискация
conflict *n* конфликт
conflict *v* конфликтовать
conflicting *adj* противоречащий
conform *v* согласовывать
conformist *adj* конформистский
conformity *n* соответствие
confound *v* смущать
confront *v* противостоять
confrontation *n* столкновение
confuse *v* смешивать
confusing *adj* сбивающий с толку
confusion *n* смущение
congenial *adj* сходный
congested *adj* переполненный
congestion *n* скопление
congratulate *v* поздравлять
congregate *v* собирать
congregation *n* собрание
congress *n* конгресс
conjecture *n* догадка
conjugal *adj* супружеский
conjugate *v* соединяться
conjure up *v* воображать
connect *v* соединить

connection *n* соединение
connive *v* потворствовать
connote *v* ассоциироваться
conquer *v* завоёвывать
conqueror *n* завоеватель
conquest *n* завоевание
conscience *n* совесть
conscious *adj* сознательный
consciousness *n* сознание
conscript *n* призывник
consecrate *v* посвящать
consecutive *adj* последовательный
consensus *n* согласие
consent *v* соглашаться
consent *n* согласие
consequence *n* последствие
consequent *adj* логичный
conservation *n* сохранение
conservative *adj* консервативный
conserve *v* охранять
conserve *n* варенье
consider *v* рассматривать
considerable *adj* значительный
considerate *adj* внимательный
consideration *n* размышление
consignment *n* партия товара
consist *v* заключаться
consistency *n* постоянство
consistent *adj* плотный; последовательный
consolation *n* утешение

console _v_ утешать
consolidate _v_ объединять
consonant _n_ согласный звук
conspicuous _adj_ видный
conspiracy _n_ заговор
conspirator _n_ заговорщик
constancy _n_ устойчивость
constant _adj_ постоянный
constellation _n_ созвездие
consternation _n_ оцепенение
constipation _n_ запор
constitute _v_ составлять
constitution _n_ конституция
constrain _v_ принуждать
constraint _n_ принуждение
construct _v_ сооружать
construction _n_ строительство
constructive _adj_ строительный
consul _n_ консул
consulate _n_ консульство
consult _v_ советоваться
consultation _n_ консультация
consume _v_ истреблять
consumer _n_ потребитель
consumption _n_ потребление
contact _v_ касаться
contact _n_ контакт
contagious _adj_ заразный
contain _v_ содержать
container _n_ контейнер
contaminate _v_ загрязнять
contamination _n_ загрязнение

contemplate _v_ созерцать
contemporary _adj_ современный
contempt _n_ презрение
contend _v_ бороться
contender _n_ соперник
content _adj_ довольный
contentious _adj_ спорный
contents _n_ оглавление
contest _n_ дискуссия
contestant _n_ соперник
context _n_ контекст
continent _n_ континент
continental _adj_ континентальный
contingency _n_ случайность
contingent _adj_ случайный
continuation _n_ продолжение
continue _v_ продолжать
continuity _n_ неразрывность
continuous _adj_ непрерывный
contour _n_ контур
contraband _n_ контрабанда
contract _v_ заключать договор
contract _n_ договор
contradict _v_ противоречить
contradiction _n_ противоречие
contrast _n_ контраст
contribute _v_ содействовать
contribution _n_ вклад
contributor _n_ жертвователь
contrition _n_ раскаяние
control _n_ контроль
control _v_ контролировать

C

controversial *adj* сомнительный
controversy *n* дебаты
convene *v* созывать
convenience *n* удобство
convenient *adj* удобный
convent *n* монастырь
convention *n* собрание
conventional *adj* обыкновенный
converge *v* сходиться
conversation *n* разговор
converse *v* разговаривать
conversely *adv* обратно
conversion *n* превращение
convert *v* преобразовывать
convert *n* новообращённый
convey *v* перевозить
convict *v* осудить; убедить
conviction *n* осуждение
convince *v* убеждать
convincing *adj* убедительный
convoluted *adj* спиралевидный
convoy *n* сопровождение
convulse *v* вызывать судороги
convulsion *n* судороги
cook *v* готовить
cook *n* повар
cookie *n* печенье
cooking *n* кулинария
cool *adj* прохладный
cool *v* охлаждать
cool down *v* охлаждать
cooling *adj* охлаждение

coolness *n* прохлада
cooperate *v* сотрудничать
cooperation *n* кооперация
cooperative *adj* совместный
coordinate *v* согласовывать
coordinator *n* координатор
cop *n* мент
cope *v* справиться
copper *n* медь
copy *v* копировать
copy *n* экземпляр
copyright *n* авторское право
cord *n* шнур; связка
cordial *adj* сердечный
cordless *adj* беспроводный
cordon *n* кордон
cordon off *v* оцеплять
core *n* центр
cork *n* пробка
corn *n* зерно
corner *n* угол; перекресток
cornerstone *n* угловой камень
cornet *n* корнет
corollary *n* вывод
coronary *adj* коронарный
coronation *n* коронация
corporal *adj* телесный
corporal *n* капрал
corporation *n* корпорация
corpse *n* труп
corpulent *adj* дородный
corpuscle *n* частица

correct v исправлять
correct adj правильный
correction n исправление
correlate v сопоставлять
correspond v соответствовать
correspondent n корреспондент
corridor n коридор
corroborate v подтверждать
corrode v разъедать
corrupt v развращать
corrupt adj испорченный
corruption n гниение; коррупция
cosmetic n косметика
cosmic adj космический
cosmonaut n космонавт
cost iv стоить
cost n цена
costly adj дорогостоящий
cottage n загородный дом
cotton n хлопок
couch n диван
cough n кашель
cough v кашлять
council n совет
counsel v советовать
counsel n обсуждение
counselor n советник
count v считать
count n вычисление
countenance n выражение лица
counter n прилавок
counter v противоречить

counteract v препятствовать
counterfeit v подделывать
counterfeit adj фальшивый
counterpart n дубликат
countess n графиня
countless adj бесчисленный
country n страна; деревня
countryman n земляк
countryside n сельская местность
county n графство
coup n неожиданный успех
couple n пара; муж и жена
coupon n купон
courage n мужество
courageous adj мужественный
courier n курьер
course n курс
court n суд; двор
court v ухаживать
courteous adj любезный
courtesy n любезность
courthouse n здание суда
courtship n ухаживание
cousin n двоюродный брат
cove n бухточка
covenant n завет
cover n крышка
cover v накрывать
cover up v прятать
coverage n сфера действия
covert adj затаённый
coverup n укрывательство**

covet *v* домогаться
cow *n* корова
coward *n* трус
cowardice *n* трусость
cowardly *adv* трусливо
cowboy *n* ковбой
cozy *adj* уютный
crab *n* краб
crack *n* треск
crack *v* трещать; стрелять
cradle *n* колыбель
craft *n* ремесло; ловкость
craftsman *n* мастер
cram *v* впихивать
cramp *n* спазм
crane *n* журавль
crank *n* кривошип
cranky *adj* неисправный
crap *n* чепуха
crappy *adj* дрянной
crash *n* грохот; авария
crash *v* грохотать
crass *adj* бестолковый
crater *n* кратер
crave *v* жаждать
craving *n* страстное желание
crawl *v* ползать
crayon *n* пастель
craziness *n* сумасшествие
crazy *adj* сумасшедший
creak *v* скрипеть
creak *n* скрип

cream *n* сливки
creamy *adj* сливочный
crease *n* складка; граница
crease *v* сминать
create *v* создавать
creation *n* сотворение
creative *adj* творческий
creativity *n* творчество
creator *n* создатель
creature *n* создание
credibility *n* вероятность
credible *adj* вероятный
credit *n* доверие
creditor *n* кредитор
creed *n* вероисповедание
creek *n* бухта
creep *v* ползать
creepy *adj* вызывающий страх
cremate *v* кремировать
crematorium *n* крематорий
crest *n* гребешок
crevice *n* трещина
crew *n* экипаж
crib *n* стойло
cricket *n* сверчок; крикет
crime *n* преступление
criminal *adj* криминальный
cripple *adj* ущербный
cripple *v* травмировать
crisis *n* кризис
crisp *adj* хрустящий
crispy *adj* хрустящий

criterion *n* критерий
critical *adj* критический
criticism *n* критика
criticize *v* критиковать
crockery *n* посуда
crocodile *n* крокодил
crony *n* закадычный друг
crook *n* жулик
crooked *adj* изогнутый
crop *n* урожай
cross *n* крест
cross *v* пересекать
cross out *v* вычёркивать
crossing *n* перечёркивание
crossword *n* кроссворд
crow *n* ворона
crow *v* кукарекать
crowbar *n* лом
crowd *n* толпа
crowd *v* толпиться
crowded *adj* переполненный
crown *n* корона
crown *v* короновать
crucial *adj* решающий
crucifix *n* распятие
crucify *v* распинать
crude *adj* сырая нефть
cruel *adj* жестокий
cruelty *n* жестокость
cruise *v* совершать круиз
crumb *n* крошка
crumble *v* раскрошить

crunchy *adj* хрусткий
crusade *n* крестовый поход
crusader *n* крестоносец
crush *v* дробить
crust *n* корка; сухарь
crutch *n* стойка
cry *n* крик
cry *v* кричать
cry out *v* требовать
crying *n* вопль
crystal *n* кристалл
cub *n* детеныш зверя
cube *n* куб
cubic *adj* кубический
cubicle *n* кабина
cucumber *n* огурец
cuddle *v* обнимать
cuff *n* манжета
cuisine *n* кухня
culminate *v* завершиться
culpability *n* виновность
culprit *n* обвиняемый
cult *n* поклонение
cultivate *v* возделывать
cultivation *n* культивация
cultural *adj* культурный
culture *n* культура
cumbersome *adj* громоздкий
cunning *adj* лукавый
cup *n* чашка
cupboard *n* буфет
curable *adj* излечимый

C

C

curator _n_ смотритель
curb _v_ обуздывать
curb _n_ обуздание
curdle _v_ коагулировать
cure _v_ исцелять
cure _n_ лечение
curfew _n_ комендантский час
curiosity _n_ любопытство
curious _adj_ любопытный
curl _v_ виться
curl _n_ локон
curly _adj_ кудрявый
currency _n_ валюта
current _adj_ текущий
curse _v_ проклинать
curtail _v_ сокращать
curtain _n_ занавеска
curve _n_ дуга
curve _v_ изгибать
cuss _v_ сквернословить
custodian _n_ хранитель
custody _n_ опекунство
custom _n_ обычай
customary _adj_ обычный
customer _n_ покупатель
customs _n_ таможня
cut _n_ разрез
cut _iv_ резать
cut back _v_ повторить
cut down _v_ сокращать
cut off _v_ отрезать
cut out _v_ вырезать

cutter _n_ резчик
cyanide _n_ цианид
cycle _n_ цикл
cyclist _n_ велосипедист
cyclone _n_ циклон
cylinder _n_ цилиндр
cynic _adj_ циничный
cynicism _n_ цинизм
cypress _n_ кипарис
cyst _n_ пузырь
czar _n_ царь

D

dad _n_ папочка
dagger _n_ кинжал
daily _adv_ ежедневно
dam _n_ дамба
damage _n_ вред
damage _v_ повреждать
damaging _adj_ вредный
damn _v_ проклинать
damnation _n_ проклятие
damp _adj_ влажный
dampen _v_ ослаблять
dance _n_ танец
dance _v_ танцевать
dancing _n_ танцы

dandruff *n* перхоть
danger *n* опасность
dangerous *adj* опасный
dangle *v* болтать
dare *v* отваживаться
dare *n* вызов
daring *adj* отчаянный
dark *adj* тёмный
darken *v* темнеть
darkness *n* темнота
darling *adj* любимый
darn *v* штопать
dart *n* дротик
dash *v* бросаться
dashing *adj* лихой
data *n* данные
database *n* база данных
date *n* дата; время
date *v* датировать
daughter *n* дочь
daughter-in-law *n* невестка, сноха
daunt *v* обуздывать
daunting *adj* запугивающий
dawn *n* рассвет
day *n* день
daydream *v* мечтать наяву
daze *v* ошеломить
dazed *adj* ошеломлённый
dazzle *v* слепить
dazzling *adj* ослепляющий
de luxe *adj* роскошный

deacon *n* дьякон
dead *adj* мёртвый
dead end *n* тупик
deaden *v* притуплять
deadlock *adj* тупиковый
deadly *adj* смертельный
deaf *adj* глухой
deafen *v* оглушать
deafening *adj* оглушительный
deafness *n* глухота
deal *iv* торговать
deal *n* сделка
dealer *n* дилер
dean *n* декан
dear *adj* дорогой
dearly *adv* нежно
death *n* смерть
death toll *n* жертвы, потери
death trap *n* гиблое место
deathbed *n* смертное ложе
debase *v* ухудшать
debatable *adj* дискуссионный
debate *v* обсуждать
debate *n* дискуссия
debit *n* дебет
debrief *v* спрашивать
debris *n* обломки
debt *n* долг
debtor *n* должник
debunk *v* разоблачать
debut *n* дебют
decade *n* десяток

D

decadence *n* упадок
decapitate *v* обезглавливать
decay *v* гнить
decay *n* гниение
deceased *adj* покойный
deceit *n* обман
deceitful *adj* лживый
deceive *v* обманывать
December *n* декабрь
decent *adj* пристойный
deception *n* обман
deceptive *adj* обманчивый
decide *v* решать
deciding *adj* решающий
decimal *adj* десятичный
decimate *v* истреблять
decipher *v* декодировать
decision *n* решение
decisive *adj* решающий
deck *n* палуба
declaration *n* декларация
declare *v* заявлять
declension *n* наклон
decline *v* спускаться вниз
decline *n* падение
decompose *v* гнить
décor *n* декорация
decorate *v* украшать
decorative *adj* декоративный
decorum *n* декорум
decrease *v* уменьшаться
decrease *n* уменьшение

decree *n* декрет
decree *v* издавать декрет
decrepit *adj* дряхлый
dedicate *v* посвящать
dedication *n* посвящение
deduce *v* выводить
deduct *v* вычитать
deduction *n* вычет
deed *n* действие
deem *v* мыслить
deep *adj* глубокий
deepen *v* углублять
deer *n* олень
deface *v* ухудшать
defame *v* клеветать
defeat *v* завоёвывать
defeat *n* поражение
defect *n* недостаток
defect *v* изменить
defection *n* провал
defective *adj* дефективный
defend *v* защищать
defendant *n* ответчик
defender *n* защитник
defense *n* защита
defenseless *adj* незащищённый
defer *v* задерживать
defiance *n* вызов
defiant *adj* вызывающий
deficiency *n* нехватка
deficient *adj* недостающий
deficit *n* дефицит

defile v портить
define v определять
definite adj определённый
definition n определение
definitive adj окончательный
deflate v выпускать
defraud v лишать обманом
defray v оплачивать
defrost v размораживать
deft adj ловкий
defy v вызывать
degenerate v вырождаться
degenerate adj вырождающийся
degeneration n вырождение
degradation n разжалование
degrade v ухудшаться
degrading adj унизительный
degree n степень
dehydrate v обезвоживать
deign v снизойти
deity n божество
dejected adj подавленный
delay v откладывать
delay n задержка
delegate v уполномачивать
delegate n делегат
delegation n делегация
delete v вычеркивать
deliberate v обдумывать
deliberate adj неслучайный
delicacy n утончённость
delicate adj утончённый

delicious adj восхитительный
delight n удовольствие
delight v радовать
delightful adj очаровательный
delinquency n виновность
delinquent n правонарушитель
deliver v доставлять
delivery n поставка; роды
delude v обманывать
deluge n потоп
delusion n обман
demand v требовать
demand n требование
demanding adj требующий
demean v унижаться
demeaning adj унизительный
demeanor n поведение
demented adj сумасшедший
demise n кончина
democracy n демократия
democratic adj демократический
demolish v уничтожать
demolition n разрушение
demon n демон
demonstrate v демонстрировать
demonstrative adj показательный
den n берлога
denial n отказ
denigrate v наговаривать
Denmark n Дания
denominator n знаменатель
denote v отмечать

D

denounce *v* обвинять
dense *adj* плотный; глупый
density *n* плотность
dent *v* вмятина
dent *n* оставлять вмятину
dental *adj* зубной
dentist *n* зубной врач
dentures *n* зубной протез
deny *v* отрицать
deodorant *n* дезодорант
depart *v* уходить
department *n* отдел
departure *n* отъезд
depend *v* зависеть
dependable *adj* надежный
dependence *n* зависимость
dependent *adj* зависящий
depict *v* рисовать
deplete *v* истощать
deplorable *adj* плачевный
deplore *v* оплакивать
deploy *v* развертываться
deployment *n* развертывание
deport *v* высылать
deportation *n* высылка
depose *v* низложить
deposit *n* депозит
depot *n* склад
deprave *adj* развращать
depravity *n* развращенность
depreciate *v* обесцениваться
depreciation *n* обесценивание

depress *v* подчинять
depressing *adj* тягостный
depression *n* депрессия
deprivation *n* лишение
deprive *v* отбирать
deprived *adj* малоимущий
depth *n* глубина
derail *v* сходить с рельсов
derailment *n* крушение
deranged *adj* перепутанный
derelict *adj* покинутый
deride *v* высмеивать
derivative *adj* вторичный
derive *v* получать
derogatory *adj* умаляющий
descend *v* спускаться
descendant *n* потомок
descent *n* спуск; падение
describe *v* описывать
description *n* описание
descriptive *adj* описательный
desecrate *v* оскорблять
desegregate *v* объединять
desert *n* пустыня
desert *v* покидать
deserted *adj* заброшенный
deserter *n* дезертир
deserve *v* заслуживать
deserving *adj* заслуживающий
design *n* замысел; эскиз
designate *v* объявлять
desirable *adj* желанный

desire *n* желание
desire *v* желать
desist *v* переставать
desk *n* рабочий стол
desolate *adj* одинокий
desolation *n* опустошение
despair *n* отчаяние
desperate *adj* безысходный
despicable *adj* презренный
despise *v* презирать
despite *c* вопреки
despondent *adj* унылый
despot *n* деспот
despotic *adj* деспотический
dessert *n* десерт
destination *n* предназначение
destiny *n* судьба
destitute *adj* брошенный
destroy *v* разрушать
destroyer *n* разрушитель
destruction *n* разрушение
destructive *adj* разрушительный
detach *v* отделять
detachable *adj* отделяемый
detail *n* подробность
detail *v* детализировать
detain *v* задерживать
detect *v* обнаруживать
detective *n* детектив
detector *n* обнаружитель
detention *n* задержание
deter *v* удерживать

detergent *n* моющее средство
deteriorate *v* повреждать
deterioration *n* повреждение
determine *v* определять
deterrence *n* устрашение
detest *v* ненавидеть
detestable *adj* отвратительный
detonate *v* взрывать
detonation *n* детонация
detonator *n* детонатор
detour *n* обход
detriment *n* ущерб
detrimental *adj* губительный
devaluation *n* обесценение
devalue *v* обесценивать
devastate *v* опустошать
devastating *adj* опустошительный
devastation *n* опустошение
develop *v* развивать
development *n* развитие
deviation *n* отклонение
device *n* устройство
devil *n* дьявол
devious *adj* отдалённый
devise *v* разрабатывать
devoid *adj* лишённый
devote *v* посвящать
devotion *n* преданность
devour *v* жадно есть
devout *adj* благочестивый
dew *n* роса
diabetes *n* диабет

D

diabetic *adj* диабетический
diabolical *adj* дьявольский
diagnose *v* ставить диагноз
diagnosis *n* диагноз
diagonal *adj* диагональный
diagram *n* диаграмма
dial *n* циферблат
dial *v* звонить
dial tone *n* длинный гудок
dialect *n* диалект
dialogue *n* диалог
diameter *n* диаметр
diamond *n* алмаз
diaper *n* орнамент
diarrhea *n* понос
diary *n* ежедневник
dice *n* игральные кости
dictate *v* диктовать
dictator *n* диктатор
dictatorial *adj* диктаторский
dictatorship *n* диктатура
dictionary *n* словарь
die *v* умирать
die out *v* вымирать
diet *n* питание, диета
differ *v* отличаться
difference *n* отличие
different *adj* непохожий
difficult *adj* трудный
difficulty *n* трудность
diffuse *v* рассеивать
dig *iv* копать

digest *v* усваивать
digestion *n* пищеварение
digit *n* цифра
dignify *v* облагораживать
dignity *n* достоинство
digress *v* отступать
dike *n* ров
dilemma *n* дилемма
diligence *n* прилежание
diligent *adj* прилежный
dilute *v* разбавлять
dim *adj* тусклый
dim *v* тускнеть
dime *n* монета в 10 центов
dimension *n* измерение
diminish *v* уменьшать
dine *v* обедать
diner *n* вагон-ресторан
dining room *n* столовая
dinner *n* обед
dinosaur *n* динозавр
diocese *n* епархия
diphthong *n* дифтонг
diploma *n* диплом
diplomacy *n* дипломатия
diplomat *n* дипломат
dire *adj* жуткий
direct *adj* прямой
direct *v* направлять
direction *n* направление
director *n* директор
directory *n* справочник

dirt *n* грязь
dirty *adj* грязный
disability *n* бессилие
disadvantage *n* неудобство
disagree *v* расходиться
disagreeable *adj* неприятный
disagreement *n* разногласие
disappear *v* исчезать
disappearance *n* исчезновение
disappoint *v* разочаровывать
disappointment *n* разочарование
disapproval *n* неодобрение
disapprove *v* не одобрять
disarm *v* обезоруживать
disarmament *n* разоружение
disaster *n* бедствие
disastrous *adj* бедственный
disband *v* рассеиваться
disbelief *n* неверие
disburse *v* платить
discard *v* избавляться
discern *v* разглядеть
discharge *v* разгружать
discharge *n* разгрузка
disciple *n* ученик
discipline *n* дисциплина
disclaim *v* отказываться
disclose *v* обнаруживать
discomfort *n* неудобство
disconnect *v* разъединять
discontent *adj* недовольный
discontinue *v* останавливать

discord *n* разногласие
discount *n* скидка
discount *v* сокращать
discourage *v* обескураживать
discouragement *n* разочарование
discourtesy *n* невоспитанность
discover *v* обнаруживать
discovery *n* открытие
discredit *v* не доверять
discreet *adj* осмотрительный
discrepancy *n* различие
discretion *n* отделение
discriminate *v* различать
discrimination *n* дискриминация
discuss *v* обсуждать
discussion *n* дискуссия
disdain *n* пренебрежение
disease *n* болезнь
disembark *v* высаживать
disenchanted *adj* разочарованный
disentangle *v* развязывать
disfigure *v* обезображивать
disgrace *n* бесчестье
disgrace *v* бесчестить
disgraceful *adj* позорный
disgruntled *adj* раздражённый
disguise *v* маскировать
disguise *n* маскировка
disgust *n* отвращение
dish *n* блюдо
dishonest *adj* нечестный
dishonesty *n* нечестность

dishonor *n* бесславие
dishonorable *adj* постыдный
disintegrate *v* расщеплять
disintegration *n* расщепление
disinterested *adj* безучастный
disk *n* диск
dislike *n* неприязнь
dislocate *v* передвигать
dislodge *v* перемещать
disloyal *adj* нелояльный
disloyalty *n* нелояльность
dismal *adj* мрачный
dismantle *v* раздевать
dismay *n* испуг
dismay *v* пугать
dismiss *v* отпускать
dismount *v* спешиваться
disobedient *adj* непокорный
disobey *v* не подчиняться
disorder *n* беспорядок
disown *v* отрицать
disparity *n* несоответствие
dispatch *v* посылать
dispel *v* разгонять
dispensation *n* распределение
dispense *v* раздавать
dispersal *n* рассеивание
disperse *v* рассеивать
displace *v* перемещать
display *n* показ
display *v* показывать
displease *v* сердить

displeasing *adj* неприятный
disposable *adj* доступный
disposal *n* размещение
dispose *v* размещать
disprove *v* опровергать
dispute *n* диспут
dispute *v* дискутировать
disregard *v* пренебрегать
disrepair *n* неисправность
disrespect *n* неуважение
disrupt *v* разрывать
disruption *n* разрушение
dissatisfied *adj* недовольный
disseminate *v* разбрасывать
dissent *v* возражать
dissident *adj* инакомыслящий
dissimilar *adj* непохожий
dissipate *v* рассеивать
dissolute *adj* беспутный
dissolution *n* таяние снега
dissolve *v* растворять
dissuade *v* отговаривать
distance *n* расстояние
distant *adj* дальний
distaste *n* отвращение
distasteful *adj* противный
distill *v* дистиллировать
distinct *adj* отдельный
distinction *n* различение
distinctive *adj* отличительный
distinguish *v* различить
distort *v* искажать

distortion *n* искажение
distract *v* отвлекать
distraught *adj* смятенный
distress *n* недомогание
distressing *adj* огорчительный
distribute *v* распределять
distribution *n* раздача
district *n* район
distrust *n* недоверие
distrust *v* не доверять
distrustful *adj* недоверчивый
disturb *v* тревожить
disturbance *n* беспокойство
disturbing *adj* беспокоящий
disunity *n* разногласие
disuse *n* неупотребление
ditch *n* канава
dive *v* нырять
diver *n* ныряльщик
diverse *adj* иной
diversify *v* разнообразить
diversion *n* отклонение
diversity *n* разнообразие
divert *v* отводить
divide *v* делить
dividend *n* дивиденд
divine *adj* божественный
diving *n* ныряние
divinity *n* божественность
divisible *adj* кратный
division *n* деление
divorce *n* развод

divorce *v* разводиться
divorcee *n* разведенный муж
divulge *v* разглашать
dizziness *n* головокружение
do *iv* делать
docile *adj* восприимчивый
dock *n* док
dock *v* входить в док
doctor *n* врач
doctrine *n* доктрина
document *n* документ
documentation *n* документация
dodge *v* уклоняться
dog *n* собака
dogmatic *adj* догматический
dole out *v* скупиться
doll *n* кукла
dollar *n* доллар
dolphin *n* дельфин
domestic *adj* домашний
dominate *v* доминировать
domination *n* доминирование
dominion *n* господство
donate *v* жертвовать
donation *n* пожертвование
donkey *n* осёл
donor *n* даритель
doom *n* рок
doomed *adj* обречённый
door *n* дверь
doorbell *n* дверной звонок
doorstep *n* порог

doorway *n* дверной проём
dope *n* наркотик, дурман
dope *v* давать наркотики
dormitory *n* общежитие
dosage *n* дозировка
dossier *n* досье
dot *n* точка
double *adj* двойной
double *v* удваивать
double-check *v* перепроверить
double-cross *v* перехитрить
doubt *n* сомнение
doubt *v* сомневаться
dough *n* тесто
dove *n* голубь
down *adv* вниз
downcast *adj* нисходящий
downfall *n* крушение
downhill *adv* вниз
downpour *n* ливень
downsize *v* сокращать
downstairs *adv* внизу
down-to-earth *adj* практичный
downtrodden *adj* растоптанный
dowry *n* приданое
doze *n* сонливость
doze *v* дремать
dozen *n* дюжина
draft *n* черновик; призыв
draft *v* составлять проект
draftsman *n* составитель
drag *v* тянуть

dragon *n* дракон
drain *v* осушать
drainage *n* дренаж
dramatic *adj* драматический
dramatize *v* инсценировать
drape *n* драпировка
draw *n* рисунок; тяга
draw *iv* рисовать; тащить
drawback *n* препятствие
drawer *n* выдвижной ящик
drawing *n* рисование
dread *v* страшиться
dreaded *adj* страшный
dreadful *adj* ужасный
dream *iv* сниться, мечтать
dream *n* сон, мечта
dress *n* платье
dress *v* одеваться
dresser *n* комод с зеркалом
dressing *n* одевание
dried *adj* засохший
drift *v* гнать
drift apart *v* отдаляться
drifter *n* дрифтер
drill *v* сверлить; муштровать
drill *n* сверло
drink *iv* пить
drink *n* питье
drinkable *adj* годный для питья
drinker *n* пьяница
drip *v* капать
drip *n* капанье

drive *n* езда; дорога
drive *iv* ехать
drive at *v* намереваться
drive away *v* усердно работать
driver *n* водитель
driveway *n* проезд
drizzle *v* моросить
drizzle *n* мелкий дождь
drop *n* капля; падение
drop *v* капать; ронять
drop in *v* присоединяться
drop off *v* высаживать
drop out *v* выбывать
drought *n* засуха
drown *v* тонуть
drowsy *adj* засыпающий
drug *n* лекарство, наркотик
drugstore *n* аптека
drum *n* барабан; цилиндр
drunk *adj* напившийся
drunkenness *n* пьянство
dry *v* сушить
dry *adj* сухой
dryer *n* сушилка
dual *adj* двойной
dubious *adj* сомнительный
duchess *n* герцогиня
duck *n* утка
duck *v* пригнуться; нырять
duct *n* канал
due *adj* должный
duel *n* дуэль

dues *n* пошлины
duke *n* герцог
dull *adj* тупой
dumb *adj* немой
dummy *n* макет; мишень
dummy *adj* подставной
dump *v* выгружать
dump *n* свалка
dung *n* фекалии
dungeon *n* склеп
dupe *v* одурачивать
duplicate *v* снимать копию
duplication *n* удваивание
durable *adj* надёжный
during *pre* в течение
dusk *n* сумерки
dust *n* пыль
dusty *adj* пыльный
Dutch *adj* голландский
duty *n* долг
dwarf *n* карлик
dwell *iv* обитать
dwelling *n* жилище
dwindle *v* сокращаться
dye *v* окрашивать
dye *n* окраска
dying *adj* умирающий
dynamic *adj* динамичный
dynamite *n* динамит
dynasty *n* династия

each *adj* каждый
each other *adj* друг друга
eagerness *n* рвение
eagle *n* орёл
ear *n* ухо; колос
earache *n* боль в ухе
early *adv* рано
earmark *v* клеймо в ухе
earn *v* зарабатывать
earnestly *adv* убедительно
earnings *n* заработок
earphones *n* наушники
earring *n* серьга
earth *n* земля
earthquake *n* землетрясение
earwax *n* ушная сера
ease *v* облегчать
ease *n* облегчение
easily *adv* легко
east *n* восток
Easter *n* Пасха
eastern *adj* восточный
easterner *n* житель Востока
easy *adj* легкий
eat *iv* кушать
eat away *v* съедать
eavesdrop *v* подслушивать
ebb *v* отступать
eccentric *adj* эксцентричный

echo *n* эхо
eclipse *n* затмение
ecology *n* экология
economical *adj* экономичный
economize *v* экономить
economy *n* экономика
ecstasy *n* экстаз
ecstatic *adj* экстатический
edge *n* грань
edgy *adj* заострённый
edible *adj* съедобный
edifice *n* большой дом
edit *v* редактировать
edition *n* издание
educate *v* воспитывать
eerie *adj* зловещий
effect *n* результат
effective *adj* эффективный
effectiveness *n* эффективность
efficiency *n* эффективность
efficient *adj* эффективный
effort *n* усилие
effusive *adj* экспансивный
egg *n* яйцо
egg white *n* белок
egoism *n* эгоизм
egoist *n* эгоист
eight *adj* восемь
eighteen *adj* восемнадцать
eighth *adj* восьмой
eighty *adj* восемьдесят
either *adj* любой

either *adv* также
eject *v* извергать
elapse *v* проходить
elastic *adj* эластичный
elated *adj* ликующий
elbow *n* локоть
elder *n* старец
elderly *adj* пожилой
elect *v* избирать
election *n* выборы
electric *adj* электрический
electrician *n* электрик
electricity *n* электричество
electronic *adj* электронный
elegance *n* изящество
elegant *adj* изысканный
element *n* элемент
elementary *adj* примитивный
elephant *n* слон
elevate *v* поднимать
elevation *n* повышение
eleven *adj* одиннадцать
eleventh *adj* одиннадцатый
eligible *adj* имеющий право
eliminate *v* исключать
elm *n* вяз
eloquence *n* красноречие
else *adv* кроме
elude *v* избежать
elusive *adj* неуловимый
emaciated *adj* истощённый
emanate *v* исходить

emancipate *v* освобождать
embalm *v* бальзамировать
embark *v* грузиться
embarrass *v* затруднять
embassy *n* посольство
embellish *v* украшать
embers *n* неугасшие чувства
embezzle *v* проматывать
embitter *v* озлоблять
emblem *n* символ
embody *v* воплощать
emboss *v* выбивать
embrace *v* обниматься
embrace *n* объятия
embroider *v* вышивать
embroidery *n* вышивание
embroil *v* запутывать
embryo *n* зародыш
emerald *n* изумруд
emerge *v* появляться
emigrant *n* эмигрант
emigrate *v* эмигрировать
emission *n* выделение
emit *v* испускать
emotion *n* эмоция
emperor *n* император
emphasis *n* ударение
emphasize *v* подчёркивать
empire *n* империя
employ *v* нанимать
employee *n* служащий
employer *n* работодатель

employment *n* служба
empress *n* императрица
emptiness *n* пустота
empty *adj* пустой
empty *v* освобождать
enchant *v* очаровывать
encircle *v* окружать
enclave *n* анклав
enclose *v* огораживать
enclosure *n* огораживание
encompass *v* окружать
encounter *v* встретиться
encourage *v* поддерживать
encroach *v* вторгаться
encyclopedia *n* энциклопедия
end *n* конец
end *v* завершать
end up *v* заканчиваться
endanger *v* рисковать
endeavor *v* пытаться
endeavor *n* попытка
ending *n* завершение
endless *adj* бесконечный
endorse *v* рекомендовать
endure *v* вытерпеть
enemy *n* враг
energetic *adj* энергичный
energy *n* энергия
enforce *v* принуждать
engage *v* занимать
engaged *adj* занятый
engagement *n* встреча

engine *n* двигатель
engineer *n* инженер
England *n* Англия
English *adj* английский
engrave *v* гравировать
engraving *n* гравировка
engrossed *adj* поглощённый
engulf *v* поглощать
enhance *v* увеличивать
enjoy *v* наслаждаться
enjoyable *adj* приятный
enjoyment *n* наслаждение
enlarge *v* увеличиваться
enlargement *n* увеличение
enlighten *v* просвещать
enormous *adj* громадный
enough *adv* достаточно
enrage *v* разъярять
enrich *v* обогащать
enroll *v* вступать в члены
enrollment *n* регистрация
ensure *v* обеспечивать
entail *v* вызывать
entangle *v* запутывать
enter *v* входить
enterprise *n* предприятие
entertain *v* развлекать
entertainment *n* развлечение
enthrall *v* покорять
enthralling *adj* захватывающий
enthusiasm *n* энтузиазм
entice *v* соблазнять

enticement *n* заманивание
enticing *adj* заманчивый
entire *adj* целый
entirely *adv* всецело
entrance *n* вход
entreat *v* умолять
entree *n* вход
entrust *v* вверять
entry *n* вход
enumerate *v* перечислять
envelop *v* обёртывать
envelope *n* конверт
envious *adj* завистливый
envisage *v* обдумывать
envoy *n* посланник
envy *n* зависть
envy *v* завидовать
epidemic *n* эпидемия
epilepsy *n* эпилепсия
episode *n* эпизод
epistle *n* послание
epitaph *n* эпитафия
epitomize *v* конспектировать
epoch *n* эпоха
equal *adj* равный
equality *n* равенство
equate *v* приравнять
equation *n* уравнение
equator *n* экватор
equilibrium *n* равновесие
equip *v* снаряжать
equipment *n* оснащение

equivalent *adj* равнозначный
era *n* эра
eradicate *v* истреблять
erase *v* стирать
erect *v* сооружать
erect *adj* вертикальный
err *v* заблуждаться
errand *n* поручение
erroneous *adj* ошибочный
error *n* ошибка
erupt *v* извергать
eruption *n* извержение
escalate *v* обострять
escalator *n* эскалатор
escapade *n* эскапада
escape *v* бежать
escort *n* конвой
esophagus *n* пищевод
especially *adv* особенно
espionage *n* разведка
essay *n* эссе
essence *n* сущность
essential *adj* неотъемлемый
establish *v* учреждать
estate *n* имение
esteem *v* почитать
estimate *v* оценивать
estimation *n* почтение; оценка
estranged *adj* отдельный
estuary *n* дельта реки
eternity *n* вечность
ethical *adj* этический

E

ethics *n* этика
etiquette *n* этикет
euphoria *n* эйфория
Europe *n* Европа
European *adj* европейский
evacuate *v* опорожнять
evade *v* ускользать
evaluate *v* оценивать
evaporate *v* испарять
evasion *n* увиливание
evasive *adj* уклончивый
eve *n* канун
even *adj* равный
even if *c* даже если
even more *c* более того
evening *n* вечер
event *n* событие
eventuality *n* случайность
eventually *adv* в конце концов
ever *adv* вечно
everlasting *adj* вечный
every *adj* каждый
everybody *pro* все
everyday *adj* ежедневный
everyone *pro* все
everything *pro* всё
evict *v* выселять
evidence *n* очевидность
evil *n* зло
evil *adj* злой
evoke *v* пробуждать
evolution *n* эволюция

evolve *v* развивать
exact *adj* точный
exaggerate *v* преувеличивать
exalt *v* возвеличивать
examination *n* обследование
examine *v* осматривать
example *n* пример
exasperate *v* возмущать
excavate *v* копать
exceed *v* превышать
exceedingly *adv* весьма
excel *v* превосходить
excellence *n* совершенство
excellent *adj* отличный
except *pre* за исключением
exception *n* исключение
exceptional *adj* исключительный
excerpt *n* выдержка
excess *n* чрезмерность
excessive *adj* чрезмерный
exchange *v* обменивать
excite *v* побуждать
excitement *n* возбуждение
exciting *adj* возбуждающий
exclaim *v* восклицать
exclude *v* исключать
excruciating *adj* мучительный
excursion *n* экскурсия
excuse *v* извиняться
excuse *n* извинение
execute *v* осуществлять
exemplary *adj* образцовый

exemplify _v_ иллюстрировать
exempt _adj_ свободный
exemption _n_ освобождение
exercise _n_ упражнение
exercise _v_ упражняться
exert _v_ прилагать усилия
exertion _n_ напряжение
exhaust _v_ исчерпывать
exhausting _adj_ утомительный
exhaustion _n_ изнеможение
exhibit _v_ показывать
exhibition _n_ выставка
exhilarating _adj_ веселящий
exhort _v_ уговаривать
exile _v_ высылать
exile _n_ высылка
exist _v_ существовать
existence _n_ существование
exit _n_ выход
exodus _n_ исход
exonerate _v_ освобождать
exorbitant _adj_ безмерный
exorcist _n_ экзорцист
exotic _adj_ экзотический
expand _v_ растягиваться
expansion _n_ увеличение
expect _v_ ожидать
expectancy _n_ ожидание
expectation _n_ ожидание
expedition _n_ экспедиция
expel _v_ исключать
expenditure _n_ расходование

expense _n_ затрата
expensive _adj_ дорогостоящий
experience _n_ опыт
experiment _n_ эксперимент
expert _adj_ опытный
expiate _v_ искупать
expiation _n_ искупление
expiration _n_ экспирация
expire _v_ закончиться
explain _v_ объяснять
explicit _adj_ ясный
explode _v_ взрываться
exploit _v_ пользоваться
exploit _n_ подвиг
exploitation _n_ эксплуатация
explore _v_ исследовать
explorer _n_ исследователь
explosion _n_ взрыв
explosive _adj_ взрывчатый
export _v_ экспортировать
expose _v_ показывать
exposed _adj_ незащищённый
express _n_ экспресс; курьер
expression _n_ выражение
expressly _adv_ определенно
expropriate _v_ конфисковать
expulsion _n_ увольнение
exquisite _adj_ изысканный
extend _v_ простираться
extension _n_ удлинение
extent _n_ степень
extenuating _adj_ смягчающий

exterior *adj* наружный
exterminate *v* искоренять
external *adj* внешний
extinct *adj* потухший
extinguish *v* гасить
extort *v* вымогать
extortion *n* вымогательство
extra *adv* дополнительно
extract *v* извлекать
extradite *v* выдавать
extradition *n* экстрадиция
extraneous *adj* посторонний
extravagance *n* сумасбродство
extravagant *adj* расточительный
extreme *adj* крайний
extremist *adj* экстремист
extremities *n* конец
extricate *v* объяснять
exude *v* выделяться
exult *v* ликовать
eye *n* глаз
eyebrow *n* бровь
eye-catching *adj* броский
eyeglasses *n* очки
eyelash *n* ресничка
eyelid *n* веко
eyesight *n* зрение
eyewitness *n* свидетель

fable *n* басня
fabric *n* ткань
fabricate *v* придумвать
fabulous *adj* сказочный
face *n* лицо
face up to *v* принимать
facet *n* грань; аспект
facilitate *v* облегчать
fact *n* факт
factor *n* фактор
factory *n* завод
factual *adj* фактический
faculty *n* способность
fad *n* прихоть
fade *v* вянуть
faded *adj* увядший
fail *v* недоставать
failure *n* неудача
faint *v* падать в обморок
faint *n* обморок
faint *adj* ослабевший
fair *n* ярмарка
fair *adj* красивый
fairness *n* честность
fairy *n* фея
faith *n* вера; верность
faithful *adj* верный
fake *v* подделывать
fake *adj* поддельный

fall *n* падение
fall *iv* падать
fall back *v* отступать
fall behind *v* отставать
fall through *v* проваливаться
fallacy *n* обман
fallout *n* осадки
falsehood *n* фальшь
falsify *v* подделывать
falter *v* спотыкаться
fame *n* известность
familiar *adj* привычный
family *n* семья
famine *n* голод
famous *adj* знаменитый
fan *n* вентилятор
fanatic *adj* фанатический
fancy *adj* причудливый
fang *n* клык
fantastic *adj* фантастический
fantasy *n* фантазия
far *adv* далеко
faraway *adj* дальний
farce *n* фарс
fare *n* тариф
farewell *n* прощание
farm *n* ферма
farmer *n* фермер
farmyard *n* двор фермы
farther *adv* отдаленно
fascinate *v* восхищать
fashion *n* мода

fashionable *adj* модный
fast *adj* быстрый
fasten *v* прикреплять
fat *n* жир
fat *adj* жирный
fatal *adj* фатальный
fate *n* судьба
fateful *adj* роковой
father *n* отец
fatherhood *n* отцовство
father-in-law *n* свёкор, тесть
fatherly *adj* отцовский
fathom out *v* понять
fatigue *n* усталость
fatty *adj* жирный
faucet *n* вентиль
fault *n* ошибка
faulty *adj* неисправный
favor *n* расположение
favorable *adj* благоприятный
favorite *adj* излюбленный
fear *n* страх
fearful *adj* страшный
feasible *adj* выполнимый
feast *n* пир
feat *n* подвиг
feather *n* перо
feature *n* особенность
February *n* февраль
fed up *adj* раздраженный
federal *adj* федеральный
fee *n* плата

F

F

feeble *adj* немощный
feed *iv* кормить
feedback *n* обратная связь
feel *iv* чувствовать
feeling *n* чувство
feelings *n* чувства
feet *n* ступни
feign *v* притворяться
fellow *n* парень
fellowship *n* товарищество
female *n* женщина; самка
feminine *adj* женский
fence *n* забор
fencing *n* огораживание
fend *v* отражать
fend off *v* предотвращать
ferment *n* фермент
ferocious *adj* жестокий
ferocity *n* жестокость
ferry *n* переправа
fertile *adj* плодородный
fertility *n* плодородие
fertilize *v* удобрять
fervent *adj* горячий
fester *v* гноиться
festive *adj* праздничный
festivity *n* праздник
fetid *adj* вонючий
fetus *n* плод
feud *n* вражда
fever *n* жар
few *adj* немногие

fewer *adj* меньше
fiancé *n* жених
fiber *n* волокно
fickle *adj* непостоянный
fiction *n* выдумка
fictitious *adj* выдуманный
fiddle *n* скрипка
fidelity *n* преданность
field *n* поле
fierce *adj* свирепый
fiery *adj* огненный
fifteen *adj* пятнадцать
fifth *adj* пятый
fifty *adj* пятьдесят
fifty-fifty *adv* поровну
fig *n* инжир
fight *iv* сражаться
fight *n* бой
fighter *n* воин
figure *n* фигура
figure out *v* вычислять
file *v* регистрировать
file *n* папка, файл
fill *v* наполнять
filling *n* наполнение
film *n* фильм
filter *n* фильтр
filter *v* фильтровать
filth *n* грязь
filthy *adj* запачканный
fin *n* плавник
final *adj* заключительный

finalize *v* заканчивать
finance *v* финансы
financial *adj* финансовый
find *iv* находить
find out *v* узнать
fine *n* конец
fine *v* штрафовать
fine *adv* тонко; хорошо
fine *adj* тонкий; хороший
fine print *n* мелкий шрифт
finger *n* палец
fingernail *n* ноготь
fingerprint *n* отпечаток пальца
fingertip *n* кончик пальца
finish *v* кончать
Finland *n* Финляндия
Finnish *adj* финский
fire *v* зажигать; стрелять
fire *n* огонь
firecracker *n* фейерверк
firefighter *n* пожарник
fireman *n* пожарный
fireplace *n* камин
firewood *n* дрова
fireworks *n* фейерверк
firm *adj* крепкий
firm *n* фирма
firmness *n* стойкость
first *adj* первый
fish *n* рыба
fisherman *n* рыбак
fishy *adj* рыбный

fist *n* кулак
fit *n* подгонка
fit *v* соответствовать
fitting *adj* подходящий
five *adj* пять
fix *v* устанавливать
fjord *n* фьорд
flag *n* флаг
flagpole *n* флагшток
flamboyant *adj* цветистый
flame *n* пламя
flammable *adj* огнеопасный
flank *n* бочок
flare *n* вспышка
flare-up *v* вспыхивать
flash *n* вспышка
flashlight *n* сигнальный огонь
flashy *adj* вульгарный
flat *n* плоскость
flat *adj* плоский
flatten *v* выравнивать
flatter *v* льстить
flattery *n* лесть
flaunt *v* щеголять
flavor *n* вкус
flaw *n* трещина
flawless *adj* безупречный
flea *n* блоха
flee *iv* убегать
fleece *n* овечья шерсть
fleeting *adj* стремительный
flesh *n* тело**

F

F

flex v изгибать
flexible adj гибкий
flicker v мерцать
flier n лётчик
flight n полёт; бегство
flimsy adj ломкий
flirt v флиртовать
float v всплывать
flock n клок; стадо, стая
flog v пороть
flood v нахлынуть
floodgate n ворота шлюза
flooding n затопление
floor n пол
flop n глухой удар
floss n пушок
flour n мука
flourish v цвести
flow v течь
flow n течение
flower n цветок
flu n грипп
fluctuate v колебаться
fluently adv бегло
fluid n жидкость
flunk v уклоняться
flush v наполнять
flute n флейта
flutter v перепархивать
fly iv летать
fly n муха
foam n пена

focus n фокус
foe n враг
fog n туман
foggy adj туманный
foil v мешать
fold v складывать
folder n папка
folks n люди
folksy adj народный
follow v следовать
follower n последователь
folly n глупость
fond adj любящий
fondle v ласкать
fondness n нежность
food n еда
fool v дурачить
fool adj глупый
foot n ступня
football n футбол
footnote n сноска
footprint n след
footstep n след
footwear n обувь
for pre для
forbid iv запрещать
force n сила
force v заставлять
forceful adj могущественный
forcibly adv принудительно
forefront n передовая линия
foreground n передний план

forehead *n* лоб
foreign *adj* иностранный
foreigner *n* иностранец
foreman *n* мастер
foremost *adj* передний
foresee *iv* предвидеть
foreshadow *v* предвещать
foresight *n* предвидение
forest *n* лес
foretaste *n* предвкушение
foretell *v* прогнозировать
forever *adv* навсегда
forewarn *v* предостерегать
foreword *n* введение
forfeit *v* поплатиться
forge *v* выковывать
forgery *n* подделка
forget *v* забывать
forgivable *adj* простительный
forgive *v* прощать
forgiveness *n* прощение
fork *n* вилка
form *n* форма
formal *adj* формальный
formality *n* формальность
formalize *v* оформлять
formally *adv* официально
format *n* формат
formation *n* образование
former *adj* бывший
formerly *adv* раньше
formidable *adj* грозный

formula *n* формула
forsake *iv* оставлять
fort *n* форт
forthcoming *adj* ожидаемый
forthright *adj* прямой
fortify *v* укреплять
fortitude *n* стойкость
fortress *n* крепость
fortunate *adj* счастливый
fortune *n* счастье
forty *adj* сорок
forward *adv* вперед
fossil *n* ископаемое
foster *v* воспитывать
foul *adj* грязный
foundation *n* фундамент
founder *n* основатель
foundry *n* литейный цех
fountain *n* фонтан
four *adj* четыре
fourteen *adj* четырнадцать
fourth *adj* четвертый
fox *n* лиса
foxy *adj* лисий
fraction *n* дробь
fracture *n* перелом
fragile *adj* ломкий
fragment *n* обломок
fragrance *n* аромат
fragrant *adj* ароматный
frail *adj* хрупкий
frailty *n* хрупкость

frame *n* каркас; рама
frame *v* обрамлять
framework *n* структура
France *n* Франция
franchise *n* право голоса
frank *adj* откровенный
frankly *adv* откровенно
frankness *n* откровенность
frantic *adj* безумный
fraternal *adj* братский
fraud *n* мошенничество
freckle *n* веснушка
freckled *adj* веснушчатый
free *v* освобождать
free *adj* свободный
freedom *n* свобода
freeze *iv* обледенеть
freight *n* фрахт
French *adj* французский
frenetic *adj* буйный
frenzied *adj* бешеный
frenzy *n* бешенство
frequency *n* частота
frequent *adj* частый
frequent *v* часто посещать
fresh *adj* свежий
freshen *v* свежеть
freshness *n* свежесть
friar *n* монах
friction *n* трение
Friday *n* пятница
fried *adj* жареный

friend *n* друг
friendship *n* дружба
fries *n* картофель фри
frigate *n* фрегат
fright *n* страх
frighten *v* пугать
frightening *adj* устрашающий
frigid *adj* холодный
fringe *n* бахрома
frog *n* лягушка
from *pre* от, из, с
front *n* фронт; фасад; лоб
front *adj* передний
frontage *n* передний фасад
frontier *n* рубеж
frost *n* мороз
frosty *adj* морозный
frown *v* насупиться
frozen *adj* замороженный
frugal *adj* бережливый
frugality *n* бережливость
fruit *n* плод
fruitful *adj* плодоносный
fruity *adj* фруктовый
frustrate *v* расстраивать
frustration *n* крушение
fry *v* жарить
frying pan *n* сковорода
fuel *n* топливо
fuel *v* разжигать
fugitive *n* беглец
fulfill *v* выполнять

fulfillment *n* выполнение
full *adj* полный
fully *adv* полностью
fumes *n* дым, газы
fumigate *v* окуривать
fun *n* веселье
function *n* функция
fund *n* фонд
fund *v* финансировать
fundamental *adj* основной
funds *n* средства
funeral *n* похороны
fungus *n* грибок
funny *adj* забавный
fur *n* мех
furious *adj* взбешённый
furiously *adv* бешено
furnace *n* очаг
furnish *v* доставлять
furnishings *n* меблировка
furniture *n* мебель
furor *n* фурор
furrow *n* борозда
furry *adj* меховой
further *adv* вдали
furthermore *adv* к тому же
fury *n* неистовство
fuse *n* плавка
fusion *n* расплавление
fuss *n* протест
fussy *adj* вычурный
futile *adj* бесполезный

futility *n* тщетность
future *n* будущее
fuzzy *adj* пушистый

G

gag *n* затычка
gag *v* затыкать
gage *v* ручаться
gain *v* добывать
gain *n* прибыль
gal *n* девчонка
galaxy *n* галактика
gale *n* шторм
gallant *adj* галантный
gallery *n* галерея
gallon *n* галлон
gallop *v* скакать галопом
gallows *n* виселица
game *n* игра
gang *n* комплект
gangrene *n* гангрена
gangster *n* гангстер
gap *n* пролом
garage *n* гараж
garbage *n* мусор
garden *n* сад
gardener *n* садовник

gargle *v* полоскать
garland *n* гирлянда
garlic *n* чеснок
garment *n* предмет одежды
garnish *v* гарнировать
garnish *n* гарнир
garrison *n* гарнизон
garrulous *adj* болтливый
garter *n* подвязка
gas *n* газ
gash *n* порез
gasoline *n* бензин
gasp *v* задыхаться
gastric *adj* желудочный
gate *n* ворота
gather *v* собираться
gathering *n* собрание
gauge *v* измерять
gauze *n* газ
gaze *v* вглядываться
gear *n* механизм
geese *n* гуси
gender *n* род
gene *n* ген
general *n* генерал
generalize *v* обобщать
generate *v* порождать
generation *n* поколение
generator *n* генератор
generic *adj* родовой
generosity *n* щедрость
genetic *adj* генетический

genial *adj* общительный
genius *n* гений
genocide *n* геноцид
genteel *adj* благородный
gentle *adj* кроткий
gentleman *n* джентльмен
gentleness *n* мягкость
genuine *adj* подлинный
geography *n* география
geology *n* геология
geometry *n* геометрия
germ *n* эмбрион; микроб
German *adj* немецкий
Germany *n* Германия
germinate *v* прорастать
gerund *n* герундий
gestation *n* беременность
gesticulate *v* жестикулировать
gesture *n* жест
get *iv* получить
get along *v* уживаться
get back *v* вернуться
get by *v* принимать
get down *v* подбить
get down to *v* приняться за
get in *v* прийти, сажать
get off *v* отправляться
get out *v* выведывать
get over *v* прийти в себя
get together *v* собираться
get up *v* подниматься
geyser *n* гейзер

ghastly *adj* жуткий

ghost *n* привидение

giant *n* великан

gift *n* дар

gifted *adj* талантливый

gigantic *adj* гигантский

giggle *v* хихикать

gimmick *n* ухищрение

ginger *n* имбирь

giraffe *n* жираф

girl *n* девочка

girlfriend *n* подружка

give *iv* дать

give away *v* проговориться

give back *v* возвращать

give in *v* уступать

give out *v* выдавать

give up *v* отказаться

glacier *n* ледник

glad *adj* радостный

gladiator *n* гладиатор

glamorous *adj* обаятельный

glance *v* взглянуть

glance *n* быстрый взгляд

gland *n* железа

glare *n* блеск

glass *n* стекло

glasses *n* очки

gleam *n* слабый свет

gleam *v* мерцать

glide *v* скользить

glimmer *n* мерцание

glimpse *n* проблеск

glimpse *v* мелькнуть

glitter *v* блестеть

globe *n* шар

globule *n* шарик

gloom *n* мрак

gloomy *adj* мрачный

glorify *v* прославлять

glory *n* слава

gloss *n* лоск

glossary *n* глоссарий

glossy *adj* глянцевитый

glove *n* перчатка

glow *v* светиться

glucose *n* глюкоза

glue *n* клей

glue *v* приклеивать

glut *n* избыток

glutton *n* обжора

gnaw *v* грызть

go *iv* идти

go ahead *v* продолжаться

go away *v* заканчиваться

go back *v* возвращаться

go down *v* понижаться

go in *v* вступать

go on *v* продолжать

go out *v* выходить

go over *v* приниматься

go through *v* быть принятым

go under *v* тонуть

go up *v* переходить

G

G

goad *v* подгонять
goal *n* цель; гол
goalkeeper *n* вратарь
goat *n* козел
gobble *v* пожирать
God *n* Бог
goddess *n* богиня
godless *adj* безбожный
goggles *n* защитные очки
gold *n* золото
golden *adj* золотой
good *adj* хороший
good-looking *adj* красивый
goodness *n* добродетель
goods *n* товары
goof *v* бездельничать
goof *n* тупица
goose *n* гусь
gorge *n* горло
gorgeous *adj* вычурный
gorilla *n* горилла
gory *adj* окровавленный
gospel *n* Евангелие
gossip *v* сплетничать
gossip *n* сплетня
gout *n* подагра
govern *v* управлять
government *n* правительство
governor *n* правитель
gown *n* платье
grab *v* хватать
grace *n* благодать

graceful *adj* вежливый
gracious *adj* милосердный
grade *n* стадия, ранг
gradual *adj* постепенный
graft *v* прививать
graft *n* прививка
grain *n* зерно
gram *n* грамм
grammar *n* грамматика
grand *adj* большой
grandchild *n* внук
granddad *n* дедушка
grandfather *n* дедушка
grandmother *n* бабушка
grandson *n* внук
grandstand *n* трибуна
granite *n* гранит
granny *n* бабуля
grant *v* жаловать
grant *n* грант
grape *n* виноград
grapefruit *n* грейпфрут
graphic *adj* графический
grasp *n* хватка
grasp *v* хватать; понимать
grass *n* трава
grassroots *n* источник
grateful *adj* благодарный
gratify *v* удовлетворять
gratifying *adj* приятный
gratitude *n* благодарность
gratuity *n* пособие

grave *adj* серьезный
grave *n* могила
gravel *n* гравий
gravely *adv* серьёзно
gravestone *n* могильная плита
graveyard *n* кладбище
gravitate *v* тяготеть
gravity *n* тяжесть
gravy *n* подливка
gray *adj* серый
grayish *adj* сероватый
graze *v* задевать
graze *n* соприкосновение
grease *v* замасливать
grease *n* жир
greasy *adj* засаленный
great *adj* великий
greatness *n* величие
Greece *n* Греция
greed *n* жадность
greedy *adj* жадный
Greek *adj* греческий
green *adj* зеленый
greenhouse *n* оранжерея
Greenland *n* Гренландия
greet *v* приветствовать
greetings *n* приветствие
gregarious *adj* стадный
grenade *n* граната
greyhound *n* борзая
grief *n* скорбь
grievance *n* обида

grieve *v* огорчать
grill *n* грилль
grim *adj* жестокий
grimace *n* гримаса
grime *n* сажа
grind *iv* молоть
grip *v* схватить
grip *n* хватка
gripe *n* захват
grisly *adj* жуткий
groan *v* стонать
groan *n* стон
groceries *n* продукты
groin *n* пах
groom *n* жених
groove *n* желобок
gross *adj* большой
grossly *adv* вульгарно
grotesque *adj* гротеск
grotto *n* грот
grouch *v* ворчать
grouchy *adj* ворчливый
ground *n* земля
ground floor *n* первый этаж
groundwork *n* основа
group *n* группа
grow *iv* расти
grow up *v* взрослеть
growl *v* рычать
grown-up *n* взрослый
growth *n* рост
grudge *n* недовольство

G

grudgingly *adv* неохотно
gruelling *adj* противный
gruesome *adj* отвратительный
grumble *v* ворчать
guarantee *v* гарантировать
guarantee *n* гарантия
guarantor *n* поручитель
guard *n* охрана
guardian *n* попечитель
guess *v* догадываться
guess *n* догадка
guest *n* гость
guidance *n* руководство
guide *v* вести
guide *n* проводник
guidebook *n* путеводитель
guidelines *n* рекомендации
guild *n* гильдия
guile *n* коварство
guillotine *n* гильотина
guilt *n* вина
guilty *adj* виновный
guise *n* наружность
guitar *n* гитара
gulf *n* залив
gull *n* чайка
gullible *adj* доверчивый
gulp *v* заглатывать
gulp *n* глотание
gulp down *v* глотать
gum *n* десна; резина
gun *n* оружие

gun down *v* застрелить
gunfire *n* орудийный огонь
gunpowder *n* порох
gust *n* порыв
gusto *n* удовольствие
gusty *adj* ветреный
gut *n* кишка
guts *n* мужество
gutter *n* канавка
guy *n* малый
guzzle *v* лопать
gymnasium *n* гимназия
gynecology *n* гинекология
gypsy *n* цыган

habit *n* привычка
habitable *adj* обитаемый
habitual *adj* привычный
hack *v* рубить
haggle *v* вздорить
hail *n* град
hail *v* приветствовать
hair *n* волосы
hairbrush *n* расческа
haircut *n* стрижка
hairdo *n* причёска

hairdresser *n* парикмахер
hairpiece *n* шиньон
hairy *adj* волосатый
half *n* половина
half *adj* половинный
hall *n* зал
hallucinate *v* ошибаться
hallway *n* коридор
halt *v* останавливаться
halve *v* делить пополам
ham *n* окорок
hamlet *n* деревушка
hammer *n* молот
hammock *n* гамак
hand *n* рука
hand in *v* возвращать
hand over *v* передавать
handbag *n* дамская сумочка
handbook *n* справочник
handcuffs *n* наручники
handful *n* пригоршня
handgun *n* пистолет
handicap *n* увечье
handkerchief *n* носовой платок
handle *v* справляться
handle *n* рукоять
handmade *adj* ручной работы
handout *n* подаяние
handrail *n* перила
handshake *n* рукопожатие
handsome *adj* красивый
handwritting *n* почерк

handy *adj* доступный
hang *iv* развешивать
hang around *v* слоняться
hang on *v* упорствовать
hang up *v* повесить
hanger *n* палач
hangup *n* проблема
happen *v* происходить
happening *n* происшествие
happiness *n* счастье
happy *adj* счастливый
harass *v* беспокоить
harassment *n* беспокойство
harbor *n* гавань
hard *adj* твердый
harden *v* твердеть
hardly *adv* едва
hardness *n* твердость
hardship *n* трудность
hardy *adj* мужественный
hare *n* заяц
harm *v* причинять вред
harm *n* вред
harmful *adj* вредный
harmless *adj* безвредный
harmonize *v* согласовывать
harmony *n* гармония
harp *n* арфа
harpoon *n* гарпун
harrowing *adj* горестный
harsh *adj* жесткий
harshly *adv* жестко

H

harshness *n* жесткость

harvest *n* жатва

hashish *n* гашиш

hassle *v* надоедать

hassle *n* препятствие

haste *n* спешка

hasten *v* спешить

hastily *adv* поспешно

hasty *adj* быстрый

hat *n* шляпа

hatchet *n* топор

hate *v* ненавидеть

hateful *adj* ненавистный

hatred *n* ненависть

haughty *adj* высокомерный

haul *v* тащить

haunt *v* навещать

have *iv* иметь

have to *v* надлежать

haven *n* гавань

havoc *n* опустошение

hawk *n* ястреб

hay *n* сено

haystack *n* стог сена

hazard *n* риск

hazardous *adj* рискованный

haze *n* легкий туман

hazelnut *n* фундук

hazy *adj* туманный

he *pro* он

head *n* голова

head for *v* направляться

headache *n* головная боль

heading *n* заголовок

head-on *adv* передней частью

headphones *n* наушники

headquarters *n* штаб-квартира

headway *n* успех

heal *v* исцелять

healer *n* исцелитель

health *n* здоровье

healthy *adj* здоровый

heap *n* груда

heap *v* нагромождать

hear *iv* слышать

hearing *n* слух

hearsay *n* молва

hearse *n* катафалк

heart *n* сердце

heartbeat *n* пульсация сердца

heartburn *n* изжога

hearten *v* воодушевлять

hearth *n* домашний очаг

heartless *adj* безжалостный

hearty *adj* сердечный

heat *v* нагреваться

heat *n* жара

heater *n* печь

heathen *n* язычник

heating *n* нагревание

heatstroke *n* тепловой удар

heatwave *n* тепловая волна

heaven *n* небеса

heavenly *adj* небесный

heaviness *n* тяжесть
heavy *adj* тяжёлый
heckle *v* трепать
hectic *adj* лихорадочный
heed *v* учитывать
heel *n* пятка
height *n* высота
heighten *v* повышать
heinous *adj* гнусный
heir *n* наследник
heiress *n* наследница
heist *n* воровство
helicopter *n* вертолёт
hell *n* ад
hello *e* привет
helm *n* штурвал
helmet *n* каска
help *v* помогать
help *n* помощь
helper *n* помощник
helpful *adj* полезный
helpless *adj* бепомощный
hem *n* рубец
hemisphere *n* полушарие
hemorrhage *n* кровоизлияние
hen *n* курица
hence *adv* отсюда
her *adj* её
herald *v* возвещать
herald *n* глашатай
here *adv* здесь
hereafter *adv* ниже

hereby *adv* настоящим
heresy *n* ересь
heretic *adj* еретический
heritage *n* наследие
hermetic *adj* герметический
hermit *n* отшельник
hernia *n* грыжа
hero *n* герой
heroic *adj* героический
heroin *n* героин
heroism *n* героизм
hers *pro* её
herself *pro* сама
hesitate *v* сомневаться
hesitation *n* сомнение
heyday *n* зенит
hiccup *n* икота
hidden *adj* спрятанный
hide *iv* прятаться
hideaway *n* укрытие
hierarchy *n* иерархия
high *adj* высокий
highlight *n* световой эффект
highly *adv* весьма
Highness *n* высочество
highway *n* магистраль
hijacker *n* налётчик
hike *v* гулять
hike *n* прогулка
hilarious *adj* веселый
hill *n* холм
hillside *n* склон холма

hilltop *n* вершина холма
hilly *adj* холмистый
hilt *n* рукоятка
hinder *v* задерживать
hindrance *n* препятствие
hinge *v* зависеть
hinge *n* петля
hint *n* намёк
hint *v* намекать
hip *n* бедро
hire *v* нанимать
his *adj* его
his *pro* его
hiss *v* шипеть
historian *n* историк
history *n* история
hit *n* толчок; удача
hit *iv* ударять
hit back *v* нападать на
hitch *n* рывок
hitch up *v* запрягать
hitherto *adv* до сих пор
hive *n* улей
hoard *v* запасать
hoarse *adj* охрипший
hoax *n* мистификация
hobby *n* хобби
hog *n* боров
hoist *v* поднимать
hoist *n* поднятие
hold *iv* держать
hold back *v* воздерживаться

hold on to *v* держаться за
hold out *v* выдерживать
hold up *v* выставлять
hole *n* дыра
holiday *n* праздник
holiness *n* святость
Holland *n* Голландия
hollow *adj* пустой
holocaust *n* жертвование
holy *adj* святой
homage *n* почтение
home *n* дом
homeland *n* отечество
homeless *adj* бездомный
homely *adj* обыденный
hometown *n* родной город
homicide *n* убийство
homily *n* проповедь
honest *adj* честный
honesty *n* честность
honey *n* мед
honeymoon *n* медовый месяц
honk *v* кричать
honor *n* почет
hood *n* капюшон
hoodlum *n* хулиган
hoof *n* копыто
hook *n* крюк; приманка
hooligan *n* хулиган
hop *v* подпрыгивать
hope *n* надежда
hopeful *adj* надеющийся

H

hopefully *adv* с надеждой
hopeless *adj* безнадежный
horizon *n* горизонт
horizontal *adj* горизонтальный
hormone *n* гормон
horn *n* рог
horrendous *adj* ужасный
horrible *adj* жуткий
horrify *v* ужасать
horror *n* ужас
horse *n* лошадь
hose *n* шланг
hospital *n* больница
hospitality *n* гостеприимство
host *n* хозяин
hostage *n* заложник
hostess *n* хозяйка
hostile *adj* вражеский
hostility *n* враждебность
hot *adj* горячий
hotel *n* гостиница
hound *n* гончая
hour *n* час
house *n* дом
household *n* семейство
housewife *n* домохозяйка
housework *n* работа по дому
hover *v* порхать
how *adv* как
however *c* однако
howl *v* выть
howl *n* вой

hub *n* ступица
huddle *v* толпиться
hug *v* обнимать
hug *n* объятие
huge *adj* огромный
hull *n* скорлупа
hum *v* жужжать
human *adj* человеческий
human being *n* человек
humankind *n* человечество
humble *adj* кроткий
humbly *adv* кротко
humid *adj* влажный
humidity *n* влажность
humiliate *v* унижать
humility *n* смирение
humor *n* юмор
hunch *n* толчок
hunchback *n* горбун
hunched *adj* сутулый
hundred *adj* сто
hundredth *adj* сотый
hunger *n* голод
hungry *adj* голодный
hunt *v* охотиться
hunter *n* охотник
hunting *n* охота
hurdle *n* плетень
hurl *v* швырять
hurricane *n* ураган
hurriedly *adv* поспешно
hurry *v* торопить

H

hurry up *v* торопиться
hurt *iv* ранить
hurt *adj* поврежденный
hurtful *adj* вредный
husband *n* муж
hush *n* тишина
hush up *v* скрывать
husky *adj* эскимосский
hustle *n* подгонять
hut *n* хата
hydrogen *n* водород
hyena *n* гиена
hygiene *n* гигиена
hymn *n* церковный гимн
hyphen *n* дефис
hypnosis *n* гипноз
hypnotize *v* гипнотизировать
hypocrisy *n* лицемерие
hypocrite *n* лицемер
hypothesis *n* гипотеза
hysteria *n* истерия
hysterical *adj* истерический

I *pro* я
ice *n* лёд
ice cream *n* мороженое
ice cube *n* кусочек льда
iceberg *n* айсберг
icebox *n* холодильник
icon *n* икона
icy *adj* ледяной
idea *n* идея
ideal *adj* идеальный
identical *adj* идентичный
identify *v* отождествлять
identity *n* идентичность
ideology *n* идеология
idiom *n* идиома
idiot *n* идиот
idiotic *adj* идиотский
idle *adj* неработающий
idol *n* идол
if *c* если
ignite *v* воспламенять
ignore *v* игнорировать
ill *adj* больной
illegal *adj* незаконный
illegible *adj* неразборчивый
illicit *adj* незаконный
illiterate *adj* неграмотный
illness *n* болезнь
illogical *adj* нелогичный

illuminate v освещать
illusion n иллюзия
illustrate v иллюстрировать
illustration n иллюстрация
illustrious adj знаменитый
image n изображение
imagination n воображение
imagine v воображать
imbalance n неустойчивость
imitate v подражать
imitation n подражание
immaculate adj опрятный
immature adj незрелый
immaturity n незрелость
immense adj безмерный
immensity n безмерность
immerse v погружать
immersion n погружение
immigrant n иммигрант
immigrate v иммигрировать
immigration n иммиграция
imminent adj неотвратимый
immobile adj недвижимый
immobilize v парализовать
immoral adj аморальный
immorality n аморальность
immortal adj бессмертный
immortality n бессмертие
immunity n иммунитет
immunize v иммунизировать
immutable adj неизменный
impact n толчок

impact v толкать
impair v ослаблять
impatience n нетерпение
impatient adj нетерпеливый
impeccable adj безгрешный
impediment n препятствие
impending adj нависающий
imperfection n несовершенство
imperial adj имперский
imperialism n империализм
impersonal adj обезличенный
impertinence n наглость
impertinent adj наглый
impetuous adj страстный
implacable adj неумолимый
implant v вживлять
implement v осуществлять
implicate v спутывать
implication n вовлечение
implore v умолять
imply v предполагать
impolite adj невежливый
import v импортировать
importance n важность
importation n импорт
impose v помещать
imposing adj внушительный
imposition n обложение
impossible adj невозможный
impotent adj бессильный
impound v запирать
impoverished adj бедный

I

impressive *adj* впечатляющий
improbable *adj* невероятный
impromptu *adv* экспромтом
improper *adj* неуместный
improve *v* улучшать
improvement *n* улучшение
impulse *n* импульс
impulsive *adj* импульсивный
impunity *n* безнаказанность
impure *adj* нечистый
in *pre* в
in depth *adv* тщательно
inability *n* неспособность
inaccessible *adj* недоступный
inaccurate *adj* неточный
inadequate *adj* неадекватный
inadmissible *adj* недопустимый
inappropriate *adj* неуместный
inasmuch as *c* поскольку
inauguration *n* инаугурация
incalculable *adj* неисчислимый
incapable *adj* неспособный
incense *n* фимиам
incentive *n* побуждение
inception *n* начало
incessant *adj* беспрестанный
inch *n* дюйм
incident *n* случай
incidentally *adv* случайно
incision *n* надрезание
incite *v* подстрекать
inclination *n* наклон

incline *v* наклоняться
include *v* включать
inclusive *adj* содержащий
incoherent *adj* бессвязный
income *n* доход
incoming *adj* входящий
incompatible *adj* несовместимый
incompetent *adj* некомпетентный
incomplete *adj* недостаточный
inconsistent *adj* несовместимый
incontinence *n* несдержанность
inconvenient *adj* неудобный
incorporate *v* объединяться
incorrect *adj* неверный
incorrigible *adj* неисправимый
increase *v* увеличивать
increase *n* увеличение
incredible *adj* маловероятный
increment *n* возрастание
incriminate *v* обвинять
incur *v* вытекать
incurable *adj* неизлечимый
indecency *n* неприличие
indecisive *adj* нерешающий
indeed *adv* несомненно
indemnify *v* застраховать
independence *n* независимость
independent *adj* независимый
index *n* индекс
indicate *v* указывать
indication *n* указание
indict *v* обвинять

indifference *n* равнодушие
indifferent *adj* безразличный
indigent *adj* лишённый
indirect *adj* непрямой
indispensable *adj* обязательный
indisposed *adj* нездоровый
indisputable *adj* бесспорный
indivisible *adj* неделимый
indoctrinate *v* внушать
induce *v* побуждать
indulge *v* потворствовать
industrious *adj* трудолюбивый
inefficient *adj* неэффективный
inept *adj* нелепый
inequality *n* разница
inevitable *adj* неизбежный
inexpensive *adj* недорогой
inexperienced *adj* неопытный
inexplicable *adj* необъяснимый
infallible *adj* безошибочный
infamous *adj* позорный
infancy *n* младенчество
infant *n* младенец
infantry *n* пехота
infect *v* заражать
infection *n* инфекция
infectious *adj* заразный
infer *v* заключать
inferior *adj* подчиненный
infested *adj* зараженный
infidelity *n* неверие
infiltrate *v* фильтровать

infiltration *n* инфильтрация
infinite *adj* бесконечный
infirmary *n* лазарет
inflammation *n* воспламенение
inflate *v* накачивать
inflation *n* инфляция
inflexible *adj* негибкий
inflict *v* наносить
influence *n* влияние
influential *adj* влиятельный
influenza *n* грипп
influx *n* приток
inform *v* информировать
informal *adj* неформальный
informant *n* информатор
information *n* информация
informer *n* информатор
infraction *n* нарушение
infrequent *adj* нечастый
infuriate *v* разъярять
infusion *n* вливание
ingest *v* глотать
ingot *n* слиток
ingrained *adj* пропитывающий
ingratiate *v* подлизываться
ingredient *n* компонент
inhabit *v* обитать
inhabitant *n* житель
inhale *v* вдыхать
inherit *v* наследовать
inheritance *n* наследование
inhibit *v* задерживать

I

inhuman *adj* бесчеловечный
initial *adj* начальный
initially *adv* в начале
initials *n* инициалы
initiate *v* знакомить
initiative *n* инициатива
inject *v* впрыскивать
injection *n* инъекция
injure *v* ранить
injurious *adj* вредный
injury *n* повреждение
ink *n* чернила
inkling *n* намёк
inlaid *adj* мозаичный
inland *adv* внутри страны
inland *adj* внутренний
inmate *n* житель
inn *n* гостиница
innate *adj* врождённый
inner *adj* внутренний
innocence *n* невинность
innocent *adj* невинный
innovation *n* нововведение
innuendo *n* косвенный намёк
input *n* вклад
inquest *n* следствие
inquire *v* осведомляться
inquiry *n* запрос
inquisition *n* инквизиция
insatiable *adj* ненасытный
inscription *n* надпись
insect *n* насекомое

inseparable *adj* неотделимый
insert *v* вставлять
insertion *n* введение
inside *adj* внутренний
inside *pre* внутри
inside out *adv* наизнанку
insincere *adj* неискренний
insincerity *n* неискренность
insinuate *v* вкрадываться
insinuation *n* намёк
insipid *adj* безвкусный
insist *v* настаивать
insistence *n* настойчивость
insolent *adj* высокомерный
insoluble *adj* нерастворимый
insomnia *n* бессонница
inspect *v* изучать
inspection *n* обследование
inspector *n* инспектор
inspiration *n* вдохновение
inspire *v* вдохновлять
instability *n* неустойчивость
install *v* вставлять
installation *n* установка
installment *n* очередной взнос
instance *n* случай
instant *n* мгновение
instantly *adv* немедленно
instead *adv* вместо
instigate *v* побуждать
instil *v* вливать по капле
instinct *n* инстинкт

institute *v* основывать
institution *n* организация
instruct *v* инструктировать
instructor *n* инструктор
insufficient *adj* недостаточный
insulate *v* изолировать
insulation *n* изоляция
insult *v* оскорблять
insult *n* оскорбление
insurance *n* страховка
insure *v* страховать
insurgency *n* мятеж
insurrection *n* восстание
intact *adj* нетронутый
intake *n* поглощение
integrate *v* объединять
integration *n* объединение
integrity *n* прямота
intelligent *adj* умный
intend *v* намереваться
intense *adj* интенсивный
intensify *v* усиливать
intensity *n* интенсивность
intensive *adj* напряжённый
intention *n* намерение
intercede *v* вступаться
intercept *v* служить помехой
intercession *n* заступничество
interchange *v* обмениваться
interchange *n* обмен
interest *n* интерес
interesting *adj* интересный

interfere *v* пересекать
interference *n* вмешательство
interior *adj* внутренний
interlude *n* перерыв
intermediary *n* посредник
intern *v* интернировать
interpret *v* толковать
interpretation *n* перевод
interpreter *n* переводчик
interrogate *v* расспрашивать
interrupt *v* прерывать
interruption *n* перерыв
intersect *v* пересекать
intertwine *v* переплетать
interval *n* интервал
intervene *v* вмешиваться
intervention *n* вмешательство
interview *n* интервью
intestine *n* кишечник
intimacy *n* близость
intimate *adj* близкий
intimidate *v* запугивать
intolerable *adj* невыносимый
intolerance *n* нетерпимость
intoxicated *adj* опьяненный
intravenous *adj* внутривенный
intrepid *adj* бесстрашный
intricate *adj* запутанный
intrigue *n* интрига
intriguing *adj* интригующий
intrinsic *adj* присущий
introduce *v* представлять

I

introduction *n* вступление

intrude *v* вторгаться

intruder *n* незваный гость

intrusion *n* внедрение

intuition *n* интуиция

inundate *v* затоплять

invade *v* вторгаться

invader *n* захватчик

invalid *n* инвалид

invalidate *v* аннулировать

invaluable *adj* бесценный

invent *v* изобретать

invention *n* изобретение

inventory *n* инвентаризация

invest *v* инвестировать

investigate *v* расследовать

investigation *n* расследование

investor *n* инвестор

invincible *adj* неодолимый

invisible *adj* невидимый

invitation *n* приглашение

invite *v* приглашать

invoice *n* счёт-фактура

invoke *v* упрашивать

involve *v* вовлекать

involved *v* вовлечённый

involvement *n* вовлеченность

inward *adj* внутренний

inwards *adv* внутрь

iodine *n* йод

irate *adj* взбешенный

Ireland *n* Ирландия

Irish *adj* ирландский

iron *n* железо; утюг

iron *v* гладить утюгом

ironic *adj* иронический

irony *n* ирония

irrational *adj* нелогичный

irregular *adj* нерегулярный

irrelevant *adj* неуместный

irreparable *adj* неисправимый

irresistible *adj* неотразимый

irreversible *adj* неизменяемый

irrevocable *adj* безвозвратный

irrigate *v* орошать

irrigation *n* орошение

irritate *v* раздражать

irritating *adj* раздражающий

Islamic *adj* исламский

island *n* остров

isle *n* остров

isolate *v* изолировать

isolation *n* изоляция

issue *n* издание

Italian *adj* итальянский

italics *adj* курсив

Italy *n* Италия

itch *v* чесаться

itchiness *n* зуд

item *n* пункт

itinerary *n* курс

ivory *n* слоновая кость

J

jackal n шакал

jacket n куртка

jackpot n куш

jaguar n ягуар

jail n тюрьма

jailer n тюремщик

jam n затор; джем

janitor n швейцар

January n январь

Japan n Япония

Japanese adj японский

jar n банка

jasmine n жасмин

jaw n челюсть

jealous adj ревнивый

jealousy n ревность

jeans n джинсы

jeopardize v рисковать

jerk v резко толкать

jerk adj ухабистый

jersey n свитер

Jew n еврей

jeweler n ювелир

Jewish adj еврейский

jigsaw n лобзик

job n работа

jobless adj безработный

join v присоединять

joint n сустав; узел

jointly adv совместно

joke n шутка

joke v шутить

jokingly adv шутливо

jolly adj жизнерадостный

jolt v встряхивать

jolt n тряска

journal n дневник; журнал

journalist n журналист

journey n путешествие

jovial adj величественный

joy n радость

joyful adj радостный

joyfully adv радостно

jubilant adj ликующий

Judaism n иудаизм

judge n судья

judgment n суждение

jug n кувшин

juggler n фокусник

juice n сок

juicy adj сочный

July n июль

jump v прыгать

jump n прыжок

jumpy adj неспокойный

junction n перекресток

June n июнь

jungle n джунгли

junior adj младший

junk n рухлядь

jury n присяжные

J

just *adj* справедливый
justice *n* справедливость
justify *v* оправдывать
justly *adv* справедливо
juvenile *n* юноша
juvenile *adj* юношеский

J

kangaroo *n* кенгуру
karate *n* каратэ
keep *iv* держать
keep on *v* продолжать
keg *n* бочонок
kennel *n* конура
kettle *n* чайник
key *n* ключ; клавиша
keyboard *n* клавиатура
kick *v* пинать
kickback *n* бурная реакция
kid *n* козлёнок; ребенок
kidnap *v* похищать людей
kidnapper *n* похититель
kidney *n* почка
kill *v* убивать
killer *n* убийца
killing *n* убийство
kilogram *n* килограмм

kilometer *n* километр
kilowatt *n* киловатт
kind *adj* добрый
kindle *v* зажигать
kindness *n* доброта
king *n* король
kingdom *n* царство
kinship *n* родство
kiosk *n* киоск
kiss *v* целовать
kiss *n* поцелуй
kitchen *n* кухня
kitten *n* котенок
knee *n* колено
kneecap *n* коленная чашка
knife *n* нож
knight *n* рыцарь
knit *v* вязать
knob *n* выпуклость
knock *n* стучать
knock *v* стук; неприятность
knot *n* узел
know *iv* знать
know-how *n* знание дела
knowingly *adv* намеренно
knowledge *n* знание

L

lab *n* лаборатория
label *n* этикетка
labor *n* труд
laborer *n* разнорабочий
labyrinth *n* лабиринт
lace *n* шнурок
lack *v* недоставать
lack *n* недостаток
lad *n* парень
ladder *n* лестница
laden *adj* гружёный
lady *n* дама
ladylike *adj* воспитанная
lagoon *n* лагуна
lake *n* озеро
lamb *n* ягнёнок
lame *adj* хромой
lament *v* стенать
lament *n* причитание
lamp *n* лампа
lamppost *n* фонарный столб
lampshade *n* абажур
land *n* земля
land *v* причаливать
landfill *n* свалка
landing *n* высадка
landlady *n* домовладелица
landlord *n* арендодатель
landscape *n* ландшафт

lane *n* тропинка
language *n* язык
languish *v* слабеть
lantern *n* фонарик
lap *n* подол; круг
lapse *n* упущение
larceny *n* воровство
lard *n* свиное сало
large *adj* большой
larynx *n* гортань
laser *n* лазер
lash *n* плеть; критика
lash *v* хлестать
lash out *v* наброситься
last *v* продолжаться
last *adj* последний
last name *n* фамилия
last night *adv* вчера вечером
lasting *adj* длительный
lastly *adv* наконец
latch *n* щеколда
late *adv* поздно
lately *adv* недавно
later *adv* позже
later *adj* более поздний
lateral *adj* боковой
latest *adj* самый поздний
lather *n* пена
latitude *n* широта
latter *adj* последний
laugh *v* смеяться
laugh *n* смех

laughable *adj* смешной
laughing stock *n* посмешище
laughter *n* смех
launch *n* запуск
launch *v* запускать
laundry *n* прачечная
lavatory *n* уборная
lavish *v* расточать
law *n* закон
lawful *adj* законный
lawmaker *n* законодатель
lawn *n* газон
lawsuit *n* иск
lawyer *n* юрист, адвокат
lax *adj* вялый
laxative *adj* слабительное
lay *n* расположение
lay *iv* положить
lay off *v* временно уволить
layer *n* слой
layman *n* мирянин
lay-out *n* макет
laziness *n* леность
lazy *adj* ленивый
lead *iv* вести
lead *n* руководство
leader *n* руководитель
leadership *n* руководство
leading *adj* руководящий
leaf *n* лист
leaflet *n* листочек
league *n* лига

leak *v* течь
leak *n* утечка
leakage *n* протечка
lean *adj* тощий; скудный
lean *iv* наклонять
lean back *v* откинуться
lean on *v* зависеть
leaning *n* склонность
leap *iv* прыгать
leap *n* прыжок
leap year *n* високосный год
learn *iv* учиться
learned *adj* ученый
learner *n* учащийся
learning *n* изучение
lease *v* сдавать в аренду
lease *n* аренда
leash *n* поводок
least *adj* наименьший
leather *n* кожа
leave *iv* покидать
leave out *v* пропускать
lectern *n* аналой
lecture *n* лекция
ledger *n* гроссбух
leech *n* пиявка
leftovers *n* остаток
leg *n* нога
legacy *n* наследство
legal *adj* юридический
legality *n* законность
legalize *v* легализовать

legend *n* легенда
legible *adj* разборчивый
legion *n* легион
leisure *n* досуг
lemon *n* лимон
lemonade *n* лимонад
lend *iv* одалживать
length *n* длина
lengthen *v* удлиняться
lengthy *adj* многословный
leniency *n* сострадание
lense *n* линза
Lent *n* Великий пост
lentil *n* чечевица
leopard *n* леопард
leper *n* прокаженный
leprosy *n* проказа
less *adj* меньший
lessee *n* арендатор
lessen *v* уменьшаться
lesser *adj* меньший
lesson *n* урок
lessor *n* арендодатель
let *iv* позволять
let down *v* разочаровывать
let go *v* выпускать
let in *v* допускать
let out *v* выпустить
lethal *adj* смертельный
letter *n* буква; письмо
lettuce *n* салат
leukemia *n* лейкемия

level *v* выравнивать
level *n* уровень; ступень
lever *n* рычаг
lewd *adj* похотливый
liability *n* обязательство
liable *adj* обязанный
liaison *n* контакт
liar *n* лгун
libel *n* клевета
liberate *v* освобождать
liberation *n* высвобождение
liberty *n* свобода
librarian *n* библиотекарь
library *n* библиотека
lice *n* вошь
licence *n* лицензия
license *v* разрешать
lick *v* лизать
lid *n* крышка
lie *iv* лгать
lie *v* лежать
lie *n* ложь
lieu *n* место
lieutenant *n* лейтенант
life *n* жизнь
lifeguard *n* лейб-гвардеец
lifeless *adj* бездыханный
lifestyle *n* стиль жизни
lift *v* поднимать
lift off *v* стартовать
lift-off *n* отслаивание
ligament *n* связь

light *iv* освещать
light *adj* легкий
light *n* свет
lighter *n* осветитеть
lighthouse *n* маяк
lighting *n* освещение
lightly *adv* слегка
lightning *n* молния
lightweight *n* легкий вес
likable *adj* приятный
like *pre* подобно
like *v* нравиться
likelihood *n* вероятность
likely *adv* вероятно
likeness *n* сходство
likewise *adv* подобно
liking *n* симпатия
limb *n* конечность
lime *n* известь
limestone *n* известняк
limit *n* граница; предел
limit *v* ограничивать
limitation *n* ограничение
limp *v* прихрамывать
limp *n* хромота
line *n* линия
line up *v* выстраивать
linen *n* полотно
linger *v* засиживаться
lingerie *n* дамское бельё
lingering *adj* медлительный
lining *n* подкладка

link *v* связывать
link *n* звено
lion *n* лев
lioness *n* львица
lip *n* губа
liqueur *n* ликёр
liquid *n* жидкость
liquidate *v* ликвидировать
liquidation *n* ликвидация
list *v* перечислять
list *n* список
listen *v* слушать
listener *n* слушатель
litany *n* литания
liter *n* литр
literal *adj* буквенный
literally *adv* буквально
literate *adj* грамотный
literature *n* литература
litigate *v* судиться
litigation *n* тяжба
litre *n* литр
litter *n* беспорядок
little *adj* маленький
little by little *adv* мало-помалу
liturgy *n* литургия
live *adj* живой
live *v* жить
live off *v* жить за счёт
live up *v* удовлетворять
lively *adj* живой
liver *n* печень

L

livestock *n* домашний скот
livid *adj* синевато-багровый
living room *n* гостиная
lizard *n* ящерица
load *v* грузить
load *n* груз
loaded *adj* нагруженный
loaf *n* буханка
loan *v* одалживать
loan *n* ссуда
loathe *v* питать отвращение
loathing *n* отвращение
lobby *n* вестибюль
lobster *n* омар
local *adj* местный
localize *v* локализовать
locate *v* помещать
lock *v* запирать
lock *n* замок
lock up *v* запирать
locker room *n* раздевалка
locksmith *n* слесарь
locust *n* саранча
lodge *v* останавливаться
lodging *n* приют
lofty *adj* очень высокий
log *n* бревно
log *v* заготавливать лес
log in *v* входить в систему
log off *v* выход из системы
logic *n* логика
logical *adj* логичный

loin *n* поясница
loiter *v* медлить
loneliness *n* одиночество
lonely *adj* одинокий
loner *n* одиночка
lonesome *adj* одинокий
long *adj* длинный
long for *v* тосковать
longing *n* сильное желание
longitude *n* долгота
long-standing *adj* давнишний
long-term *adj* долгосрочный
look *n* взгляд; внешность
look *v* смотреть; выглядеть
look after *v* заботиться
look at *v* посмотреть на
look down *v* смотреть свысока
look for *v* искать
look forward *v* ждать
look into *v* изучать
look out *v* быть настороже
look over *v* тщательно изучать
look through *v* просматривать
looking glass *n* зеркало
looks *n* наружность
loom *n* очертания
loophole *n* амбразура
loose *v* освобождать
loose *adj* свободный
loosen *v* ослаблять
loot *v* грабить
loot *n* добыча

L

lord *n* господин
lordship *n* светлость
lose *iv* терять
loser *n* неудачник
loss *n* потеря
lot *adv* гораздо
lotion *n* лосьон
lots *adv* много
lottery *n* лотерея
loud *adj* громкий
loudly *adv* громко
lounge *n* гостиная
louse *n* вошь
lousy *adj* вшивый
lovable *adj* симпатичный
love *v* любить
love *n* любовь
lover *n* любовник
loving *adj* любящий
low *adj* низкий
lower *adj* нижний
lowkey *adj* неброский
lowly *adj* невысокий
loyal *adj* преданный
loyalty *n* преданность
lubricate *v* смазывать
lubrication *n* смазка
lucid *adj* прозрачный
luck *n* фортуна
lucky *adj* счастливый
lucrative *adj* прибыльный
ludicrous *adj* курьёзный

luggage *n* багаж
lukewarm *adj* тепловатый
lull *n* временное затишье
lumber *n* пиломатериалы
luminous *adj* светящийся
lump *n* глыба; шишка
lump together *v* объединять
lunacy *n* лунатизм
lunatic *adj* сумасшедший
lunch *n* обед
lung *n* лёгкое
lure *v* приманивать
lush *adj* сочный
lust *v* страстно желать
lust *n* вожделение
lustful *adj* похотливый
luxurious *adj* роскошный
luxury *n* роскошь
lynch *v* линчевать
lynx *n* рысь
lyrics *n* лирика

L

machine *n* механизм
machine gun *n* пулемёт
mad *adj* безумный
madam *n* мадам
madden *v* сводить с ума
madly *adv* безумно
madman *n* безумец
madness *n* сумасшествие
magazine *n* журнал
magic *n* волшебство
magical *adj* волшебный
magician *n* маг
magistrate *n* судья
magnet *n* магнит
magnetic *adj* магнитный
magnetism *n* магнетизм
magnificent *adj* великолепный
magnify *v* преувеличивать
magnitude *n* величина
mahogany *n* красное дерево
maid *n* девушка
maiden *n* дева
mail *v* посылать по почте
mail *n* почта
mailbox *n* почтовый ящик
mailman *n* почтальон
maim *v* калечить
main *adj* основной
mainland *n* континент

mainly *adv* в основном
maintain *v* поддерживать
maintenance *n* поддержание
majestic *adj* величественный
majesty *n* величественность
major *n* майор
major *adj* значительный
majority *n* большинство
make *n* тип
make *iv* делать
make up *v* придумывать
maker *n* создатель
makeup *n* состав
malaria *n* малярия
male *n* мужчина; самец
malevolent *adj* злобный
malfunction *n* неисправная работа
malice *n* злоба
malign *v* клеветать
malignancy *n* вредоносность
malignant *adj* злобный
mall *n* торговый центр
malnutrition *n* недоедание
mammal *n* млекопитающее
mammoth *n* мамонт
man *n* человек, мужчина
manage *v* управлять
management *n* управление
manager *n* руководитель
mandate *n* мандат
mandatory *adj* обязательный
maneuver *n* манёвр

M

manger n кормушка
mangle v калечить
manhandle v тащить
manhunt n облава
maniac adj маниакальный
manifest v проявлять
manipulate v манипулировать
mankind n человечество
manliness n мужественность
manly adj мужественный
manner n способ
mannerism n манерность
manners n манеры
manpower n рабочая сила
manual n руководство
manual adj ручной
manufacture v производить
manure n компост
manuscript n манускрипт
many adj многие
map n карта
marble n мрамор
march v граничить;
маршировать
march n граница; марш
March n март
mare n кобыла
margin n поле
marginal adj приграничный
marinate v мариновать
marine adj морской
marital adj брачный

mark n метка
mark v ставить знак
mark down v снизить цену
marker n маркер
market n рынок
marksman n меткий стрелок
marmalade n конфитюр
marriage n брак
married adj женатый, замужняя
marrow n костный мозг
marry v жениться
Mars n Марс
marshal n маршал
martyr n мученик
martyrdom n мученичество
marvel n чудо
marvelous adj удивительный
marxist adj марксистский
masculine adj мужской
mash v разминать
mask n маска
masochism n мазохизм
mason n каменщик
mass n масса; большинство
massacre n резня
massage n массаж
massage v массировать
masseur n массажист
masseuse n массажистка
massive adj массивный
mast n мачта
master n хозяин

M

master *v* господствовать
mastermind *n* выдающийся ум
mastermind *v* тайно руководить
masterpiece *n* шедевр
mastery *n* власть
mat *n* коврик
match *n* спичка
match *v* соответствовать
mate *n* мат
material *n* вещество; сведения
materialism *n* материализм
maternal *adj* материнский
maternity *n* материнство
math *n* математика
matrimony *n* супружество
matter *n* вещество; значение
mattress *n* матрац
mature *adj* зрелый
maturity *n* зрелость
maul *v* сильно ударять
maxim *n* максима
maximum *adj* максимальный
May *n* май
may *iv* мочь
may-be *adv* может быть
mayhem *n* нанесение увечья
mayor *n* мэр
maze *n* лабиринт
meadow *n* луг
meager *adj* тощий
meal *n* еда
mean *iv* иметь в виду

mean *adj* неприятный
meaning *n* значение
meanness *n* низость
means *n* средство
meantime *adv* тем временем
meanwhile *adv* между тем
measles *n* корь
measure *v* измерять
measurement *n* измерение
meat *n* мясо
meatball *n* фрикаделька
mechanic *n* механик
mechanism *n* механизм
mechanize *v* механизировать
medal *n* медаль
medallion *n* медальон
meddle *v* вмешиваться
mediate *v* посредничать
mediator *n* посредник
medication *n* лечение
medicinal *adj* лекарственный
medicine *n* медицина
medieval *adj* средневековый
mediocre *adj* посредственный
meditate *v* обдумывать
meditation *n* раздумье
medium *adj* средний
meek *adj* кроткий
meekness *n* кротость
meet *iv* встречать
meeting *n* собрание
melancholy *n* меланхолия

mellow *adj* сочный
mellow *v* созревать
melodic *adj* мелодичный
melody *n* мелодия
melon *n* дыня
melt *v* таять
member *n* член
membership *n* членство
membrane *n* перепонка
memo *n* заметка
memoirs *n* мемуары
memorable *adj* незабываемый
memory *n* память
men *n* мужчины
menace *n* угроза
mend *v* чинить
meningitis *n* менингит
menopause *n* менопауза
menstruation *n* менструация
mental *adj* умственный
mentality *n* менталитет
mentally *adv* умственно
mention *v* упоминать
mention *n* упоминание
menu *n* меню
merchandise *n* товары
merchant *n* торговец
merciful *adj* милосердный
merciless *adj* безжалостный
mercury *n* ртуть
mercy *n* милосердие
merely *adv* только

M

merge *v* сливаться
merger *n* поглощение
merit *n* заслуга
merit *v* заслуживать
mermaid *n* русалка
merry *adj* восхитительный
mesh *n* петля
mesmerize *v* гипнотизировать
mess *n* беспорядок
mess up *v* испортить
message *n* сообщение
messenger *n* вестник
Messiah *n* Мессия
messy *adj* грязный
metal *n* металл
metaphor *n* метафора
meteor *n* метеор
meter *n* счётчик; метр
method *n* метод
meticulous *adj* мелочный
metric *adj* метрический
metropolis *n* столица
Mexican *adj* мексиканский
mice *n* мыши
microbe *n* микроб
microphone *n* микрофон
microscope *n* микроскоп
midday *n* полдень
middle *n* середина
middleman *n* посредник
midget *n* карлик
midnight *n* полночь

midsummer *n* середина лета
midwife *n* акушерка
mighty *adj* могущественный
migraine *n* мигрень
migrant *n* мигрант
migrate *v* мигрировать
mild *adj* тихий
mildew *n* плесень
mile *n* миля
militant *adj* воинственный
milk *n* молоко
milky *adj* молочный
mill *n* мельница
millennium *n* тысячелетие
milligram *n* миллиграмм
millimeter *n* миллиметр
million *n* миллион
millionaire *n* миллионер
mince *v* крошить
mincemeat *n* фарш
mind *v* возражать
mind *n* разум
mindful *adj* помнящий
mine *n* шахта
mine *pro* мой
minefield *n* минное поле
miner *n* горняк
mineral *n* минерал
mingle *v* смешиваться
miniature *n* миниатюра
minimum *n* минимум
miniskirt *n* мини-юбка

minister *n* министр; священник
minister *v* помогать
ministry *n* духовенство
minor *adj* незначительный
minority *n* меньшинство
mint *n* мята
mint *v* чеканить
minus *adj* отрицательный
minute *n* минута
miracle *n* чудо
miraculous *adj* чудотворный
mirage *n* мираж
mirror *n* зеркало
misbehave *v* плохо вести себя
miscarry *v* терпеть неудачу
mischief *n* вред
mischievous *adj* озорной
misdemeanor *n* мисдиминор
miser *n* скряга
miserable *adj* жалкий
misery *n* невзгода
misfortune *n* неудача
misgiving *n* опасение
misleading *adj* обманчивый
misprint *n* опечатка
miss *v* упустить
miss *n* потеря
missile *n* ракета
missing *adj* недостающий
mission *n* миссия
missionary *n* миссионер
mist *n* мгла

mistake *iv* ошибаться
mistake *n* ошибка
mistaken *adj* ошибочный
mister *n* господин
mistress *n* хозяйка
mistrust *n* недоверие
mistrust *v* не доверять
misty *adj* туманный
mitigate *v* смягчать
mix *v* перемешивать
mixed-up *adj* запутанный
mixer *n* смеситель
mixture *n* смесь
mix-up *n* неразбериха
moan *v* стонать
moan *n* стон
mob *v* толпиться
mob *n* сборище
mobile *adj* мобильный
mobilize *v* мобилизовать
mobster *n* бандит
mock *v* насмехаться
mockery *n* насмешка
mode *n* режим
model *n* модель
moderate *adj* умеренный
moderation *n* смягчение
modern *adj* современный
modest *adj* скромный
modesty *n* скромность
module *n* модуль
moisten *v* увлажнять

moisture *n* влажность
molar *n* коренной зуб
mold *v* плесневеть
mold *n* плесень
mole *n* родинка; крот
molecule *n* молекула
molest *v* заигрывать
mom *n* мама
moment *n* момент
momentarily *adv* моментально
momentous *adj* важный
monarch *n* монарх
monarchy *n* монархия
monastery *n* монастырь
monastic *adj* монастырский
Monday *n* понедельник
money *n* деньги
monitor *v* контролировать
monk *n* монах
monkey *n* обезьяна
monogamy *n* единобрачие
monologue *n* монолог
monopoly *n* монополия
monotonous *adj* монотонный
monotony *n* монотонность
monster *n* чудовище
monstrous *adj* чудовищный
month *n* месяц
monthly *adv* ежемесячно
monument *n* памятник
monumental *adj* огромный
mood *n* настроение

M

moody *adj* угрюмый
moon *n* луна
moor *v* причаливать
mop *v* мыть
moral *adj* нравственный
moral *n* мораль
morality *n* нравственность
more *adj* больший
moreover *adv* кроме того
morning *n* утро
moron *n* болван
morphine *n* морфий
morsel *n* маленький кусочек
mortal *adj* смертный
mortality *n* смертельность
mortar *n* ступа
mortgage *n* ипотека
mortification *n* смирение
mortify *v* подавлять
mortuary *n* морг
mosaic *n* мозаика
mosque *n* мечеть
mosquito *n* комар
moss *n* мох
most *adj* наибольший
mostly *adv* главным образом
motel *n* мотель
moth *n* мотылек
mother *n* мать
motherhood *n* материнство
mother-in-law *n* теща, свекровь
motion *n* движение

motionless *adj* неподвижный
motivate *v* побуждать
motive *n* мотив
motor *n* двигатель
motorcycle *n* мотоцикл
motto *n* девиз
mouldy *adj* заплесневелый
mount *n* гора
mount *v* восходить
mountain *n* гора
mountainous *adj* гористый
mourn *v* скорбеть
mourning *n* скорбь
mouse *n* мышь
mouth *n* рот
move *n* движение
move *v* двигать
move back *v* двигаться назад
move forward *v* продвигаться
move out *v* съезжать
move up *v* подниматься
movement *n* движение
movie *n* кинофильм
mow *v* гримасничать
much *adv* очень
mucus *n* слизь
mud *n* грязь
muddle *n* путаница
muddy *adj* грязный
muffle *v* закутывать
muffler *n* тёплый шарф
mug *n* кружка

mug v напиваться
mugging n хулиганство
mule n мул
multiple adj составной
multiplication n умножение
multiply v умножать
multitude n множество
mumble v бормотать
mummy n мумия
mumps n свинка
munch v чавкать
munitions n боеприпасы
murder n убийство
murderer n убийца
murky adj мрачный
murmur v шелестеть
murmur n шёпот
muscle n мышца
museum n музей
mushroom n гриб
music n музыка
musician n музыкант
Muslim adj мусульманский
must iv должен
mustache n усы
mustard n горчица
muster v созывать
mutate v видоизменять
mute adj немой
mutilate v калечить
mutiny n мятеж
mutually adv взаимно

muzzle v вытягивать морду
muzzle n морда
my adj мой
myopic adj близорукий
myself pro меня самого
mysterious adj таинственный
mystery n тайна
mystic adj мистический
mystify v смущать
myth n миф

N

nag v придираться
nagging adj ворчливый
nail n ноготь
naive adj наивный
naked adj голый
name n имя
namely adv а именно
nanny n нянечка
nap n короткий сон
napkin n салфетка
narcotic n наркотик
narrate v рассказывать
narrow adj узкий
narrowly adv тесно
nasty adj отвратительный

M

nation *n* нация
national *adj* национальный
nationality *n* национальность
native *adj* родной
natural *adj* природный
naturally *adv* естественно
nature *n* природа
naughty *adj* непослушный
nausea *n* морская болезнь
nave *n* неф
navel *n* пупок
navigate *v* плавать
navigation *n* навигация
navy blue *adj* тёмно-синий
near *pre* около
nearby *adj* близлежащий
nearly *adv* близко
nearsighted *adj* близорукий
neat *adj* опрятный
neatly *adv* опрятно
necessary *adj* необходимый
necessitate *v* вынуждать
necessity *n* необходимость
neck *n* шея
necklace *n* ожерелье
necktie *n* галстук
need *v* нуждаться
need *n* нужда
needle *n* игла
needless *adj* ненужный
needy *adj* нуждающийся
negative *adj* отрицательный

neglect *v* пренебрегать
negligence *n* небрежность
negligent *adj* небрежный
negotiation *n* переговоры
neighbor *n* сосед
neighborhood *n* окружение
neither *adj* никакой
neither *adv* ни тот ни другой
nephew *n* племянник
nerve *n* нерв
nervous *adj* нервный
nest *n* гнездо
net *n* сеть
Netherlands *n* Нидерланды
network *n* сеть
neurotic *adj* невротический
neutral *adj* нейтральный
neutralize *v* нейтрализовать
never *adv* никогда
nevertheless *adv* однако
new *adj* новый
newly *adv* заново
newlywed *adj* новобрачный
news *n* новость
newspaper *n* газета
newsstand *n* газетный ларек
next *adj* следующий
next door *adj* по соседству
nibble *v* грызть
nice *adj* приятный
nicely *adv* приятно
nickel *n* никель

N

nickname *n* кличка

nicotine *n* никотин

niece *n* племянница

night *n* ночь

nightfall *n* сумерки

nightgown *n* ночная рубашка

nightingale *n* соловей

nightmare *n* кошмар

nine *adj* девять

nineteen *adj* девятнадцать

ninety *adj* девяносто

ninth *adj* девятый

nip *n* щипок

nip *v* щипать

nipple *n* сосок

nitpicking *adj* придирчивый

nitrogen *n* азот

no one *pro* ни один

nobility *n* благородство

noble *adj* благородный

nobleman *n* аристократ

nobody *pro* никто

nocturnal *adj* ночной

nod *v* прозевать

noise *n* шум

noisily *adv* шумно

noisy *adj* шумный

none *pre* ни один из

nonetheless *c* тем не менее

nonsense *n* абсурд

nonsmoker *n* некурящий

nonstop *adv* без остановок

noon *n* полдень

noose *n* петля

nor *c* ни

norm *n* норма

normal *adj* нормальный

normalize *v* нормализовать

normally *adv* нормально

north *n* север

northeast *n* северо-восток

northern *adj* северный

northerner *adj* северянин

Norway *n* Норвегия

Norwegian *adj* норвежский

nose *n* нос

nostalgia *n* ностальгия

nostril *n* ноздря

nosy *adj* носатый

not *adv* нет

notably *adv* исключительно

notary *n* нотариус

notation *n* нотация

note *v* замечать

notebook *n* записная книжка

nothing *n* ничего

notice *v* уведомлять

notice *n* извещение

notification *n* извещение

notify *v* извещать

notion *n* понятие

notorious *adj* знаменитый

nourish *v* кормить

nourishment *n* кормление

novel *n* роман
novelty *n* новизна
November *n* ноябрь
novice *n* новобранец
now *adv* сейчас
nowadays *adv* в наши дни
nowhere *adv* нигде
noxious *adj* вредный
nozzle *n* насадка
nuance *n* нюанс
nuclear *adj* ядерный
nude *adj* обнаженный
nudism *n* нудизм
nudist *n* нудист
nudity *n* нагота
nuisance *n* досада
nullify *v* аннулировать
numb *adj* окоченелый
number *n* число
numbness *n* оцепенение
nun *n* монахиня
nurse *n* сиделка
nurse *v* ухаживать
nursery *n* рассадник
nurture *v* кормить
nut *n* орех; сумасброд
nutrition *n* питание
nutritious *adj* питательный

oak *n* дуб
oar *n* весло
oasis *n* оазис
oath *n* клятва
oatmeal *n* овсянка
obedience *n* послушание
obedient *adj* послушный
obese *adj* тучный
obey *v* повиноваться
object *v* возражать
object *n* предмет
objection *n* возражение
objective *n* цель
obligate *v* обязывать
obligation *n* обязательство
obligatory *adj* обязательный
oblige *v* обязывать
obliged *adj* вынужденный
oblique *adj* наклонный
obliterate *v* удалять
oblivion *n* забвение
oblivious *adj* не замечающий
oblong *adj* продолговатый
obnoxious *adj* неприятный
obscene *adj* непристойный
obscenity *n* непристойность
obscure *adj* непонятный
obscurity *n* неясность
observation *n* наблюдение

observatory *n* обсерватория
observe *v* наблюдать
obsess *v* завладевать
obsolete *adj* устарелый
obstacle *n* препятствие
obstinacy *n* упрямство
obstinate *adj* упрямый
obstruct *v* преграждать
obtain *v* получать
obvious *adj* очевидный
obviously *adv* очевидно
occasion *n* возможность
occasionally *adv* иногда
occult *adj* оккультный
occupant *n* оккупант
occupation *n* занятие
occupy *v* занимать
occur *v* случаться
ocean *n* океан
October *n* октябрь
octopus *n* осьминог
ocurrence *n* происшествие
odd *adj* нечётный; странный
oddity *n* странность
odds *n* трудности
odious *adj* гнусный
odometer *n* одометр
odor *n* запах
odyssey *n* одиссея
of *pre* из, от
off *adv* от, у
offend *v* обижать

offense *n* оскорбление
offer *v* предлагать
offer *n* предложение
offering *n* приношения
office *n* офис
officer *n* чиновник
official *adj* служебный
offset *v* возмещать
offspring *n* отпрыск
often *adv* часто
oil *n* масло; нефть
ointment *n* мазь
okay *adv* хорошо
old *adj* старый
old age *n* старость
old-fashioned *adj* старомодный
olive *n* оливка
omelette *n* омлет
omen *n* знамение
omission *n* пропуск
omit *v* пропускать
on *pre* на
once *adv* однажды
once *c* лишь
one *adj* один
oneself *pre* себя
ongoing *adj* непрерывный
onion *n* лук
onlooker *n* зритель
only *adv* только
onset *n* атака
onslaught *n* нападение

onwards *adv* вперед
opaque *adj* непрозрачный
open *v* открывать
open *adj* открытый
open up *v* открыться
opening *n* открытие
open-minded *adj* отзывчивый
openness *n* откровенность
opera *n* опера
operate *v* действовать
operation *n* операция
opinion *n* мнение
opium *n* опиум
opponent *n* конкурент
opportune *adj* благоприятный
opportunity *n* возможность
oppose *v* противиться
opposite *adv* напротив
oppress *v* угнетать
oppression *n* угнетение
opt for *v* выбирать
optical *adj* оптический
optician *n* оптик
optimism *n* оптимизм
option *n* выбор
optional *adj* необязательный
opulence *n* изобилие
or *c* или
oracle *n* оракул
orally *adv* устно
orange *n* апельсин
orangutan *n* орангутанг

orbit *n* орбита
orchard *n* фруктовый сад
orchestra *n* оркестр
ordeal *n* суровое испытание
order *n* порядок
ordinarily *adv* обыкновенно
ordinary *adj* обыкновенный
ordination *n* ординация
ore *n* руда
organ *n* орган
organism *n* организм
organist *n* органист
organization *n* организация
organize *v* организовывать
orient *n* Восток
oriental *adj* восточный
orientation *n* ориентация
origin *n* происхождение
original *adj* первоначальный
originally *adv* первоначально
originate *v* порождать
ornament *n* орнамент
ornamental *adj* декоративный
orphan *n* сирота
orphanage *n* сиротский приют
orthodox *adj* традиционный
ostentatious *adj* показной
ostrich *n* страус
other *adj* другой
otherwise *adv* иначе
otter *n* выдра
ought to *iv* должен

O.

ounce *n* унция

our *adj* наш

ours *pro* наш

ourselves *pro* себя

oust *v* выгонять

out *adv* вне

outbreak *n* вспышка

outburst *n* взрыв

outcast *adj* отверженный

outcome *n* результат

outcry *n* неистовый крик

outdated *adj* несовременный

outdo *v* превзойти

outdoor *adv* снаружи

outdoors *adv* на улице

outer *adj* внешний

outfit *n* снаряжение

outgoing *adj* уходящий

outgrow *v* перерастать

outing *n* прогулка

outlast *v* длиться дольше

outlaw *v* запрещать

outlet *n* выход; розетка

outline *n* очертание; конспект

outline *v* очертить

outlive *v* пережить

outlook *n* перспективы

outmoded *adj* старомодный

outperform *v* превосходить

outpouring *n* выливание

output *n* продукция

outrage *n* произвол

outright *adj* совершенный

outrun *v* перегонять

outset *n* начинание

outshine *v* затмить

outside *adv* снаружи

outskirts *n* окраина

outspoken *adj* откровенный

outstanding *adj* выдающийся

outstretched *adj* протянутый

outward *adj* наружный

outweigh *v* перевешивать

oval *adj* овальный

ovary *n* яичник

ovation *n* овация

oven *n* духовка

over *pre* над, выше

overall *adv* повсеместно

overbearing *adj* властный

overboard *adv* за борт

overcast *adj* хмурый

overcoat *n* пальто

overcome *v* побороть

overdo *v* перестараться

overdone *adj* преувеличенный

overdose *n* передозировка

overdue *adj* просроченный

overestimate *v* переоценивать

overhaul *v* проверять

overlook *v* обозревать

overpower *v* побеждать

overrate *v* переоценивать

override *v* отменять

overrule *v* отклонять
overseas *adv* за границей
oversee *v* наблюдать
overshadow *v* затемнять
oversight *n* недосмотр
overstate *v* преувеличивать
overstep *v* переступить
overtake *v* наверстать
overthrow *v* перебрасывать
overthrow *n* свержение
overtime *adv* сверхурочно
overturn *v* опрокидывать
overwhelm *v* переполнять
owe *v* быть должным
owing to *adv* из-за того
owl *n* сова
own *v* владеть
own *adj* собственный
owner *n* собственник
ownership *n* собственность
ox *n* бык
oxen *n* рогатый скот
oxygen *n* кислород
oyster *n* устрица

pace *v* задавать темп
pace *n* темп
pacify *v* успокаивать
pack *v* упаковывать
package *n* пакет
pact *n* пакт
pad *v* набивать
padding *n* набивка
paddle *v* грести вёслами
padlock *n* висячий замок
pagan *adj* языческий
page *n* страница; этап
pail *n* ведро
pain *n* боль
painful *adj* болезненный
painless *adj* безболезненный
paint *v* рисовать
paint *n* рисование
paintbrush *n* кисточка
painter *n* художник
painting *n* живопись
pair *n* пара
pajamas *n* пижама
pal *n* приятель
palace *n* дворец
palate *n* нёбо
pale *adj* бледный
paleness *n* бледность
palm *n* ладонь; пальма

P

palpable *adj* осязаемый
paltry *adj* пустяковый
pamper *v* баловать
pamphlet *n* брошюра
pan *n* кастрюля
pander *v* сводничать
pang *n* болевой приступ
panic *n* паника
panorama *n* панорама
panther *n* пантера
pants *n* брюки
pantyhose *n* колготки
papacy *n* папство
paper *n* бумага
paperclip *n* скрепка для бумаг
parable *n* притча
parachute *n* парашют
parade *n* парад
paradise *n* рай

paradox *n* парадокс
paragraph *n* абзац
parallel *n* параллель
paralysis *n* паралич
paralyze *v* парализовать
parameters *n* параметры
paramount *adj* верховный
parasite *n* паразит
paratrooper *n* парашютист
parcel *n* посылка
parchment *n* пергамент
pardon *v* извинять
pardon *n* извинение

parenthesis *n* скобки
parents *n* родители
parishioner *n* прихожанин
parity *n* равенство
park *v* парковать
park *n* парк
parking *n* автостоянка
parliament *n* парламент
parochial *adj* приходской
parrot *n* попугай
parsley *n* петрушка
parsnip *n* пастернак
part *v* расставаться
part *n* часть
partial *adj* частичный
partially *adv* отчасти
participate *v* участвовать
participation *n* участие
participle *n* причастие
particle *n* частица
particularly *adv* особенно
parting *n* разделение
partisan *n* партизан
partition *n* разделение
partly *adv* частично
partner *n* партнёр
partnership *n* сотрудничество
partridge *n* куропатка
party *n* сторона; партия
pass *n* проход
pass *v* проходить
pass around *v* обходить

pass away v исчезать
pass out v терять сознание
passage n проход
passenger n пассажир
passer-by n прохожий
passion n страсть
passionate adj страстный
passive adj пассивный
passport n паспорт
password n пароль
past adj прошлый
paste v приклеивать
paste n паста
pasteurize v пастеризовать
pastime n развлечение
pastor n пастор
pastoral adj пастырский
pastry n выпечка
pasture n пастбище
pat n похлопывание
patch v латать
patch n заплатка
patent n патент
patent adj патентованный
paternity n отцовство
path n тропинка
pathetic adj жалкий
patience n терпение
patient adj терпеливый
patio n патио
patriarch n патриарх
patrimony n наследство

patriot n патриот
patriotic adj патриотический
patrol n патруль
patron n покровитель
pattern n образец
pavement n тротуар
pavilion n палатка
paw n лапа
pawn v закладывать
pawnbroker n ростовщик
pay n плата
pay iv платить
pay back v отомстить
pay off v расплачиваться
paycheck n чек
payee n получатель
payment n оплата
pea n горох
peace n мир
peaceful adj мирный
peach n персик
peacock n павлин
peak n пик
peanut n арахис
pear n груша
pearl n жемчуг
peasant n крестьянин
pebble n галька
peck v клевать
peck n множество
peculiar adj своеобразный
pedagogy n педагогика

P

pedal *n* педаль

pedantic *adj* педантичный

pedestrian *n* пешеход

peel *v* очищать шкурку

peel *n* кожица

peep *v* подглядывать

peer *n* ровня

pelican *n* пеликан

pellet *n* гранула

pen *n* ручка

penalize *v* наказывать

penalty *n* наказание

penance *n* покаяние

penchant *n* склонность

pencil *n* карандаш

pendant *n* подвеска

pendulum *n* маятник

penetrate *v* проникать

penguin *n* пингвин

penicillin *n* пенициллин

peninsula *n* полуостров

penniless *adj* безденежный

penny *n* пенни

pension *n* пенсия

pentagon *n* пятиугольник

pent-up *adj* сдерживаемый

people *n* люди

pepper *n* перец

per *pre* по, из расчета на

perceive *v* воспринимать

percent *adv* одна сотая часть

perception *n* восприятие

perennial *adj* многолетний

perfect *adj* совершенный

perfection *n* совершенство

perforate *v* перфорировать

perforation *n* перфорация

perform *v* исполнять

performance *n* выполнение

perfume *n* духи

perhaps *adv* возможно

peril *n* опасность

perilous *adj* опасный

perimeter *n* периметр

period *n* срок

perish *v* погибать

perishable *adj* тленный

perjury *n* лежать (клятва)

permanent *adj* постоянный

permeate *v* проникать

permission *n* разрешение

permit *v* разрешать

perpetrate *v* совершать

persecute *v* преследовать

persist *v* настаивать

persistence *n* настойчивость

persistent *adj* настойчивый

person *n* человек

personal *adj* личный

personality *n* личность

personnel *n* персонал

perspective *n* перспектива

perspiration *n* потение

perspire *v* потеть

persuade *v* убеждать
persuasion *n* убеждение
persuasive *adj* убедительный
pertain *v* принадлежать
pertinent *adj* уместный
perturb *v* возмущать
pervert *v* извращать
pervert *adj* извращенный
pessimism *n* пессимизм
pest *n* вредитель
pester *v* надоедать
pesticide *n* пестицид
petal *n* лепесток
petite *adj* маленькая
petition *n* петиция
petrified *adj* ископаемый
petroleum *n* нефть
pettiness *n* мелочность
petty *adj* маловажный
pew *n* церковная скамья
phantom *n* призрак
pharmacist *n* аптекарь
pharmacy *n* аптека
phase *n* фаза
pheasant *n* фазан
phenomenon *n* явление
philosopher *n* философ
philosophy *n* философия
phobia *n* фобия
phone *n* телефон
phoney *adj* поддельный
phosphorus *n* фосфор

photo *n* фотография
photocopy *n* фотокопия
photographer *n* фотограф
phrase *n* фраза
physically *adv* физически
physician *n* врач
physics *n* физика
pianist *n* пианист
piano *n* пианино
pick *v* выбирать
pick up *v* подбирать
pickpocket *n* вор-карманник
pickup *n* погрузка
picture *n* картина
picture *v* изображать
picturesque *adj* живописный
pie *n* пирог
piece *n* часть
piecemeal *adv* по частям
pier *n* дамба
pierce *v* прокалывать
piercing *n* прокол
piety *n* благочестие
pig *n* свинья
pigeon *n* голубь
piggy bank *n* копилка
pile *v* складывать в кучу
pile *n* куча
pile up *v* накапливать
pilfer *v* воровать
pilgrim *n* паломник
pilgrimage *n* паломничество

P

pill *n* таблетка
pillage *v* грабеж
pillar *n* столб
pillow *n* подушка
pillowcase *n* наволочка
pilot *n* пилот
pimple *n* прыщ
pin *n* булавка
pincers *n* клещи
pinch *v* щипать
pinch *n* щипок
pine *n* сосна
pineapple *n* ананас
pink *adj* розовый
pinpoint *v* указать точно
pint *n* пинта
pioneer *n* пионер
pious *adj* набожный
pipe *n* труба
pipeline *n* трубопровод
piracy *n* пиратство
pirate *n* пират
pistol *n* пистолет
pit *n* яма
pitchfork *n* вилы
pitfall *n* ловушка; ошибка
pitiful *adj* плачевный
pity *n* жалость
placard *n* плакат
placate *v* умиротворять
place *n* место
placid *adj* безмятежный

plague *n* эпидемия
plain *n* равнина
plain *adj* ясный
plainly *adv* ясно
plaintiff *n* истец
plan *v* запланировать
plan *n* план
plane *n* плоскость
planet *n* планета
plant *v* сажать
plant *n* растение
plaster *n* пластырь
plastic *n* пластмасса
plate *n* тарелка
plateau *n* плато
platform *n* платформа
platinum *n* платина
platoon *n* взвод
plausible *adj* благовидный
play *v* играть; исполнять
play *n* игра; спектакль
player *n* игрок
playful *adj* игривый
plea *n* тяжба
plead *v* умолять
pleasant *adj* приятный
please *v* угождать
pleasing *adj* приятный
pleasure *n* удовольствие
pleat *n* складка
pleated *adj* складчатый
pledge *n* клятва

plentiful *adj* изобилующий

plenty *n* достаток

pliable *adj* гибкий

pliers *n* щипчики

plot *v* составлять план

plot *n* план; заговор

plow *v* пахать

ploy *n* хитрость

pluck *v* срывать

plug *v* затыкать

plug *n* пробка

plum *n* слива

plumber *n* водопроводчик

plumbing *n* слесарные работы

plummet *v* бросать

plump *adj* пухлый

plunder *v* разорять

plunge *v* нырять; вовлекать

plunge *n* ныряние

plus *pre* плюс

plush *adj* плюш

plutonium *n* плутоний

pneumonia *n* пневмония

pocket *n* карман

poem *n* поэма

poet *n* поэт

poetry *n* поэзия

poignant *adj* едкий

point *n* точка; пункт

point *v* указывать

poise *n* устойчивость

poison *v* отравлять

poison *n* яд

poisoning *n* отравление

poisonous *adj* ядовитый

Poland *n* Польша

polar *adj* полярный

pole *n* столб

police *n* полиция

policeman *n* полицейский

policy *n* политика

Polish *adj* польский

polish *n* блеск

polish *v* начищать

polite *adj* вежливый

politeness *n* вежливость

politician *n* политик

politics *n* политика

poll *n* голосование

pollen *n* пыльца

pollute *v* загрязнять

pollution *n* загрязнение

polygamist *adj* полигамный

polygamy *n* полигамия

pomegranate *n* гранат

pomposity *n* помпезность

pond *n* пруд

ponder *v* обдумывать

pontiff *n* римский папа

pool *n* лужа; бассейн

pool *v* присоединять

poor *n* бедный

poorly *adv* бедно

Pope *n* римский папа

P

poppy *n* мак
popular *adj* популярный
populate *v* населять
population *n* население
porcelain *n* фарфор
porch *n* крыльцо
porcupine *n* дикобраз
pore *n* пора
pork *n* свинина
porous *adj* пористый
port *n* гавань
portable *adj* портативный
portent *n* знамение
porter *n* носильщик
portion *n* порция
portrait *n* портрет
portray *v* изображать
Portugal *n* Португалия
Portuguese *adj* португальский
pose *v* позировать
pose *n* поза
posh *adj* шикарный
position *n* позиция
positive *adj* позитивный
possess *v* владеть
possession *n* владение
possibility *n* вероятность
possible *adj* вероятный
post *n* шест; почта
postage *n* почтовая оплата
postcard *n* открытка
poster *n* плакат

posterity *n* потомство
postman *n* почтальон
postpone *v* откладывать
postponement *n* отсрочка
pot *n* горшок; катрюля
potato *n* картофель
potent *adj* могущественный
potential *adj* потенциальный
pothole *n* выбоина
poultry *n* домашняя птица
pound *v* избивать
pound *n* фунт
pour *v* лить
poverty *n* бедность
powder *n* порошок
power *n* сила
powerful *adj* могучий
powerless *adj* бессильный
practical *adj* практический
practice *n* практика
practise *v* упражняться
practising *adj* практикующий
prairie *n* прерия
praise *v* хвалить
praise *n* хвала
praiseworthy *adj* похвальный
prank *n* проказа
prawn *n* креветка
pray *v* молиться
prayer *n* молитва
preach *v* проповедовать
preacher *n* проповедник

preaching *n* проповедь
preamble *n* преамбула
precarious *adj* ненадежный
precede *v* предшествовать
precedent *n* прецедент
precept *n* принцип
precious *adj* драгоценный
precipice *n* обрыв
precipitate *v* низвергать
precise *adj* точный
precision *n* точность
precursor *n* предтеча
predicament *n* затруднение
predict *v* предсказывать
prediction *n* предсказание
predilection *n* пристрастие
predominate *v* доминировать
preface *n* предисловие
prefer *v* предпочитать
preference *n* предпочтение
prefix *n* приставка
pregnancy *n* беременность
pregnant *adj* беременная
prehistoric *adj* доисторический
prejudice *n* предубеждение
prelude *n* прелюдия
premature *adj* недоношенный
premier *adj* первый
premise *n* предпосылка
premises *n* недвижимость
preoccupation *n* озабоченность
preoccupy *v* поглощать

preparation *n* подготовка
prepare *v* готовить
preposition *n* предлог
prerequisite *n* предпосылка
prerogative *n* прерогатива
prescribe *v* предписывать
prescription *n* рецепт
presence *n* присутствие
present *adj* присутствующий
present *v* преподносить
presentation *n* презентация
preserve *v* сохранять
presidency *n* президентство
president *n* президент
press *n* пресс; пресса
press *v* нажимать
pressing *adj* тягостный
pressure *v* заставлять
pressure *n* давление
prestige *n* престиж
presume *v* предполагать
presuppose *v* полагать
presupposition *n* допущение
pretend *v* притворяться
pretense *n* притворство
pretension *n* претензия
pretty *adj* прелестный
prevail *v* превалировать
prevent *v* предотвращать
previous *adj* предыдущий
prey *n* добыча
price *n* цена

P

pricey *adj* дорогой
prick *v* проколоть
pride *n* гордость
priest *n* священник
priestess *n* жрица
priesthood *n* священство
primacy *n* превосходство
prime *adj* основной
primitive *adj* примитивный
prince *n* принц
princess *n* принцесса
principal *adj* главный
principle *n* принцип
print *v* печатать
print *n* печать
printer *n* принтер
printing *n* печатание
prior *adj* прежний
priority *n* приоритет
prism *n* призма
prison *n* тюрьма
prisoner *n* заключенный
privacy *n* уединение
private *adj* частный
privilege *n* привилегия
prize *n* приз
probability *n* вероятность
probable *adj* вероятный
probe *v* опробовать
probing *n* зондирование
problem *n* проблема
procedure *n* процедура

proceed *v* продолжать
proceeds *n* выручка
process *v* перерабатывать
process *n* процесс
procession *n* процессия
proclaim *v* провозглашать
proclamation *n* декларация
procrastinate *v* откладывать
procreate *v* порождать
procure *v* добывать
prod *v* протыкать
prodigious *adj* непомерный
prodigy *n* чудо
produce *v* производить
produce *n* продукция
product *n* продукт
production *n* производство
profane *adj* нечестивый
profess *v* признавать
profession *n* профессия
professor *n* профессор
proficiency *n* опытность
proficient *adj* опытный
profile *n* профиль
profit *v* приносить выгоду
profit *n* выгода
profitable *adj* выгодный
profound *adj* глубокий
program *n* программа
programmer *n* программист
progress *v* развиваться
progress *n* прогресс

P

prohibit v запрещать
prohibition n запрет
project v проектировать
project n проект
projectile n снаряд
prologue n пролог
prolong v продолжать
promenade n прогулка
prominent adj выдающийся
promise n обещание
promote v продвигать
prompt adj проворный
prone adj склонный
pronoun n местоимение
pronounce v произносить
proof n доказательство
propaganda n пропаганда
propagate v размножать
propel v толкать вперёд
propensity n пристрастие
proper adj подходящий
property n имущество
prophecy n пророчество
prophet n пророк
proportion n пропорция
proposal n предложение
propose v предлагать
proposition n предложение
prose n проза
prosecute v преследовать
prosecutor n прокурор
prospect n шанс

prosper v процветать
prosperity n преуспевание
prosperous adj процветающий
prostrate v поверженный
protect v защищать
protection n защита
protein n белок
protest v протестовать
protest n протест
protocol n протокол
prototype n прототип
protract v продлевать
protracted adj затянувшийся
protrude v высовываться
proud adj гордый
proudly adv гордо
prove v доказывать
proven adj доказанный
proverb n пословица
provide v обеспечивать
providence n провидение
providing that c при условии что
province n провинция
provision n обеспечение
provisional adj временный
provocation n провокация
provoke v провоцировать
prow n нос
prowl v красться
prowler n вор
proximity n близость
prudence n благоразумие

P

prudent *adj* благоразумный
prune *v* подрезать
prune *n* чернослив
prurient *adj* похотливый
pseudonym *n* псевдоним
psychiatrist *n* психиатр
psychiatry *n* психиатрия
psychic *adj* душевный
psychology *n* психология
psychopath *n* психопат
public *adj* общественный
publication *n* публикация
publicity *n* публичность
publicly *adv* публично
publish *v* публиковать
publisher *n* издатель
pudding *n* пудинг
puerile *adj* юношеский
puff *n* дуновение
puffy *adj* порывистый
pull *v* тянуть
pull down *v* сбрасывать
pull out *v* выходить
pulley *n* блок
pulp *n* мякоть
pulpit *n* кафедра
pulsate *v* пульсировать
pulse *n* пульс
pulverize *v* измельчать
pump *v* накачивать
pump *n* насос
pumpkin *n* тыква

punch *n* удар кулаком
punctual *adj* пунктуальный
puncture *n* прокалывание
punish *v* наказывать
punishable *adj* наказуемый
punishment *n* наказание
pupil *n* ученик
puppet *n* кукла
puppy *n* щенок
purchase *v* покупать
purchase *n* покупка
pure *adj* чистый
puree *n* пюре
purgatory *n* чистилище
purge *n* очищение
purge *v* прочищать
purification *n* очистка
purify *v* очищать
purity *n* чистота
purple *adj* сиреневый
purpose *n* цель
purposely *adv* намеренно
purse *n* дамская сумочка
pursue *v* преследовать
pursuit *n* преследование
pus *n* гной
push *v* толкать
pushy *adj* назойливый
put *iv* ставить
put aside *v* откладывать
put away *v* отказаться
put off *v* выключать

race

put out *v* выгонять
put up *v* строить
put up with *v* выносить
putrid *adj* гнилой
puzzle *n* головоломка
pyramid *n* пирамида
python *n* питон

quagmire *n* трясина
quail *n* перепел
quake *v* трястись
quality *n* качество
qualm *n* беспокойство
quandary *n* затруднение
quantity *n* количество
quarrel *v* ссориться
quarrel *n* ссора
quarrelsome *adj* задиристый
quarry *n* каменоломня
quarter *n* четверть
quarterly *adj* квартальный
quarters *n* помещение
quash *v* аннулировать
queen *n* королева
queer *adj* чудной
quell *v* подавлять

quench *v* тушить
quest *n* поиск
question *v* спрашивать
question *n* вопрос
questionable *adj* сомнительный
questionnaire *n* анкета
queue *n* очередь
quick *adj* быстрый
quicken *v* ускорять
quickly *adv* быстро
quicksand *n* зыбучий песок
quiet *adj* тихий
quietness *n* тишина
quilt *n* лоскутное одеяло
quit *iv* оставлять
quite *adv* вполне
quiver *v* трястись
quiz *v* проводить опрос
quotation *n* цитирование
quote *v* цитировать

R

rabbi *n* раввин
rabbit *n* кролик
rabies *n* бешенство
raccoon *n* енот
race *n* раса

racism *n* расизм
racist *adj* расистский
racket *n* ракетка; грохот
radar *n* радиолокатор
radiation *n* радиация
radiator *n* радиатор
radical *adj* радикальный
radio *n* радио
radish *n* редиска
radius *n* радиус
raffle *n* лотерея
raft *n* плот
rag *n* тряпка
rage *n* ярость
ragged *adj* зазубренный
raid *n* налёт; облава
raid *v* вторгаться
raider *n* налётчик
rail *n* перила; рейка
railroad *n* железная дорога
rain *n* дождь
rain *v* падать дождем
rainbow *n* радуга
raincoat *n* плащ
rainfall *n* ливень
rainy *adj* дождливый
raise *n* поднятие
raise *v* поднимать
raisin *n* изюм
rake *n* грабли
rally *n* сплочение
ram *n* баран

ram *v* врезаться
ramification *n* разветвление
ramp *n* уклон
rampage *v* неистовствовать
rampant *adj* необузданный
ramson *n* черемша
ranch *n* ранчо
rancor *n* злоба
randomly *adv* беспорядочно
range *n* ряд
rank *n* ряд; ранг
rank *v* располагать в ряд
ransack *v* обыскивать
rape *v* изнасиловать
rape *n* изнасилование
rapid *adj* скорый
rapist *n* насильник
rare *adj* редкий
rarely *adv* редко
rascal *n* жулик
rash *v* спешить
rash *n* поспешность
raspberry *n* малина
rat *n* крыса
rate *n* норма; ставка
rather *adv* скорее
ratification *n* ратификация
ratify *v* ратифицировать
ratio *n* пропорция
ration *v* нормировать
ration *n* рацион
rational *adj* разумный

R

rattle v грохотать
ravage v уничтожать
ravage n уничтожение
rave v бредить
raven n ворон
ravine n овраг
raw adj сырой
ray n луч
raze v разрушать
razor n бритва
reach v достигать
reach n досягаемость
react v реагировать
reaction n реакция
read iv читать
reader n читатель
readiness n готовность
reading n чтение
ready adj готовый
real adj реальный
realism n реализм
reality n реальность
realize v реализовывать
really adv действительно
realm n царство
realty n недвижимость
reap v пожинать
rear v выращивать
rear n задняя часть
rear adj задний
reason v обосновывать
reason n причина

reasonable adj благоразумный
reasoning n рассуждение
reassure v заверять
rebate n скидка
rebel v бунтовать
rebel n мятежник
rebellion n сопротивление
rebirth n возрождение
rebound v отскакивать
rebuff v противостоять
rebuff n отпор
rebuke v упрекать
rebuke n упрёк
rebut v опровергать
recall v помнить
recant v отрекаться
recap v резюмировать
recede v отступать
receipt n получение
receive v получить
recent adj недавний
reception n получение
receptionist n регистратор
recess n перерыв
recession n снижение
recharge v перезаряжать
recipe n рецепт
reciprocal adj взаимный
recital n концерт
recite v рассказывать
reckless adj необдуманный
reckon v подсчитывать

R

reckon on v рассчитывать
reclaim v перевоспитывать
recline v прислонять
recluse n затворник
recognition n узнавание
recognize v узнавать
recollect v вспоминать
recollection n воспоминание
recompense v возмещать
recompense n возмещение
reconcile v примирить
reconstruct v перестраивать
record v записывать
record n запись; рекорд
recorder n магнитофон
recording n регистрация
recount n пересчет
recovery n возврат
recreate v воссоздавать
recreation n отдых
recruit v вербовать
recruit n призывник
recruitment n вербовка
rectangle n прямоугольник
rectify v исправлять
rector n ректор
rectum n прямая кишка
recuperate v поправляться
recur v возвращаться
recurrence n повторение
red adj красный
red tape n бюрократизм

redden v краснеть
redeem v выкупать
redemption n выкуп
redo v переделывать
redouble v удваивать
redress v исправлять
reduce v сокращать
redundant adj чрезмерный
reed n тростник
reef n риф
reel n бобина; вращение
reelect v переизбирать
reentry n повторный вход
refer to v ссылаться на
referee n арбитр
reference n справка
referendum n референдум
refill v наполнять снова
refinance v рефинансировать
refine v рафинировать
reflect v отражать
reflection n отражение
reflexive adj рефлексивный
reform v реформировать
reform n реформа
refrain v воздерживаться
refresh v освежать
refreshing adj освежающий
refreshment n отдых
refrigerate v хранить в холоде
refuel v дозаправиться
refuge n убежище

refugee *n* беженец
refund *v* возмещать
refund *n* возмещение
refurbish *v* обновлять
refusal *n* отказ
refuse *v* отказывать
refuse *n* отходы
refute *v* опровергать
regain *v* восстанавливать
regal *adj* королевский
regard *v* расценивать
regarding *pre* относительно
regardless *adv* безотносительно
regards *n* приветствие
regeneration *n* возрождение
regent *n* регент
regime *n* режим
regiment *n* полк
region *n* регион
regional *adj* региональный
register *v* регистрировать
registration *n* регистрация
regret *v* сожалеть
regret *n* сожаление
regularity *n* закономерность
regularly *adv* регулярно
regulate *v* регулировать
regulation *n* регулирование
rehearsal *n* репетиция
rehearse *v* репетировать
reign *v* царствовать
reign *n* царствование

reimburse *v* возмещать
rein *v* удерживать
rein *n* поводья
reindeer *n* северный олень
reinforce *v* усиливать
reinforcements *n* усиление
reiterate *v* повторять
reject *v* отвергать
rejection *n* отказ
rejoin *v* воссоединяться
relapse *n* рецидив
related *adj* связанный
relative *adj* относительный
relative *n* родственник
relax *v* расслаблять
relay *v* сменять
release *v* освобождать
relegate *v* низводить
relent *v* уступать
relentless *adj* безжалостный
relevant *adj* уместный
reliable *adj* надёжный
reliance *n* уверенность
relic *n* реликвия
relief *n* облегчение
relieve *v* облегчать
religion *n* религия
religious *adj* религиозный
relinquish *v* отступать
relish *v* наслаждаться
relive *v* возродиться
relocate *v* перемещать

relocation *n* перемещение
reluctant *adj* неохотный
reluctantly *adv* неохотно
rely on *v* надеяться
remain *v* оставаться
remainder *n* остаток
remaining *adj* остающийся
remains *n* остатки
remake *v* переделывать
remark *v* делать замечание
remark *n* замечание
remarkable *adj* замечательный
remedy *v* излечивать
remedy *n* лекарство
remember *v* помнить
remembrance *n* воспоминание
remind *v* напоминать
reminder *n* напоминание
remission *n* отпущение грехов
remit *v* прощать
remnant *n* остаток
remodel *v* реконструировать
remote *adj* отдаленный
removal *n* перемещение
remove *v* передвигать
remunerate *v* вознаграждать
renew *v* обновлять
renewal *n* обновление
renounce *v* отказываться
renovate *v* реставрировать
renovation *n* реконструкция
renowned *adj* прославленный

rent *v* арендовать
rent *n* аренда
repair *v* ремонтировать
reparation *n* репарация
repatriate *v* репатриировать
repay *v* отплачивать
repayment *n* оплата
repeal *v* аннулировать
repeal *n* аннулирование
repeat *v* повторять
repel *v* отбрасывать
repent *v* каяться
repentance *n* покаяние
repetition *n* повторение
replace *v* заменять
replacement *n* замена
replay *n* воспроизведение
replenish *v* пополняться
replete *adj* наполненный
replica *n* реплика
replicate *v* воспроизводить
reply *v* отвечать
reply *n* ответ
report *v* отчитываться
report *n* отчет
reportedly *adv* по сообщениям
reporter *n* докладчик
repose *v* полагаться
repose *n* передышка
represent *v* представлять
repress *v* подавлять
repression *n* подавление

reprint v переиздавать
reprint n переиздание
reprisal n репрессалия
reproach v укорять
reproach n укор
reproduce v порождать
reproduction n размножение
reptile n рептилия
republic n республика
repudiate v отрекаться
repugnant adj отвратительный
repulse v отбивать
repulse n отражение
repulsive adj противный
reputation n репутация
request v просить
request n просьба
require v требовать
requirement n требование
rescue v спасать
rescue n спасение
research v исследовать
research n исследование
resemblance n сходство
resemble v походить
resent v негодовать
resentment n негодование
reservation n резервирование
reserve v запасать
reservoir n резервуар
reside v проживать
residence n местожительство

residue n осадок
resign v уступать
resilient adj пружинистый
resist v сопротивляться
resistance n сопротивление
resolution n резолюция
resolve v разрешить
resort v прибегать к
resounding adj гулкий
resource n ресурс
respect v уважать
respect n уважение
respiration n дыхание
respite n передышка
respond v отвечать
response n ответ
responsible adj ответственный
responsive adj отзывчивый
rest v отдыхать
rest n отдых
rest room n комната отдыха
restaurant n ресторан
restful adj спокойный
restitution n возврат
restless adj беспокойный
restoration n восстановление
restore v восстанавливать
restrain v сдерживать
restraint n сдержанность
restrict v ограничивать
result n результат
resume v возобновлять

R

resumption *n* возобновление
resuscitate *v* воскрешать
retain *v* удерживать
retaliate *v* отплачивать
retaliation *n* возмездие
retarded *adj* замедленный
retention *n* удерживание
retire *v* отступать
retirement *n* отступление
retract *v* втягивать
retreat *v* отходить
retreat *n* отступление
retrieval *n* возвращение
retrieve *v* отыскать
return *v* возвращаться
return *n* возвращение
reunion *n* воссоединение
reveal *v* обнаруживать
revealing *adj* разоблачающий
revel *v* пировать
revelation *n* откровение
revenge *v* отомстить
revenge *n* месть
revenue *n* выручка
reverence *n* почтение
reverse *n* обратная сторона
reversible *adj* обратимый
revert *v* возвращаться
review *n* рецензия
revise *v* рецензировать
revision *n* ревизия
revive *v* оживать

revoke *v* отменять
revolt *v* восставать
revolt *n* бунт
revolting *adj* отвратительный
revolve *v* вращаться
revolver *v* револьвер
revue *n* обозрение
revulsion *n* отвращение
reward *v* награждать
reward *n* награда
rewarding *adj* стоящий
rheumatism *n* ревматизм
rhinoceros *n* носорог
rhyme *n* рифма
rhythm *n* ритм
rib *n* ребро
ribbon *n* лента
rice *n* рис
rich *adj* богатый
rid of *iv* избавляться
riddle *n* загадка
ride *iv* ехать верхом
ridge *n* гребень горы
ridicule *v* высмеивать
ridicule *n* насмешка
ridiculous *adj* нелепый
rifle *n* винтовка
rift *n* трещина
right *adv* правильно
right *adj* правильный
right *n* право
rigid *adj* жесткий

R

rigor *n* строгость
rim *n* обод; оправа
ring *iv* звонить
ring *n* кольцо; звон
ringleader *n* зачинщик
rinse *v* полоскать
riot *v* бунтовать
riot *n* бунт
rip *v* рваться
rip apart *v* разбивать
rip off *v* вымогать
ripe *adj* зрелый
ripen *v* зреть
ripple *n* зыбь
rise *iv* вставать
risk *v* рисковать
risk *n* риск
risky *adj* рискованный
rite *n* обряд
rival *n* конкурент
rivalry *n* конкуренция
river *n* река
rivet *v* приковывать
riveting *adj* захватывающий
road *n* дорога
roam *v* бродить
roar *v* реветь
roar *n* рев
roast *v* жарить в печи
roast *n* жаркое
rob *v* грабить
robber *n* грабитель

robbery *n* грабеж
robe *n* халат
robust *adj* крепкий
rock *n* камень
rocket *n* ракета
rocky *adj* каменистый
rod *n* ветка
rodent *n* грызун
roll *v* катить
romance *n* романс
roof *n* крыша
room *n* комната; место
roomy *adj* просторный
rooster *n* петух
root *n* корень
rope *n* веревка
rosary *n* розарий
rose *n* роза
rosy *adj* розовый
rot *v* гнить
rot *n* гниение
rotate *v* вращаться
rotation *n* вращение
rotten *adj* гнилой
rough *adj* грубый
round *adj* круглый
roundup *n* сводка новостей
rouse *v* пробуждать
rousing *adj* воодушевляющий
route *n* маршрут
routine *n* обычный порядок
row *v* располагать в ряд

R

row *n* ряд
rowdy *adj* буйный
royal *adj* королевский
rub *v* тереть
rubber *n* резина
rubbish *n* мусор
rubble *n* булыжник
ruby *n* рубин
rudder *n* руль
rude *adj* невежливый
rudeness *n* грубость
rudimentary *adj* элементарный
rug *n* ковёр
ruin *v* разрушать
ruin *n* крах
rule *v* править
rule *n* правило
ruler *n* правитель; линейка
rum *n* ром
rumble *v* громыхать
rumble *n* грохот
rumor *n* молва
run *iv* бежать
run away *v* избегать
run into *v* сталкиваться
run out *v* кончаться
run over *v* сбить
run up *v* увеличиваться
runner *n* бегун; лезвие
rupture *n* разрыв
rupture *v* разрывать
rural *adj* сельский

R

ruse *n* приём
rush *v* мчаться
Russia *n* Россия
Russian *adj* русский
rust *v* ржаветь
rust *n* ржавчина
rustic *adj* деревенский
rust-proof *adj* нержавеющий
rusty *adj* ржавый
ruthless *adj* безжалостный
rye *n* рожь

S

sabotage *v* саботировать
sabotage *n* саботаж
sack *v* класть в мешок
sack *n* мешок; ограбление
sacrament *n* таинство
sacred *adj* священный
sacrifice *n* жертва
sacrilege *n* кощунство
sad *adj* грустный
sadden *v* печалить
saddle *n* седло
sadist *n* садист
sadness *n* печаль
safety *n* безопасность

sail *v* плавать
sail *n* парус
sailboat *n* парусник
sailor *n* матрос
saint *n* святой
salad *n* салат
salary *n* зарплата
sale *n* продажа
sale slip *n* товарный чек
salesman *n* продавец
saliva *n* слюна
salmon *n* лосось
saloon *n* салун
salt *n* соль
salty *adj* соленый
salvage *v* спасать
salvation *n* спасение
same *adj* тот же самый
sample *n* образец
sanctify *v* освящать
sanction *v* санкционировать
sanction *n* санкция
sanctity *n* святость
sanctuary *n* святилище
sand *n* песок
sandal *n* сандалия
sandpaper *n* наждачная бумага
sandwich *n* бутерброд
sane *adj* здравый
sanity *n* здравомыслие
sap *n* жизненные соки
sap *v* иссушать

saphire *n* сапфир
sarcasm *n* сарказм
sarcastic *adj* саркастический
sardine *n* сардина
satanic *adj* сатанинский
satellite *n* спутник
satire *n* сатира
satisfy *v* удовлетворять
saturate *v* пропитывать
Saturday *n* суббота
sauce *n* соус
saucepan *n* кастрюля
saucer *n* блюдце
sausage *n* колбаса
savage *adj* дикий
savagery *n* дикость
save *v* спасать; копить
savings *n* сбережения
savior *n* спаситель
savor *v* наслаждаться
saw *iv* пилить
saw *n* пила
say *iv* говорить
saying *n* высказывание
scald *v* обжигать
scale *v* взвешивать
scale *n* чаша весов
scalp *n* скальп
scam *n* афера
scan *v* просматривать
scandal *n* скандал
scandalize *v* шокировать

S

scapegoat *n* козёл отпущения
scar *n* шрам
scarce *adj* недостаточный
scarcely *adv* едва
scarcity *n* недостаток
scare *v* напугать
scare *n* испуг
scare away *v* отпугивать
scarf *n* шарф
scary *adj* страшный
scatter *v* рассеивать
scenario *n* сценарий
scene *n* обстановка; сцена
scenery *n* декорации сцены
scenic *adj* сценический
scent *n* аромат
sceptic *adj* скептический
schedule *v* планировать
schedule *n* расписание
scheme *n* схема; интрига
schism *n* схизма
scholar *n* учёный
scholarship *n* учёность
school *n* школа
science *n* наука
scientific *adj* научный
scientist *n* учёный
scissors *n* ножницы
scoff *v* насмехаться
scold *v* бранить
scolding *n* выговор
scooter *n* детский самокат

scope *n* пределы
scorch *v* обжигать
score *n* счет
scorn *v* презирать
scornful *adj* презрительный
scorpion *n* скорпион
scoundrel *n* негодяй
scour *v* отчищать
scourge *n* плеть
scout *n* разведчик
scramble *v* пробираться
scrap *n* клочок
scrap *v* списывать
scrape *v* скоблить
scratch *v* царапать
scratch *n* царапина
scream *v* визжать
scream *n* визг
screech *v* визжать
screen *n* экран; прикрытие
screen *v* ставить экран
screw *v* привинчивать
screw *n* шуруп
screwdriver *n* отвертка
scribble *v* черкнуть
script *n* сценарий
scroll *n* свиток
scrub *v* скрести
scruples *n* сомнения
scrupulous *adj* скрупулёзный
scuffle *n* драка
sculptor *n* скульптор**

S

sculpture n скульптура
sea n море
seafood n морепродукты
seagull n чайка
seal v запечатывать
seal n печать; тюлень
seal off v запаивать наглухо
seam n шов
seamless adj бесшовный
seamstress n швея
search v искать
search n поиск
seashore n морской берег
seaside adj морской курорт
season n время года
seasonal adj сезонный
seasoning n приправа
seat n сиденье
secede v отделяться
secluded adj уединенный
seclusion n уединение
second n секунда
secrecy n секретность
secret n секрет
secretary n секретарь
secretly adv скрытно
sect n секта
section n секция
sector n сектор
secure v охранять
secure adj безопасный
security n безопасность

seduce v соблазнять
seduction n обольщение
see iv видеть
seed n семя
seedless adj бессемянный
seek iv искать
seem v казаться
see-through adj прозрачный
segment n часть
segregate v отделять
segregation n отделение
seize v схватить
seizure n захват
seldom adv редко
select v выбирать
selection n выбор
self-concious adj застенчивый
self-esteem n самооценка
self-interest n своекорыстие
selfish adj эгоистичный
selfishness n эгоизм
self-respect n самоуважение
sell iv продавать
seller n продавец
sellout n распродажа
semblance n подобие
semester n семестр
seminary n семинария
senate n сенат
senator n сенатор
send iv посылать
sender n отправитель

S

senile *adj* страческий
senior *adj* старший
seniority *n* старшинство
sensation *n* ощущение
sense *v* ощущать
sense *n* чувство; сознание
sensible *adj* благоразумный
sensitive *adj* чувствительный
sensual *adj* чувственный
sentence *v* приговаривать
sentence *n* приговор
sentry *n* караул
separate *v* отделять
separate *adj* отдельный
separation *n* отделение
September *n* сентябрь
sequel *n* продолжение
serenade *n* серенада
serene *adj* ясный
serenity *n* ясность
sergeant *n* сержант
series *n* ряд
serious *adj* серьезный
seriousness *n* серьёзность
sermon *n* проповедь
serpent *n* змей
serum *n* сыворотка
servant *n* слуга
serve *v* служить
service *n* служба
service *v* обслуживать
session *n* сессия

set *n* набор
set *iv* класть
set about *v* начинать
set off *v* отправляться
set out *v* выставлять
set up *up* устанавливать
setback *n* отступление
setting *n* окружение
settle *v* урегулировать
settle down *v* угомониться
settlement *n* поселение
settler *n* поселенец
setup *n* осанка
seven *adj* семь
seventeen *adj* семнадцать
seventh *adj* седьмой
seventy *adj* семьдесят
sever *v* разлучать
several *adj* некоторые
severance *n* разрыв
severe *adj* строгий
severity *n* строгость
sew *v* шить
sewage *n* сточные воды
sewer *n* швея
sewing *n* шитьё
sex *n* пол; секс
sexuality *n* сексуальность
shabby *adj* поношенный
shack *n* лачуга
shackle *n* кандалы
shade *n* тень; оттенок

S

shadow *n* тень
shady *adj* затененный
shake *iv* трясти
shaken *adj* потрясенный
shaky *adj* трясущийся
shallow *adj* мелкий
sham *n* притворство
shambles *n* разруха
shame *v* стыдить
shame *n* стыд
shameful *adj* постыдный
shameless *adj* бесстыдный
shape *v* придавать форму
shape *n* форма
share *v* делить
share *n* доля; акция
shareholder *n* акционер
shark *n* акула
sharp *adj* острый; резкий
sharpen *v* заострять
sharpener *n* точилка
shatter *v* раздробить
shave *v* брить
she *pro* она
shear *iv* стричь
shed *iv* проливать
sheep *n* овца
sheets *n* простыни
shelf *n* полка
shell *n* раковина
shellfish *n* моллюск
shelter *v* приютить

shelter *n* приют
shelves *n* полки
shepherd *n* пастух
sherry *n* херес
shield *v* заслонять
shield *n* щит
shift *n* сдвиг; смена
shift *v* перемещать
shine *iv* светить
shiny *adj* блестящий
ship *n* корабль
shipment *n* груз
shipyard *n* верфь
shirk *v* красться
shirt *n* рубашка
shiver *v* трепетать
shiver *n* трепет
shock *v* поражать
shock *n* потрясение; удар
shocking *adj* потрясающий
shoddy *adj* поддельный
shoe *n* туфля, ботинок
shoot *iv* стрелять
shoot down *v* сбить
shop *v* делать покупки
shop *n* магазин
shopping *n* покупка товаров
shore *n* берег
short *adj* короткий
shortage *n* нехватка
shortcoming *n* отсутствие
shorten *v* укорачивать

S

shorthand *n* стенография
shortly *adv* коротко
shorts *n* шорты
shortsighted *adj* близорукий
shot *n* выстрел; росток
shotgun *n* дробовик
shoulder *n* плечо
shout *v* кричать
shout *n* крик
shouting *n* крики
shove *v* толкать
shove *n* толчок
shovel *n* лопата
show *iv* показывать
show off *v* красоваться
show up *v* обнаруживаться
shower *n* душ; ливень
shrapnel *n* шрапнель
shred *v* шинковать
shred *n* клочок
shriek *v* орать
shriek *n* визг
shrimp *n* креветка
shrine *n* склеп
shrink *iv* сокращать
shroud *n* саван
shrouded *adj* скрытый
shrub *n* куст
shrug *v* пожимать
shudder *n* дрожь
shudder *v* вздрагивать
shuffle *v* перемешивать

shun *v* беречься
shut *iv* закрывать
shut off *v* выключать
shut up *v* замолчать
shy *adj* застенчивый
shyness *n* застенчивость
sick *adj* больной
sicken *v* заболевать
sickening *adj* тошнотворный
sickle *n* серп
sickness *n* болезнь
side *n* сторона
sideburns *n* бакенбарды
sidewalk *n* тротуар
sideways *adv* в сторону
siege *n* осада
siege *v* осаждать
sift *v* просеивать
sigh *n* вздох
sigh *v* вздыхать
sight *n* зрение
sign *v* подписывать
sign *n* знак
signal *n* сигнал
signature *n* подпись
significance *n* значение
significant *adj* значительный
signify *v* значить
silence *n* тишина
silent *adj* безмолвный
silhouette *n* силуэт
silk *n* шелк

S

silly *adj* глупый

silver *n* серебро

similar *adj* подобный

similarity *n* сходство

simple *adj* простой

simplicity *n* простота

simplify *v* упрощать

simply *adv* просто

simulate *v* притворяться

sin *v* грешить

sin *n* грех

since *c* так как

since *pre* с тех пор

since then *adv* с того времени

sincere *adj* искренний

sincerity *n* искренность

sinful *adj* греховный

sing *iv* петь

singer *n* певец

single *n* неженатый

single *adj* единичный

singular *adj* исключительный

sinister *adj* зловещий

sink *iv* тонуть

sink in *v* оседать

sinner *n* грешник

sip *v* прихлёбывать

sip *n* маленький глоток

sir *n* сэр

siren *n* сирена

sirloin *n* филей

sister *n* сестра

sister-in-law *n* невестка, золовка

sit *iv* сидеть

site *n* место

sitting *n* заседание

situated *adj* расположенный

situation *n* ситуация

six *adj* шесть

sixteen *adj* шестнадцать

sixth *adj* шестой

sixty *adj* шестьдесят

sizable *adj* существенный

size *n* размер

size up *v* оценивать

skate *n* конек

skeleton *n* скелет

skeptic *adj* скептический

sketch *v* делать набросок

sketch *n* набросок

sketchy *adj* схематичный

ski *v* ходить на лыжах

skill *n* умение

skillful *adj* искусный

skim *v* снимать

skin *v* покрывать

skin *n* кожа

skinny *adj* худой

skip *v* скакать

skip *n* скачок

skirmish *n* перестрелка

skirt *n* юбка

skull *n* череп

sky *n* небо

S

skyscraper *n* небоскреб
slab *n* плита
slack *adj* вялый
slacken *v* ослаблять
slacks *n* слаксы
slam *v* захлопывать
slander *n* злословие
slanted *adj* наклонный
slap *n* шлепок
slap *v* шлёпать
slash *n* порез
slash *v* резать
slate *n* сланец
slaughter *v* забивать
slaughter *n* убой
slave *n* раб
slavery *n* рабство
slay *iv* убивать
sleazy *adj* непрочный
sleep *iv* спать
sleep *n* сон
sleeve *n* рукав
sleeveless *adj* без рукавов
sleigh *n* санки
slender *adj* стройный
slice *v* нарезать
slice *n* ломтик
slide *iv* скользить
slightly *adv* немного
slim *adj* стройный
slip *v* скользить
slip *n* скольжение

slipper *n* тапочки
slippery *adj* скользкий
slit *iv* разрезать
slob *n* неряха
slogan *n* лозунг
slope *n* наклон
sloppy *adj* мокрый
slot *n* щель
slow *adj* медленный
slow down *v* замедлять
slowly *adv* медленно
sluggish *adj* вялый
slum *n* трущобы
slump *v* проваливаться
slur *v* позорить
sly *adj* коварный
smack *n* вкус
smack *v* чмокать
small *adj* маленький
small print *n* мелкий шрифт
smallpox *n* оспа
smart *adj* умный
smash *v* крушить
smear *n* мазок
smear *v* размазывать
smell *iv* пахнуть
smelly *adj* вонючий
smile *v* улыбаться
smile *n* улыбка
smith *n* кузнец
smoke *v* дымиться; курить
smoked *adj* дымчатый

S

smoker n курильщик
smoking gun n явная улика
smooth v разглаживать
smooth adj гладкий
smoothly adv гладко
smoothness n гладкость
smother v душить
smuggler n контрабандист
snail n улитка
snake n змея
snapshot n снимок
snare v поймать в ловушку
snare n ловушка
snatch v хватать
sneak v подкрадываться
sneeze v чихать
sneeze n чиханье
sniff v нюхать
sniper n снайпер
snitch v доносить
snooze v дремать
snore v храпеть
snore n храп
snow v идет снег
snow n снег
snowfall n снегопад
snowflake n снежинка
snub v унижать
snub n пренебрежение
soak v замачивать
soak in v впитываться
soak up v промокать

soar v парить
sob v рыдать
sob n рыдание
sober adj трезвый
sociable adj контактный
socialism n социализм
socialize v общаться
society n общество
sock n носок
sod n дёрн
soda n сода
sofa n диван
soft adj мягкий
soften v смягчать
softly adv мягко
softness n мягкость
soggy adj сырой
soil v пачкать
soil n почва
soiled adj запачканный
solace n утешение
solar adj солнечный
solder v запаивать
soldier n солдат
sold-out adj распроданный
sole n подошва
sole adj единственный
solely adv единственно
solemn adj священный
solicit v упрашивать
solid adj твёрдый
solidarity n солидарность

S

solitary *adj* одиночный
solitude *n* одиночество
soluble *adj* растворимый
solution *n* раствор
solve *v* решать
solvent *adj* растворяющий
somber *adj* мрачный
some *adj* некоторый
somebody *pro* кто-нибудь
someday *adv* когда-нибудь
somehow *adv* как-нибудь
someone *pro* кто-нибудь
something *pro* что-нибудь
sometimes *adv* иногда
someway *adv* как-нибудь
somewhat *adv* кое-что
son *n* сын
song *n* песня
son-in-law *n* зять
soon *adv* вскоре
soothe *v* успокаивать
sorcerer *n* колдун
sorcery *n* колдовство
sore *n* рана
sore *adj* болезненный
sorrow *n* скорбь
sorrowful *adj* скорбный
sorry *adj* сожалеющий
sort *n* сорт
sort out *v* решать
soul *n* душа
sound *n* звук

sound *v* звучать
sound out *v* выведывать
soup *n* суп
sour *adj* кислый
source *n* источник
south *n* юг
southeast *n* юго-восток
southern *adj* южный
southerner *n* южанин
southwest *n* юго-запад
souvenir *n* сувенир
sovereign *adj* верховный
sovereignty *n* суверенитет
soviet *adj* советский
sow *iv* сеять
space *n* пространство
space out *v* растягивать
spacious *adj* обширный
spade *n* лопата
Spain *n* Испания
span *v* отмерять
span *n* интервал; пядь
Spaniard *n* испанец
Spanish *adj* испанский
spank *v* шлепать
spanking *n* порка
spare *v* беречь; уделять
spare *adj* запасной
spare part *n* запчасть
sparingly *adv* скупо
spark *n* искра
spark off *v* вызывать

S

spark plug *n* свеча зажигания
sparkle *v* искриться
sparrow *n* воробей
sparse *adj* редкий
spasm *n* спазм
speak *iv* говорить
speaker *n* оратор; динамик
spear *n* копье
spearhead *v* наконечник
special *adj* особенный
specialty *n* специализация
species *n* вид
specific *adj* специфический
specimen *n* образец
speck *n* крапинка
spectacle *n* зрелище
spectator *n* наблюдатель
speculate *v* обдумывать
speculation *n* спекуляция
speech *n* речь
speechless *adj* немой
speed *iv* мчаться
speed *n* скорость
speedily *adv* стремительно
speedy *adj* стремительный
spell *n* заклинание
spelling *n* правописание
spend *iv* тратить
spending *n* расходы
sperm *n* сперма
sphere *n* сфера
spice *n* специя

spicy *adj* острый
spider *n* паук
spiderweb *n* паутина
spill *iv* проливать
spill *n* пролитая жидкость
spin *iv* прясть; крутиться
spine *n* позвоночник
spinster *n* прядильщица
spirit *n* дух
spiritual *adj* духовный
spit *iv* плевать
spite *n* злость
spiteful *adj* злобный
splash *v* брызгать
splendid *adj* роскошный
splendor *n* сверкание
splint *n* шина
splinter *n* лучина
splinter *v* раскалывать
split *n* трещина; раскол
split *iv* раскалывать
split up *v* разделяться
spoil *v* портить
spoils *n* останки
sponge *n* губка
sponsor *n* спонсор
spontaneity *n* спонтанность
spontaneous *adj* спонтанный
spooky *adj* зловещий
spool *n* шпулька
spoon *n* ложка
spoonful *n* полная ложка

S

sporadic *adj* спорадический

sport *n* спорт

sportman *n* спортсмен

sporty *adj* спортивный

spot *v* пятнать

spot *n* пятно; прыщик

spotless *adj* чистый

spouse *n* супруг

sprain *v* вывихнуть

sprawl *v* растянуться

spray *v* брызгать

spread *iv* расстилать

spring *iv* скакать

spring *n* весна; пружина

springboard *n* трамплин

sprinkle *v* брызгать

sprout *v* расти

spruce up *v* чистить

spur *v* пришпоривать

spur *n* шпора; стимул

spy *v* шпионить

spy *n* шпион

squalid *adj* запущенный

squander *v* расточать

square *adj* квадратный

square *n* квадрат; клетка

squash *v* раздавливать

squeak *v* пищать

squeaky *adj* писклявый

squeeze *v* сжимать

squid *n* кальмар

squirrel *n* белка

stab *v* колоть

stab *n* удар ножом

stability *n* стабильность

stable *adj* устойчивый

stable *n* конюшня

stack *n* стопка

staff *n* кадры

stage *n* сцена; стадия

stage *v* инсценировать

stagger *v* шататься

stagnant *adj* застойный

stagnate *v* застаиваться

stagnation *n* застой

stain *v* окрашивать

stain *n* пятно

stair *n* ступенька

staircase *n* лестница

stairs *n* ступени

stake *n* кол; столб; ставка

stake *v* укреплять стойкой

stale *adj* черствый

stalemate *n* пат

stalk *v* выслеживать

stalk *n* цветоножка

stall *n* стойло

stall *v* стопориться

stammer *v* заикаться

stamp *v* штамповать

stamp *n* штамп

stamp out *v* затаптывать

stampede *n* паническое бегство

stand *iv* стоять

S

stand *n* подставка
stand for *v* поддерживать
stand out *v* выделяться
stand up *v* защищать
standard *n* стандарт
standing *n* положение
standpoint *n* позиция
standstill *adj* бездействующий
staple *n* скоба
star *n* звезда
starch *n* крахмал
starchy *adj* крахмальный
stare *v* уставиться
stark *adj* неистовый
start *v* начинать
start *n* начало
startle *v* испугать
startled *adj* испуганный
starvation *n* голодание
starve *v* голодать
state *n* состояние; штат
state *v* заявлять
statement *n* заявление
station *n* станция
stationary *adj* стационарный
statistic *n* статистика
statue *n* статуя
status *n* статус
statute *n* закон
staunch *adj* стойкий
stay *v* останавливаться
stay *n* пребывание

steady *adj* устойчивый
steak *n* кусок мяса
steal *iv* воровать
stealthy *adj* незаметный
steam *n* пар
steel *n* сталь
steep *adj* крутой
stem *n* ствол
stem *v* происходить
stench *n* вонь
step *n* шаг; след
step down *v* понижать
step out *v* выходить
step up *v* усиливать
stepbrother *n* сводный брат
step-by-step *adv* постепенно
stepdaughter *n* падчерица
stepfather *n* отчим
stepladder *n* стремянка
stepmother *n* мачеха
stepsister *n* сводная сестра
stepson *n* пасынок
sterile *adj* бесплодный
sterilize *v* стерилизовать
stern *n* корма
stern *adj* суровый
sternly *adv* сурово
stewardess *n* стюардесса
stick *n* втыкать
stick *iv* приклеивать
stick out *v* высовываться
sticker *n* наклейка

S

sticky *adj* липкий

stiff *adj* жесткий

stiffness *n* жесткость

stifle *v* душить

stifling *adj* душный

still *adj* неподвижный

still *adv* по-прежнему

stimulant *n* стимулятор

stimulate *v* стимулировать

stimulus *n* стимул

sting *iv* жалить

sting *n* жало; укус

stinging *adj* жгучий

stingy *adj* скупой

stink *iv* вонять

stink *n* вонь

stinking *adj* зловонный

stipulate *v* обусловливать

stir *v* размешивать

stir up *v* побуждать

stitch *v* пришивать

stitch *n* стежок

stock *v* снабжать

stock *n* запас; акции

stocking *n* накопление

stockpile *n* резерв

stockroom *n* кладовая

stoic *adj* стоический

stomach *n* желудок, живот

stone *n* камень

stone *v* бросать камни

stool *n* табурет

stop *v* останавливаться

stop *n* остановка

stop by *v* заглянуть

storage *n* хранение

store *v* хранить

store *n* магазин

stork *n* аист

storm *n* шторм

stormy *adj* штормовой

story *n* рассказ; история

stove *n* печь

straight *adj* прямой

straighten out *v* исправить

strain *v* натягивать

strain *n* натяжение

strained *adj* растянутый

strainer *n* сито

strait *n* пролив

stranded *adj* скрученный

strange *adj* странный

stranger *n* незнакомец

strangle *v* задушить

strap *n* ремень

strategy *n* стратегия

straw *n* солома

strawberry *n* клубника

stray *adj* заблудившийся

stray *v* заблудиться

stream *n* ручей; течение

street *n* улица

streetcar *n* трамвай

streetlight *n* уличный фонарь

S

strength n сила
strengthen v укрепляться
strenuous adj энергичный
stress n напряжение
stressful adj стрессовый
stretch n растяжение
stretch v растягиваться
stretcher n носилки
strict adj строгий
stride iv шагать
strife n борьба
strike n удар
strike iv ударяться
strike out v исключать
strike up v заиграть
striking n поразительный
string n веревка; ряд
stringent adj обязательный
strip n полоса
strip v раздевать
stripe n полоса
striped adj полосатый
strive iv пытаться
stroke n удар
stroll v прогуливаться
strong adj сильный
structure n структура
struggle v бороться
struggle n борьба
stub n пень; окурок
stubborn adj упрямый
student n студент

study v изучать
stuff n материал
stuff v набивать
stuffing n начинка
stuffy adj душный
stumble v спотыкаться
stun v оглушить ударом
stunning adj оглушающий
stupendous adj громадный
stupid adj глупый
stupidity n глупость
sturdy adj прочный
stutter v заикаться
style n стиль
subdue v подчинять
subdued adj подчиненный
subject v подчинять
subject n предмет; субъект
sublime adj величайший
submerge v окунать
submissive adj покорный
submit v подчиняться
subpoena v вызывать в суд
subscribe v подписываться
subscription n подписка
subsequent adj последующий
subsidize v субсидировать
subsidy n субсидия
subsist v прокормить
substance n вещество
substantial adj существенный
substitute v заменять

S

substitute *n* заместитель
subtitle *n* подзаголовок
subtle *adj* неуловимый
subtract *v* вычитать
subtraction *n* вычитание
suburb *n* пригород
subway *n* тоннель, метро
succeed *v* сменять
success *n* успех
successful *adj* удачный
successor *n* преемник
succulent *adj* сочный
succumb *v* поддаваться
such *adj* такой
suck *v* сосать
sucker *adj* сосун
sudden *adj* внезапный
suddenly *adv* вдруг
suffer *v* страдать
suffer from *v* страдать от
suffering *n* страдание
sufficient *adj* достаточный
suffocate *v* задыхаться
sugar *n* сахар
suggest *v* предлагать
suggestion *n* предложение
suggestive *adj* намекающий
suicide *n* самоубийство
suit *n* костюм
suitable *adj* подходящий
suitcase *n* чемодан
sullen *adj* мрачный

sulphur *n* сера
sum *n* сумма
sum up *v* обобщать
summarize *v* подводить итог
summary *n* резюме
summer *n* лето
summit *n* вершина
summon *v* вызвать
sumptuous *adj* роскошный
sun *n* солнце
sunburn *n* загар
Sunday *n* воскресенье
sundown *n* закат
sunken *adj* затонувший
sunny *adj* солнечный
sunrise *n* восход
sunset *n* закат
superb *adj* великолепный
superfluous *adj* избыточный
superior *adj* высший
superiority *n* старшинство
supermarket *n* супермаркет
superpower *n* сверхдержава
supersede *v* вытеснять
superstition *n* суеверие
supervise *v* заведовать
supervision *n* заведование
supper *n* ужин
supple *adj* эластичный
supplier *n* поставщик
supplies *n* запасы
supply *v* поставлять

S

support v поддерживать
supporter n приверженец
suppose v полагать
supposing c если бы
supposition n предположение
suppress v пресекать
supremacy n верховенство
supreme adj верховный
sure adj уверенный
surely adv конечно
surface n поверхность
surge n большая волна
surgeon n хирург
surgical adv хирургический
surname n фамилия
surpass v превосходить
surplus n избыток
surprise v удивлять
surprise n удивление
surrender v сдаваться
surrender n капитуляция
surround v окружать
surroundings n окрестности
surveillance n надзор
survey n опрос
survival n выживание
survive v выдержать
susceptible adj восприимчивый
suspect v подозревать
suspend v подвешивать
suspenders n подтяжки
suspense n неизвестность

suspension n приостановка
suspicion n подозрение
sustain v поддерживать
sustenance n поддержка
swallow v глотать
swamp n болото
swamped adj заболоченный
swan n лебедь
swap v обменивать
swap n обмен
swarm n рой, толпа
sway v качать
swear iv клясться
sweat n пот
sweat v потеть
sweater n свитер
Sweden n Швеция
Sweedish adj шведский
sweep iv подметать
sweet adj сладкий
sweeten v подслащивать
sweetness n сладость
sweets n сласти
swell iv опухать
swelling n опухоль
swift adj быстрый
swim iv плавать
swimmer n пловец
swimming n плавание
swindle v обманывать
swindle n надувательство
swindler n жулик

swing *iv* качать
swing *n* колебание
Swiss *adj* швейцарский
switch *v* переключать
switch *n* выключатель
switch off *v* выключать
switch on *v* включать
Switzerland *n* Швейцария
swivel *v* поворачиваться
swollen *adj* опухший
sword *n* меч
swordfish *n* меч-рыба
syllable *n* слог
symbol *n* символ
symbolic *adj* символический
symmetry *n* симметрия
sympathize *v* сочувствовать
sympathy *n* сочувствие
symphony *n* симфония
symptom *n* симптом
synagogue *n* синагога
synod *n* синод
synonym *n* синоним
synthesis *n* синтез
syphilis *n* сифилис
syringe *n* спринцовка
syrup *n* сироп
system *n* система

table *n* стол; таблица
tablecloth *n* скатерть
tablet *n* табличка
tack *n* кнопка
tackle *v* энергично браться
tact *n* такт
tactful *adj* тактичный
tactical *adj* тактический
tactics *n* тактика
tag *n* ярлык
tail *n* хвост
tail *v* идти следом
tailor *n* портной
tainted *adj* испорченный
take *iv* брать
take apart *v* разбирать
take away *v* убирать
take back *v* возвращать
take in *v* принимать
take off *v* снимать
take out *v* вынимать
take over *v* перенимать
tale *n* сказка
talent *n* талант
talk *v* говорить
talkative *adj* разговорчивый
tall *adj* высокий
tame *v* приручать
tangent *n* касательная

tangerine *n* мандарин

tangible *adj* вещественный

tangle *n* путаница

tank *n* бак

tanned *adj* смуглый

tantamount to *adj* равносильный

tantrum *n* приступ гнева

tap *n* пробка

tap into *v* подключиться к

tape *n* лента

tape recorder *n* магнитофон

tapestry *n* гобелен

tar *n* смола

tarantula *n* тарантул

tardy *adv* медлительный

target *n* мишень

tariff *n* тариф

tarnish *v* тускнеть

tart *n* пирог

tartar *n* зубной камень

task *n* задача

taste *v* пробовать на вкус

taste *n* вкус

tasteful *adj* вкусный

tasteless *adj* безвкусный

tasty *adj* вкусный

tavern *n* таверна

tax *n* налог

tea *n* чай

teach *iv* учить

teacher *n* учитель

team *n* команда

teapot *n* чайник

tear *iv* рвать; мучить

tear *n* слеза

tearful *adj* плачущий

tease *v* дразнить

teaspoon *n* чайная ложка

technical *adj* технический

technician *n* техник

technique *n* техника

technology *n* технология

tedious *adj* нудный

tedium *n* скука

teenager *n* подросток

teeth *n* зубы

telegram *n* телеграмма

telepathy *n* телепатия

telephone *n* телефон

telescope *n* телескоп

television *n* телевидение

tell *iv* рассказывать

teller *n* рассказчик

temper *n* нрав

temperature *n* температура

tempest *n* буря

temple *n* храм

temporary *adj* временный

tempt *v* искушать

temptation *n* искушение

tempting *adj* заманчивый

ten *adj* десять

tenacity *n* цепкость

tenant *n* владелец

tendency *n* тенденция

tenderness *n* нежность

tennis *n* теннис

tenor *n* направление

tense *adj* напряженный

tension *n* напряжение

tent *n* палатка

tentacle *n* щупальце

tenth *n* десятая часть

tenuous *adj* тонкий

tepid *adj* тепловатый

term *n* срок

terminate *v* прекращать

terminology *n* терминология

termite *n* термит

terms *n* условия

terrace *n* терраса

terrain *n* местность

terrestrial *adj* земной

terrible *adj* ужасный

terrific *adj* ужасающий

terrify *v* ужасать

terrifying *adj* ужасающий

territory *n* территория

terror *n* террор

terrorism *n* терроризм

terrorist *n* террорист

terrorize *v* терроризировать

terse *adj* сжатый

test *v* проверять

test *n* проверка

testament *n* свидетельство

text *n* текст

textbook *n* учебник

texture *n* текстура

thank *v* благодарить

thankful *adj* благодарный

thanks *n* благодарность

that *adj* тот

thaw *v* таять

thaw *n* оттепель

theater *n* театр

theft *n* воровство

theme *n* тема

themselves *pro* себя

then *adv* тогда

theologian *n* богослов

theology *n* богословие

theory *n* теория

therapy *n* терапия

there *adv* там, туда

therefore *adv* поэтому

thermometer *n* термометр

thermostat *n* термостат

these *adj* эти

thesis *n* тезис

they *pro* они

thick *adj* толстый; густой

thicken *v* утолщать, сгущать

thickness *n* толщина

thief *n* вор

thigh *n* бедро

thin *adj* тонкий; худой

thing *n* вещь

think *iv* думать

thinly *adv* тонко

third *adj* третий

thirst *v* жаждать

thirsty *adj* жаждущий

thirteen *adj* тринадцать

thirty *adj* тридцать

this *adj* этот

thorn *n* колючка

thorny *adj* колючий

thorough *adj* тщательный

those *adj* те

though *c* хотя

thought *n* мысль

thoughtful *adj* задумчивый

thousand *adj* тысяча

thread *v* продевать нитку

thread *n* нить

threat *n* угроза

threaten *v* угрожать

three *adj* три

thresh *v* хлестать

threshold *n* порог

thrifty *adj* бережливый

thrill *n* возбуждение

thrive *v* преуспевать

throat *n* горло

throb *n* биение

throb *v* пульсировать

thrombosis *n* тромбоз

throne *n* трон

throng *n* толпа

through *pre* через

throw *iv* бросать

throw away *v* отбрасывать

throw up *v* упустить

thug *n* убийца

thunder *n* гром

thunderbolt *n* удар молнии

thunderstorm *n* гроза

Thursday *n* четверг

thus *adv* так

thwart *v* расстраивать

tickle *v* щекотать

tickle *n* щекотка

ticklish *adj* щекотливый

tide *n* прилив и отлив

tidy *adj* опрятный

tie *v* завязывать

tie *n* лента; галстук

tiger *n* тигр

tight *adj* тугой

tighten *v* затягивать

tile *n* черепица

till *v* пахать

tilt *v* наклонять

timber *n* лесоматериалы

time *n* время

time *v* назначать время

times *n* времена

timetable *n* расписание

timid *adj* робкий

timidity *n* робость

tin *n* олово

T

tiny *adj* крошечный

tip *n* кончик; наклон

tired *adj* усталый

tiredness *n* усталость

tireless *adj* неутомимый

tiresome *adj* утомительный

tissue *n* ткань

title *n* название

to *pre* к, в

toad *n* жаба

toast *v* поджаривать

toast *n* тост

toaster *n* тостер

tobacco *n* табак

today *adv* сегодня

toe *n* палец ноги

together *adv* вместе

toilet *n* туалет

token *n* жетон

tolerable *adj* терпимый

tolerance *n* терпимость

tolerate *v* выносить

toll *n* пошлина; потери

toll *v* звонить в колокол

tomato *n* помидор

tomb *n* гробница

tombstone *n* надгробие

tomorrow *adv* завтра

ton *n* тонна

tone *n* тон

tongs *n* щипцы

tongue *n* язык

tonight *adv* сегодня вечером

too *adv* тоже

tool *n* инструмент

tooth *n* зуб

toothache *n* зубная боль

toothpick *n* зубочистка

top *n* верхушка

topic *n* тема

topple *v* валиться

torch *n* фонарь

torment *v* мучить

torment *n* мучение

torrent *n* поток

torrid *adj* знойный

torso *n* торс

tortoise *n* черепаха

torture *v* пытать

torture *n* пытка

toss *v* подбрасывать

total *adj* общий

totalitarian *adj* тоталитарный

totality *n* полнота

touch *n* прикосновение

touch *v* прикасаться

touch on *v* затрагивать

touch up *v* подправлять

touching *adj* трогательный

tough *adj* жёсткий

toughen *v* ужесточать

tour *n* путешествие

tourism *n* туризм

tourist *n* турист

tournament *n* соревнование
tow *v* буксировать
tow truck *n* тягач
towards *pre* к
towel *n* полотенце
tower *n* башня
town *n* город
toxic *adj* токсический
toxin *n* токсин
toy *n* игрушка
trace *v* прослеживать
track *n* след
track *v* следить
traction *n* тяга
tractor *n* трактор
trade *n* торговля
trade *v* торговать
trademark *n* торговая марка
trader *n* торговец
tradition *n* традиция
traffic *v* торговать
tragedy *n* трагедия
tragic *adj* трагический
trail *v* протаптывать
trail *n* тропинка
trailer *n* автоприцеп
train *n* поезд
train *v* обучать
trainee *n* ученик, стажер
trainer *n* инструктор
training *n* обучение
trait *n* особенность

traitor *n* изменник
trajectory *n* траектория
tram *n* трамвай
trample *v* топтать
trance *n* транс
tranquility *n* спокойствие
transaction *n* сделка
transcend *v* превышать
transcribe *v* переписывать
transfer *v* передавать
transfer *n* передача
transfusion *n* переливание
transit *n* проезд
transition *n* перемещение
translate *v* переводить
translator *n* переводчик
transmit *v* передавать
transparent *adj* прозрачный
transplant *v* пересаживать
transport *v* перевозить
trap *n* капкан
trash *n* хлам
trash can *n* мусорное ведро
traumatic *adj* травматический
traumatize *v* травмировать
travel *v* путешествовать
traveler *n* путешественник
tray *n* поднос
treacherous *adj* вероломный
treachery *n* вероломство
tread *iv* ступать
treason *n* измена

treasure *n* сокровище
treasurer *n* казначей
treat *v* обращаться
treat *n* угощение
treatment *n* обращение
treaty *n* договор
tree *n* дерево
tremble *v* дрожать
tremendous *adj* громадный
tremor *n* дрожь
trench *n* ров
trend *n* курс
trespass *v* посягать
trial *n* испытание
triangle *n* треугольник
tribe *n* племя
tribulation *n* бедствие
tribunal *n* трибунал
tribute *n* дань
trick *v* обманывать
trick *n* обман; фокус
tricky *adj* хитрый
trigger *v* спускать курок
trim *v* подрезать
trimester *n* триместр
trip *n* поездка; промах
trip *v* споткнуться
triple *adj* тройной
tripod *n* тренога
triumph *n* триумф
triumphant *adj* победоносный
trivial *adj* тривиальный

trolley *n* тележка
troop *n* отряд
trophy *n* трофей
tropic *n* тропик
tropical *adj* тропический
trouble *n* беспокойство
trouble *v* беспокоить
troublesome *adj* беспокойный
trousers *n* брюки
trout *n* форель
truce *n* перемирие
truck *n* грузовик
trucker *n* дальнобойщик
trumpet *n* труба
trunk *n* ствол; туловище
trust *v* доверять
trust *n* доверие
truth *n* истина
truthful *adj* истинный
try *v* пытаться
tub *n* бочка
tuberculosis *n* туберкулёз
Tuesday *n* вторник
tuition *n* обучение
tulip *n* тюльпан
tumble *v* спотыкаться
tummy *n* животик
tumor *n* опухоль
tumult *n* суматоха
tumultuous *adj* шумный
tuna *n* тунец
tune *n* мелодия

tune *v* настраивать
tunic *n* туника
tunnel *n* тоннель
turbine *n* турбина
turf *n* дёрн
Turk *n* турок
Turkey *n* Турция
turmoil *n* шумный
turn *n* поворот
turn *v* поворачивать
turn back *v* возвращать
turn down *v* отвергать
turn in *v* сдавать
turn off *v* выключать
turn on *v* включать
turn out *v* выворачивать
turn up *v* подшивать
turret *n* башенка
turtle *n* черепаха
tusk *n* клык
tutor *n* репетитор
tweezers *n* пинцет
twelfth *adj* двенадцатый
twelve *adj* двенадцать
twentieth *adj* двадцатый
twenty *adj* двадцать
twice *adv* дважды
twilight *n* сумерки
twin *n* близнец
twinkle *v* мерцать
twist *v* скручивать
twist *n* изгиб; твист

twisted *adj* скрученный
twister *n* обманщик
two *n* два
tycoon *n* магнат
type *n* тип; шрифт
type *v* печатать
typical *adj* типичный
tyranny *n* тирания
tyrant *n* тиран

ugliness *n* уродство
ugly *adj* уродливый
ulcer *n* язва
ultimate *adj* окончательный
ultimatum *n* ультиматум
ultrasound *n* ультразвук
umbrella *n* зонт
unable *adj* неспособный
unanimity *n* единодушие
unarmed *adj* безоружный
unattached *adj* непривязанный
unavoidable *adj* неизбежный
unaware *adj* неведающий
unbearable *adj* невыносимый
unbeatable *adj* непобедимый
unbelievable *adj* невероятный

unbroken *adj* неразбитый
unbutton *v* расстёгивать
uncle *n* дядя
uncomfortable *adj* неудобный
uncommon *adj* необычный
uncover *v* снимать
undecided *adj* нерешённый
undeniable *adj* неоспоримый
under *pre* под
undercover *adj* секретный
underdog *n* неудачник
undergo *v* испытывать
underground *adj* подземный
underlie *v* лежать в основе
underline *v* подчёркивать
undermine *v* подрывать
underneath *pre* ниже
understand *v* понимать
understandable *adj* понятный
understanding *adj* понимающий
undertake *v* предпринимать
underwear *n* нижнее бельё
underwrite *v* подписывать
undisputed *adj* неоспоримый
undo *v* открывать
undoubtedly *adv* несомненно
undress *v* раздевать
undue *adj* непомерный
unearth *v* выкапывать
uneasiness *n* неудобство
uneasy *adj* неловкий
unemployed *adj* безработный

unemployment *n* безработица
unending *adj* бесконечный
unequal *adj* неравный
uneven *adj* неровный
unexpected *adj* неожиданный
unfailing *adj* неизменный
unfairly *adv* несправедливо
unfaithful *adj* неверный
unfamiliar *adj* незнакомый
unfasten *v* отстёгивать
unfit *adj* негодный
unfold *v* развертывать
unfriendly *adj* недружелюбный
ungrateful *adj* неблагодарный
unhappiness *n* несчастье
unhappy *adj* несчастливый
unharmed *adj* невредимый
unhealthy *adj* нездоровый
unheard-of *adj* неслыханный
unification *n* унификация
uniformity *n* единообразие
unify *v* объединять
unilateral *adj* односторонний
union *n* союз
unique *adj* уникальный
unit *n* единица
unite *v* объединять
unity *n* единство
universal *adj* универсальный
universe *n* вселенная
university *n* университет
unjustified *adj* неоправданный

unknown *adj* неизвестный
unlawful *adj* незаконный
unleaded *adj* неэтилированный
unleash *v* спускать с привязи
unless *c* если не
unlike *adj* непохожий
unlikely *adj* вряд ли
unload *v* разгружать
unlock *v* отпирать
unlucky *adj* неудачный
unmarried *adj* неженатый
unmask *v* разоблачать
unnecessary *adj* ненужный
unnoticed *adj* незамеченный
unoccupied *adj* незанятый
unpack *v* распаковывать
unpleasant *adj* неприятный
unplug *v* отключить
unpopular *adj* непопулярный
unprofitable *adj* невыгодный
unprotected *adj* незащищённый
unravel *v* распутывать
unreal *adj* ненастоящий
unrealistic *adj* нереалистичный
unreasonable *adj* неразумный
unrelated *adj* неродственный
unreliable *adj* ненадёжный
unrest *n* тревога
unsafe *adj* ненадёжный
unselfish *adj* бескорыстный
unstable *adj* нестабильный
unsteady *adj* неустойчивый

unsuccessful *adj* безуспешный
unsuitable *adj* неподходящий
unthinkable *adj* невероятный
untie *v* отвязывать
until *pre* пока
untrue *adj* неверный
unusual *adj* необыкновенный
unwillingly *adv* неохотно
unwind *v* разматывать
unwise *adj* неразумный
unwrap *v* разворачивать
upbringing *n* воспитание
upcoming *adj* предстоящий
upgrade *v* улучшать
upheaval *n* подъём
uphill *adv* идущий вверх
uphold *v* поддерживать
upholstery *n* обивка
upkeep *n* содержание
upon *pre* на, по
upper *adj* верхний
upright *adj* прямой
uprising *n* восстание
uproar *n* гул
uproot *v* выкорчевывать
upset *v* опрокидывать
upside-down *adv* вверх дном
upstairs *adv* наверх
uptight *adj* встревоженный
up-to-date *adj* современный
upturn *n* подъём
upwards *adv* вверх

urban *adj* городской
urge *n* порыв
urge *v* подгонять
urgency *n* срочность
urgent *adj* срочный
urinate *v* мочиться
urine *n* моча
urn *n* урна
us *pre* нас, нам
usage *n* употребление
use *v* использовать
use *n* использование
used to *adj* привыкший
useful *adj* полезный
usefulness *n* пригодность
useless *adj* бесполезный
user *n* потребитель
usher *n* швейцар
usual *adj* обычный
usurp *v* узурпировать
utensil *n* посуда
uterus *n* матка
utilize *v* использовать
utmost *adj* крайний
utter *v* произносить

vacancy *n* вакансия
vacant *adj* свободный
vacate *v* освобождать
vacation *n* каникулы
vaccinate *v* вакцинировать
vaccine *n* вакцина
vacillate *v* колебаться
vagrant *n* бродяга
vain *adj* тщеславный
vainly *adv* тщетно
valiant *adj* храбрый
valid *adj* действительный
validate *v* утверждать
valley *n* долина
valuable *adj* ценный
value *n* ценность
valve *n* клапан
vampire *n* вампир
van *n* фургон
vandal *n* вандал
vandalism *n* вандализм
vandalize *v* разрушать
vanguard *n* авангард
vanish *v* исчезать
vanity *n* суета
vanquish *v* побеждать
vaporize *v* испарять
variable *adj* непостоянный
varied *adj* различный

variety *n* многообразие
various *adj* различный
varnish *v* лакировать
varnish *n* лак
vary *v* менять
vase *n* ваза
vast *adj* обширный
veal *n* телятина
veer *v* поворачивать
vegetable *v* овощ
vegetarian *n* вегетарианец
vegetation *n* растительность
veil *n* вуаль
vein *n* вена
velocity *n* скорость
velvet *n* бархат
venerate *v* благоговеть
vengeance *n* месть
venison *n* оленина
venom *n* яд
vent *n* отдушина
ventilate *v* вентилировать
ventilation *n* вентиляция
venture *v* рисковать
verb *n* глагол
verbally *adv* вербально
verbatim *adv* дословно
verdict *n* вердикт
verge *n* край
verification *n* проверка
verify *v* проверять
versatile *adj* многосторонний

verse *n* стих
versed *adj* опытный
version *n* версия
versus *pre* против
vertebra *n* позвонок
very *adv* очень
vessel *n* сосуд
vest *n* жилет
vestige *n* след
veteran *n* ветеран
veterinarian *n* ветеринар
veto *v* налагать вето
viaduct *n* виадук
vibrant *adj* вибрирующий
vibrate *v* вибрировать
vibration *n* вибрация
vice *n* порок
vicinity *n* близость
vicious *adj* порочный
victim *n* жертва
victimize *v* мучить
victor *n* победитель
victorious *adj* победный
victory *n* победа
view *n* вид
view *v* осматривать
viewpoint *n* точка зрения
vigil *n* дежурство
village *n* деревня
villager *n* сельский житель
villain *n* злодей
vindicate *v* доказывать

vindictive *adj* мстительный
vine *n* виноградная лоза
vinegar *n* уксус
vineyard *n* виноградник
violate *v* нарушать
violence *n* жестокость
violent *adj* неистовый
violet *n* фиалка
violin *n* скрипка
violinist *n* скрипач
viper *n* гадюка
virgin *n* дева
virginity *n* девственность
virile *adj* мужской
virtually *adv* фактически
virtue *n* добродетель
virulent *adj* опасный
virus *n* вирус
visibility *n* видимость
visible *adj* видимый
vision *n* зрение
visit *n* посещение
visit *v* посещать
visitor *n* гость
visual *adj* зрительный
visualize *v* представлять
vital *adj* жизненный
vitality *n* жизнестойкость
vitamin *n* витамин
vivacious *adj* оживлённый
vivid *adj* яркий
vocabulary *n* словарь

vocation *n* призвание свыше
vogue *n* мода
voice *n* голос
void *adj* пустой
volatile *adj* летящий
volcano *n* вулкан
volleyball *n* волейбол
volume *n* объем; громкость
volunteer *n* доброволец
vomit *v* рвать
vomit *n* рвота
vote *v* голосовать
vote *n* голос
voting *n* голосование
vouch for *v* ручаться
voucher *n* ваучер
vow *v* клясться
vowel *n* гласный звук
voyage *n* путешествие
voyager *n* мореплаватель
vulgar *adj* вульгарный
vulgarity *n* вульгарность
vulnerable *adj* уязвимый
vulture *n* гриф

wafer n вафля

wag v качаться

wage n заработная плата

wagon n тележка

wail v выть

wail n вопль

waist n талия

wait v ждать

waiter n официант

waiting n ожидание

waitress n официантка

waive v отказываться

wake up iv будить

walk v идти

walk n ходьба

walkout n забастовка

wall n стена

wallet n бумажник

walnut n грецкий орех

walrus n морж

waltz n вальс

wander v бродить

wanderer n странник

wane v убывать

want v хотеть

war n война

ward n опекунство; район

warden n смотритель

wardrobe n гардероб

warehouse n склад

warfare n война

warm adj теплый

warm up v разогревать

warmth n тепло

warn v предупреждать

warning n предупреждение

warp v деформироваться

warrant v гарантировать

warrant n ордер

warranty n гарантия

warrior n воин

warship n военный корабль

wart n бородавка

wary adj осторожный

wash v мыть

washable adj моющийся

wasp n оса

waste v тратить впустую

waste n трата

wasteful adj расточительный

watch n часы

watch v смотреть

watch out v остерегаться

watchful adj бдительный

watchmaker n часовщик

water n вода

water v поливать

water down v разбавлять

waterfall n водопад

watermelon n арбуз

watershed n водораздел

watery *adj* водный
watt *n* ватт
wave *n* волна; взмах
waver *v* колыхаться
wavy *adj* волнистый
wax *n* воск
way *n* путь; способ
way in *n* вход
we *pro* мы
weak *adj* слабый
weaken *v* слабеть
weakness *n* слабость
wealth *n* богатство
wealthy *adj* богатый
weapon *n* орудие
wear *n* ношение; одежда
wear *iv* носить; изнашивать
wear down *v* сломить
wear out *v* изнашиваться
weary *adj* усталый
weather *n* погода
weave *iv* ткать
web *n* паутина; сеть
wed *iv* жениться
wedding *n* свадьба
wedge *n* клин
Wednesday *n* среда
weed *n* сорняк
weed *v* полоть
week *n* неделя
weekday *n* будний день
weekend *n* выходные дни

weekly *adv* еженедельно
weep *iv* плакать
weigh *v* взвешивать
weight *n* вес
weird *adj* странный
welcome *v* приветствовать
welcome *n* приветствие
weld *v* сваривать
welder *n* сварщик
welfare *n* благоденствие
well *n* добро; колодец
well-known *adj* общеизвестный
well-to-do *adj* обеспеченный
west *n* запад
western *adj* западный
westerner *adj* житель запада
wet *adj* мокрый
whale *n* кит
wharf *n* пристань
what *adj* что, какой
whatever *adj* любой
wheat *n* пшеница
wheel *n* колесо
wheelbarrow *n* тачка
wheeze *v* сопеть
when *adv* когда
whenever *adv* в любое время
where *adv* где, куда
whereas *c* тогда как
whereupon *c* вследствие чего
wherever *c* где бы ни
whether *c* ли

W

which *adj* который

while *c* пока

whim *n* прихоть

whine *v* жаловаться

whip *v* сечь; взбивать

whip *n* кнут

whirl *v* вертеть

whirlpool *n* вихрь

whiskers *n* усы

whisper *v* шептать

whisper *n* шепот

whistle *v* свистеть

whistle *n* свист

white *adj* белый

whiten *v* белить

whittle *v* строгать

who *pro* кто

whoever *pro* кто бы ни

whole *adj* целый

wholehearted *adj* искренний

wholesale *n* оптовая торговля

wholesome *adj* благотворный

whom *pro* кого, кому

why *adv* почему

wicked *adj* злой

wickedness *n* порочность

wide *adj* широкий

widely *adv* широко

widen *v* расширять

widow *n* вдова

widower *n* вдовец

width *n* ширина

wield *v* орудовать

wife *n* жена

wig *n* парик

wiggle *v* покачивать

wild *adj* дикий

wild boar *n* кабан

wilderness *n* пустыня

wildlife *n* живая природа

will *n* воля; завещание

willfully *adv* намеренно

willing *adj* готовый

willingly *adv* охотно

willingness *n* готовность

willow *n* ива

wily *adj* лукавый

win *iv* победить

win back *v* отыграть

wind *n* ветер

wind *iv* чуять; наматывать

wind up *v* заводить

winding *adj* извилистый

window *n* окно

windy *adj* ветреный

wine *n* вино

winery *n* винный завод

wing *n* крыло

wink *n* подмигивание

wink *v* подмигивать

winner *n* победитель

winter *n* зима

wipe *v* вытирать

wipe out *v* смывать

wire *n* проволока

wireless *adj* беспроводный

wisdom *n* мудрость

wise *adj* мудрый

wish *v* желать

wish *n* желание

wit *n* разум

witch *n* колдунья

witchcraft *n* колдовство

with *pre* с

withdraw *v* отодвигать

withdrawal *n* изъятие

withdrawn *adj* замкнутый

wither *v* вянуть

withhold *iv* воздерживаться

within *pre* внутри

without *pre* без

withstand *v* устоять

witness *n* свидетель

witty *adj* остроумный

wives *n* жены

wizard *n* колдун, мастер

wobble *v* пошатываться

woes *n* несчастья

wolf *n* волк

woman *n* женщина

womb *n* матка

women *n* женщины

wonder *v* удивляться

wonder *n* удивление

wonderful *adj* удивительный

wood *n* древесина, лес

wooden *adj* деревянный

wool *n* шерсть

woolen *adj* шерстяной

word *n* слово

wording *n* формулировка

work *n* работа

work *v* работать

work out *v* решать

workbook *n* учебное пособие

worker *n* рабочий

workshop *n* мастерская

world *n* мир

worldly *adj* мирской

worldwide *adj* всемирный

worm *n* червь

worn-out *adj* изношенный

worrisome *adj* беспокойный

worry *v* беспокоить

worry *n* беспокойство

worse *adj* худший

worsen *v* ухудшаться

worship *n* поклонение

worst *adj* наихудший

worth *adj* стоящий

worthless *adj* бесполезный

worthwhile *adj* полезный

worthy *adj* достойный

wound *n* рана

wound *v* ранить

woven *adj* плетеный

wrap *v* заворачивать

wrap up *v* завершать

wrapping *n* обёртка
wrath *n* гнев
wreath *n* венок
wreck *v* крушить
wreckage *n* крах
wrench *n* вывих
wrestle *v* бороться
wrestler *n* борец
wrestling *n* борьба
wretched *adj* несчастный
wring *iv* крутить
wrinkle *v* морщиться
wrinkle *n* морщина
wrist *n* запястье
write *iv* писать
write down *v* записывать
writer *n* писатель
writhe *v* скручивать
writing *n* написание
written *adj* написанный
wrong *adj* неправильный

X-mas *n* Рождество
X-ray *n* рентгеновские лучи

yacht *n* яхта
yam *n* ямс
yard *n* ярд
yarn *n* пряжа
yawn *n* зевота
yawn *v* зевать
year *n* год
yearly *adv* годовой
yearn *v* томиться
yeast *n* дрожжи
yell *v* вопить
yellow *adj* желтый
yes *adv* да
yesterday *adv* вчера
yet *c* еще
yield *v* приносить урожай
yield *n* урожай
yoke *n* ярмо
yolk *n* желток
you *pro* вы, ты
young *adj* молодой
youngster *n* юноша
your *adj* ваш, твой
yours *pro* ваш, твой
yourself *pro* себя, себе
youth *n* молодость
youthful *adj* молодой

zap *v* застрелить
zeal *n* рвение
zealous *adj* рьяный
zebra *n* зебра
zero *n* нуль

zest *n* пикантность
zinc *n* цинк
zip code *n* почтовый индекс
zipper *n* застёжка-молния
zone *n* зона
zoo *n* зоопарк
zoology *n* зоология

Z

Russian-English

Abbreviations

a - article - артикль
adj - adjective - имя прилагательное
adv - adverb - наречие
c - conjunction - союз
e - exclamation - междометие
n - noun - имя существительное
pre - preposition - предлог
pro - pronoun - местоимение
v - verb - глагол

а

а именно *adv* namely
абажур *n* lampshade
аббат *n* abbot
аббатство *n* abbey
абзац *n* paragraph
аборт *n* abortion
абрикос *n* apricot
абсолютный *adj* absolute
абстрактный *adj* abstract
абсурд *n* nonsense
абсурдный *adj* absurd
авангард *n* vanguard
авария *n* accident
август *n* August
авиакомпания *n* airline
авиапочта *n* airmail
авиация *n* aviation
автобус *n* bus
автограф *n* autograph
автомашина *n* automobile
автомобиль *n* car
автоприцеп *n* trailer
автор *n* author
автостоянка *n* parking
агент *n* agent
агентство *n* agency
агитатор *n* agitator
агностик *n* agnostic
агрессивный *adj* aggressive

агрессия *n* aggression
агрессор *n* aggressor
ад *n* hell
адаптация *n* adaptation
адаптер *n* adapter
Адвент *n* Advent
адвокат *n* attorney
адекватный *adj* adequate
адмирал *n* admiral
адрес *n* address
азот *n* nitrogen
аист *n* stork
айсберг *n* iceberg
академический *adj* academic
академия *n* academy
аквариум *n* aquarium
акведук *n* aqueduct
аккорд *n* accord
аккордеон *n* accordion
акр *n* acre
акробат *n* acrobat
аксиома *n* axiom
актер *n* actor
актив *n* assets
активация *n* activation
активность *n* activity
активный *adj* active
актрисса *n* actress
акула *n* shark
акустический *adj* acoustic
акушерка *n* midwife
акцент *n* accent

акционер *n* shareholder
акция *n* share
алгебра *n* algebra
алкоголизм *n* alcoholism
алкогольный *adj* alcoholic
аллегория *n* allegory
аллергия *n* allergy
аллея *n* alley
аллигатор *n* alligator
алмаз *n* diamond
алтарь *n* altar
алфавит *n* alphabet
алчность *n* avarice
алчный *adj* avaricious
альманах *n* almanac
альтернатива *n* alternative
альянс *n* alliance
алюминий *n* aluminum
амбар *n* barn
амбразура *n* loophole
американский *adj* American
аммиак *n* ammonia
амнезия *n* amnesia
амнистия *n* amnesty
аморальность *n* immorality
аморальный *adj* immoral
аморфный *adj* amorphous
ампутация *n* amputation
ампутировать *v* amputate
амфитеатр *n* amphitheater
анализ *n* analysis
анализировать *v* analyze

аналой *n* lectern
ананас *n* pineapple
анархист *n* anarchist
анархия *n* anarchy
анатомия *n* anatomy
ангел *n* angel
ангельский *adj* angelic
ангина *n* angina
английский *adj* English
англиканский *adj* Anglican
Англия *n* England
анекдот *n* anecdote
анемичный *adj* anemic
анемия *n* anemia
анестезия *n* anesthesia
анимация *n* animation
анкета *n* questionnaire
анклав *n* enclave
аннулирование *n* annulment
аннулировать *v* annul, nullify
анонимность *n* anonymity
анонимный *adj* anonymous
антенна *n* antenna
антибиотик *n* antibiotic
антидот *n* antidote
антилопа *n* antelope
антипатия *n* antipathy
анчоус *n* anchovy
апатия *n* apathy
апеллировать *v* appeal
апельсин *n* orange
аперитив *n* aperitif

аплодировать *v* applaud
аплодисменты *n* applause
апостол *n* apostle
апостольский *adj* apostolic
апостроф *n* apostrophe
аппеляция *n* appeal
аппендицит *n* appendicitis
аппетит *n* appetite
апрель *n* April
аптека *n* pharmacy
аптекарь *n* pharmacist
арабский *adj* Arabic
арахис *n* peanut
арбитр *n* referee
арбитраж *n* arbitration
арбуз *n* watermelon
аргумент *n* argument
арена *n* arena
арена борьбы *n* cockpit
аренда *n* lease, rent
арендатор *n* lessee
арендовать *v* rent
арендодатель *n* landlord
арест *n* arrest
арестовать *v* seize
арестовывать *v* arrest
аристократ *n* aristocrat
аристократия *n* aristocracy
арифметика *n* arithmetic
арка *n* arch
арктический *adj* arctic
армия *n* army

аромат *n* fragrance
ароматный *adj* aromatic
арсенал *n* arsenal
артерия *n* artery
артикуляция *n* articulation
артиллерия *n* artillery
артистический *adj* artistic
артишок *n* artichoke
артрит *n* arthritis
арфа *n* harp
архаичный *adj* archaic
археология *n* archaeology
архив *n* archive
архиепископ *n* archbishop
архитектор *n* architect
архитектура *n* architecture
аскетический *adj* ascetic
аспект *n* aspect, facet
аспирин *n* aspirin
ассамблея *n* assembly
ассимиляция *n* assimilation
ассортимент *n* assortment
астероид *n* asteroid
астма *n* asthma
астматический *adj* asthmatic
астролог *n* astrologer
астрология *n* astrology
астроном *n* astronomer
астрономия *n* astronomy
асфальт *n* asphalt
атака *n* attack
атаковать *v* assault

атакующий *n* attacker
атеизм *n* atheism
атеист *n* atheist
атлетический *adj* athletic
атмосфера *n* atmosphere
атмосферный *adj* atmospheric
атом *n* atom
атомный *adj* atomic
атрофия *v* atrophy
аудитория *n* auditorium
аукцион *n* auction
аукционист *n* auctioneer
аутопсия *n* autopsy
афера *n* scam
аэродром *n* airfield
аэропорт *n* airport

б

бабочка *n* butterfly
бабуля *n* granny
бабушка *n* grandmother
багаж *n* luggage
багет *n* baguette
база данных *n* database
базар *n* bazaar
базировать *v* base
базис *n* basis

бак *n* tank
бакен *n* beacon
бакенбарды *n* sideburns
бактерия *n* bacteria
балка *n* beam
балкон *n* balcony
балл *n* point
баловать *v* pamper
бальзам *n* balm
бамбук *n* bamboo
бампер *n* bumper
банальность *n* banality
банан *n* banana
бандит *n* mobster
банк *n* bank
банка *n* jar
банкет *n* banquet
банкрот *v* bankrupt
банкротство *n* bankruptcy
бар *n* bar
барабан *n* drum
баран *n* ram
барбекю *n* barbecue
баржа *n* barge
бармен *n* bartender
барменша *n* barmaid
барометр *n* barometer
баррикада *n* barricade
бархат *n* velvet
барьер *n* barrier
баскетбол *n* basketball
басня *n* fable

бассейн *n* pool, basin
бастион *n* bulwark
батальон *n* battalion
батарея *n* battery
бахрома *n* fringe
башенка *n* turret
башня *n* tower
бдительный *adj* watchful
беглец *n* fugitive
бегло *adv* fluently
бегун *n* runner
бедно *adv* poorly
бедность *n* poverty
бедный *n* poor
бедро *n* thigh, hip
бедственный *adj* disastrous
бедствие *n* disaster
бедствия *n* adversity
бежать *v* escape, run
беженец *n* refugee
без *pre* without
без остановок *adv* nonstop
без рукавов *adj* sleeveless
безбожный *adj* godless
безвкусный *adj* insipid
безвредный *adj* harmless
безграничный *adj* boundless
безгрешный *adj* impeccable
бездельник *n* bum
бездельничать *v* goof
безденежный *adj* penniless
бездетный *adj* childless

бездна *n* abyss
бездомный *adj* homeless
бездонный *adj* bottomless
бездыханный *adj* lifeless
безжалостный *adj* ruthless
беззаботный *adj* carefree
беззвучный *adj* dumb
безмерность *n* immensity
безмерный *adj* immense
безмолвный *adj* silent
безнадежный *adj* hopeless
безоблачный *adj* cloudless
безопасность *n* safety
безопасный *adj* secure
безоружный *adj* unarmed
безошибочный *adj* infallible
безработица *n* unemployment
безработный *adj* unemployed
безразличный *adj* indifferent
безумец *n* madman
безумно *adv* madly
безумный *adj* mad
безупречный *adj* flawless
безуспешный *adj* unsuccessful
безучастный *adj* disinterested
безысходный *adj* desperate
бейсбол *n* baseball
бекон *n* bacon
белить *v* whiten
белка *n* squirrel
белок *n* protein
белокурый *adj* blond

Б

белый *adj* white
бельгийский *adj* Belgian
Бельгия *n* Belgium
бенефициарий *n* beneficiary
бензин *n* gasoline
бензопила *n* chainsaw
бепомощный *adj* helpless
берег *n* beach, shore
береговая линия *n* coastline
бережливость *n* frugality
бережливый *adj* frugal, thrifty
беременная *adj* pregnant
беременность *n* pregnancy
берет *n* beret
беречь *v* protect
беречься *v* be careful
берлога *n* den
бесконечный *adj* endless
бескорыстный *adj* unselfish
бесплатный *adj* free of charge
бесплодный *adj* barren
беспокоить *v* worry
беспокойный *adj* worrisome
беспокойство *n* anxiety
беспокоящий *adj* disturbing
беспокоящийся *adj* anxious
бесполезный *adj* useless
беспорядки *n* commotion
беспорядок *n* mess
беспорядочно *adv* randomly
беспорядочный *adj* chaotic
беспрерывный *adv* ceaselessly

беспрестанный *adj* incessant
беспроводный *adj* wireless
беспутный *adj* dissolute
бессвязный *adj* incoherent
бессемянный *adj* seedless
бессилие *n* disability
бессильный *adj* powerless
бесславие *n* dishonor
бессмертие *n* immortality
бессмертный *adj* immortal
бессонница *n* insomnia
бесспорный *adj* indisputable
бесстрашный *adj* intrepid
бесстыдный *adj* shameless
бестактный *adj* brusque
бестолковый *adj* crass
бесхарактерный *adj* wimp
бесцельный *adj* aimless
бесценный *adj* invaluable
бесчеловечный *adj* brutal
бесчестить *v* disgrace
бесчестье *n* disgrace
бесчисленный *adj* countless
бесшовный *adj* seamless
бетон *n* concrete
бетонный *adj* concrete
бешено *adv* furiously
бешенство *n* frenzy; rabies
бешеный *adj* frenzied
библейский *adj* biblical
библиография *n* bibliography
библиотека *n* library

библиотекарь *n* librarian
Библия *n* bible
бигамия *n* bigamy
биение *n* throb
бизнесмен *n* businessman
бизон *n* bison
бильярд *n* billiards
бинокль *n* binoculars
бинт *n* bandage
бинтовать *v* bandage
биография *n* biography
биология *n* biology
бита *n* bat
битый *adj* beaten
бить *v* beat
бить дубинкой *v* bludgeon
бить ключом *v* spring
благовидный *adj* plausible
благоговеть *v* venerate
благодарить *v* thank
благодарность *n* gratitude
благодарный *adj* grateful
благодать *n* grace
благоденствие *n* welfare
благодетель *n* benefactor
благоприятный *adj* favorable
благоразумие *n* prudence
благоразумный *adj* sensible
благородный *adj* noble
благородство *n* nobility
благословение *n* blessing
благословлять *v* bless

благотворный *adj* beneficial
благоухающий *adj* balmy
благочестивый *adj* devout
благочестие *n* piety
блаженный *adj* blissful
блаженство *n* bliss
бледность *n* paleness
бледный *adj* pale
блендер *n* blender
блеск *n* glare
блестеть *v* glitter
блестящий *adj* shiny
близкий *adj* close, intimate
близко *adv* closely
близко от *pre* close to
близлежащий *adj* nearby
близнец *n* twin
близорукий *adj* shortsighted
близость *n* proximity
блок *n* pulley
блокада *n* blockade
блокировать *v* blockade
блокировка *n* blockage
блокнот *n* notepad
блоха *n* flea
блузка *n* blouse
блюдо *n* dish
блюдце *n* saucer
бобина *n* reel
бобр *n* beaver
Бог *n* God
богатство *n* wealth

богатый *adj* rich, wealthy
богиня *n* goddess
богослов *n* theologian
богословие *n* theology
богохульство *n* blasphemy
боеприпасы *n* ammunition
боец *n* combatant
божественность *n* divinity
божественный *adj* divine
божество *n* deity
бой *n* combat, fight
бой быков *n* bull fight
бойкотировать *v* boycott
боковой *adj* lateral
бокс *n* boxing
боксёр *n* boxer
более поздний *adj* later
более того *c* even more
болезненный *adj* painful
болезнь *n* disease
болельщик *n* fan
болото *n* swamp, bog
болтать *v* chat; dangle
болтливый *adj* garrulous
боль *n* ache, pain
боль в ухе *n* earache
больница *n* hospital
больной *adj* sick, ill
большая бочка *n* butt
большая волна *n* surge
больший *adj* more
большинство *n* majority

большой *adj* grand, large
бомба *n* bomb
бомбёжка *n* bombing
бомбить *v* bomb
борец *n* wrestler
борзая *n* greyhound
бормотать *v* mumble
боров *n* hog
борода *n* beard
бородавка *n* wart
бородатый *adj* bearded
борозда *n* furrow
бороться *v* struggle
борьба *n* wrestling
босой *adj* barefoot
босс *n* boss
ботаника *n* botany
ботинки *n* boots
ботинок *n* boot
бочка *n* tub; barrel
бочок *n* flank
бочонок *n* keg
брак *n* marriage; defect
браслет *n* bracelet
брат *n* brother
братия *n* brethren
братский *adj* brotherly
братство *n* brotherhood
брать *v* take
браузер *n* browser
брачный *adj* marital
бревно *n* log

бредить *v* rave
бренд *n* brand
бренди *n* brandy
бригада *n* brigade
бриз *n* breeze
бриллиант *adj* brilliant
Британия *n* Britain
британский *adj* British
бритва *n* razor
брить *v* shave
брифинг *n* briefing
бровь *n* eyebrow
бродить *v* roam, wander
бродяга *n* vagrant
бройлер *n* broiler
бронза *n* bronze
бронхит *n* bronchitis
броня *n* armor
бросать *v* throw
бросать вызов *v* challenge
бросать камни *v* stone
бросаться *v* dash
броский *adj* eye-catching
брошенный *adj* destitute
брошюра *n* pamphlet
брусок *n* bar
брызгать *v* sprinkle
брюки *n* pants
будильник *n* alarm clock
будить *v* wake up
будний день *n* weekday
будоражить *v* arouse

будто бы *adv* allegedly
будущее *n* future
будьте здоровы *n* cheers
буй *n* buoy
буйвол *n* buffalo
буйный *adj* rowdy
буква *n* letter
буквально *adv* literally
буквенный *adj* literal
буксировать *v* tow
булавка *n* pin
булочка *n* bun
булочная *n* bakery
булыжник *n* rubble
бульвар *n* boulevard
бумага *n* paper
бумажник *n* wallet
бункер *n* bunker; bin
бунт *n* revolt, riot
бунтовать *v* rebel, riot
буран *n* blizzard
буржуазный *adj* bourgeois
бурная реакция *n* kickback
буря *n* tempest
бутерброд *n* sandwich
бутылка *n* bottle
буфет *n* cupboard
буханка *n* loaf
бухгалтер *n* bookkeeper
бухгалтерия *n* bookkeeping
бухта *n* bay, creek
бухточка *n* cove

бывший *adj* former

бык *n* bull, ox

быстро *adv* quickly

быстрый *adj* swift, fast

быстрый взгляд *n* glance

быть *v* be

быть должным *v* owe

быть настороже *v* look out

быть принятым *v* go through

бюджет *n* budget

бюллетень *n* bulletin

бюро *n* bureau

бюрократ *n* bureaucrat

бюрократизм *n* red tape

бюрократия *n* bureaucracy

бюст *n* bust

бюстгальтер *n* bra

В

в *pre* in

в интересах *adv* behalf (on)

в конце концов *adv* eventually

в любое время *adv* whenever

в начале *adv* initially

в наши дни *adv* nowadays

в основном *adv* mainly

в сторону *adv* aside, sideways

в течение *pre* during

важность *n* importance

важный *adj* momentous

ваза *n* vase

вакансия *n* vacancy

вакцина *n* vaccine

вакцинировать *v* vaccinate

валиться *v* topple

вальс *n* waltz

валюта *n* currency

вампир *n* vampire

вандал *n* vandal

вандализм *n* vandalism

ванна *n* bath, bathtub

ванная комната *n* bathroom

варвар *n* barbarian

варварский *adj* barbaric

варварство *n* barbarism

варенье *n* conserve

варить *v* brew, cook

ватт *n* watt

вафля *n* wafer

ваш *adj* your

ваш *pro* yours

введение *n* foreword

вверх *adv* upwards

вверх дном *adv* upside-down

вверять *v* entrust

вглядываться *v* gaze

вдалеке *adv* afar

вдали *adv* further

вдова *n* widow

вдовец _n_ widower
вдоль _pre_ along
вдохновение _n_ inspiration
вдохновлять _v_ inspire
вдруг _adv_ suddenly
вдыхать _v_ inhale
вегетарианец _n_ vegetarian
ведро _n_ bucket, pail
вежливость _n_ politeness
вежливый _adj_ polite
век _n_ century
веко _n_ eyelid
великан _n_ giant
великий _adj_ great
Великий пост _n_ Lent
великолепный _adj_ superb
величайший _adj_ sublime
величие _n_ greatness
величина _n_ magnitude
велосипед _n_ bicycle
велосипедист _n_ cyclist
вена _n_ vein
венок _n_ wreath
вентилировать _v_ ventilate
вентиль _n_ faucet
вентилятор _n_ fan
вентиляция _n_ ventilation
вера _n_ faith
вербально _adv_ verbally
верблюд _n_ camel
вербовать _v_ recruit
вербовка _n_ recruitment

вердикт _n_ verdict
веревка _n_ rope, string
верить _v_ believe
верность _n_ faith
вернуться _v_ get back
верный _adj_ faithful
вероломный _adj_ treacherous
вероломство _n_ treachery
вероятно _adv_ likely
вероятность _n_ probability
вероятный _adj_ probable
версия _n_ version
вертеть _v_ whirl
вертикальный _adj_ erect
вертолёт _n_ helicopter
верующий _n_ believer
верфь _n_ shipyard
верхний _adj_ upper
верховенство _n_ supremacy
верховный _adj_ paramount
вершина _n_ summit, apex
вершина холма _n_ hilltop
вес _n_ weight
весёлый _adj_ cheerful
веселье _n_ fun
веселящий _adj_ exhilarating
весло _n_ oar
весна _n_ spring
веснушка _n_ freckle
веснушчатый _adj_ freckled
вести _v_ guide, lead
вестибюль _n_ lobby

B

B

вестник *n* messenger
весы *n* balance, scales
весьма *adv* highly
ветвь *n* branch
ветер *n* wind
ветеран *n* veteran
ветеринар *n* veterinarian
ветка *n* rod
ветреный *adj* gusty, windy
ветряная оспа *n* chicken pox
вечер *n* evening
вечно *adv* ever
вечность *n* eternity
вечный *adj* everlasting
вещественный *adj* tangible
вещество *n* matter
вещь *n* thing
вживлять *v* implant
взаимно *adv* mutually
взаимный *adj* reciprocal
взбешённый *adj* furious
взбивать *v* whip
взбираться *v* climb
взвешивать *v* weigh
взвод *n* platoon
взгляд *n* look
взглянуть *v* glance
вздорить *v* haggle
вздох *n* sigh
вздрагивать *v* shudder
вздыхать *v* sigh
взламывать *v* break open

взломщик *n* burglar
взмах *n* wave
взрослеть *v* grow up
взрослый *n* adult
взрыв *n* explosion
взрывать *v* detonate
взрываться *v* explode
взрывчатый *adj* explosive
взяточничество *n* bribery
виадук *n* viaduct
вибрация *n* vibration
вибрировать *v* vibrate
вибрирующий *adj* vibrant
вид *n* species; view
видеть *v* see
видимость *n* visibility
видимый *adj* visible
видный *adj* conspicuous
видоизменять *v* mutate
визг *n* scream, shriek
визжать *v* scream, screech
вилка *n* fork
вилы *n* pitchfork
вина *n* guilt
винный завод *n* winery
вино *n* wine
виновность *n* culpability
виновный *adj* guilty
виноград *n* grape
виноградник *n* vineyard
винтовка *n* rifle
вирус *n* virus

виселица *n* gallows
високосный год *n* leap year
висячий замок *n* padlock
витамин *n* vitamin
виться *v* curl
вихрь *n* whirlpool
вишня *n* cherry
вклад *n* contribution
включать *v* switch on
включающий *adj* inclusive
вкрадываться *v* insinuate
вкус *n* flavor, taste
вкусный *adj* tasteful, tasty
владелец *n* tenant, owner
владение *n* possession
владеть *v* own, possess
влажность *n* humidity
влажный *adj* damp, humid
вламываться *v* break in
властный *adj* overbearing
власть *n* authority
вливание *n* infusion
влияние *n* influence
влиятельный *adj* influential
вместе *adv* together
вместимость *n* capacity
вместо *adv* instead
вмешиваться *v* intervene
вмятина *v* dent
вне *adv* out
внедрение *n* intrusion
внезапно *adv* abruptly

внезапный *adj* sudden
внешний *adj* external
внешность *n* look
вниз *adv* down
внизу *adv* downstairs
внимание *n* attention
внимательный *adj* attentive
вновь *adv* again
внук *n* grandchild
внутренний *adj* interior, inner
внутри *pre* inside, within
внутри страны *adv* inland
внутривенный *adj* intravenous
внутрь *adv* inwards
внушать *v* indoctrinate
внушительный *adj* imposing
вовлекать *v* involve
вовлечение *n* implication
вовлечённый *v* involved
вода *n* water
водитель *n* driver
водный *adj* watery
водопад *n* waterfall
водопроводчик *n* plumber
водораздел *n* watershed
водород *n* hydrogen
вожделение *n* lust
возбуждающий *adj* exciting
возбуждение *n* excitement
возвеличивать *v* exalt
возвещать *v* herald
возврат *n* recovery

B

возвращать *v* give back
возвращаться *v* go back
возвращение *n* return
возгорание *n* combustion
возделывать *v* cultivate
воздержание *n* abstinence
воздух *n* air
воздушный змей *n* kite
воздушный шар *n* balloon
возлюбленная *n* sweetheart
возлюбленный *adj* beloved
возмездие *n* retaliation
возмещать *v* offset, refund
возмещение *n* recompense
возможно *adv* perhaps
возможность *n* opportunity
возможный *adj* affordable
возмущать *v* exasperate
возникать *v* arise
возобновление *n* resumption
возобновлять *v* resume
возражать *v* dissent
возражение *n* objection
возраст *n* age
возрастание *n* increment
возродиться *v* relive
возрождение *n* rebirth
воин *n* fighter, warrior
воинственный *adj* militant
вой *n* howl
война *n* war, warfare
вокруг *adv* around

вокруг *pro* about
волдырь *n* blister
волейбол *n* volleyball
волк *n* wolf
волна *n* wave
волнистый *adj* wavy
волокно *n* fiber
волосатый *adj* hairy
волосы *n* hair
волшебный *adj* magical
волшебство *n* magic
воля *n* will
вонь *n* stench, stink
вонючий *adj* fetid, smelly
вонять *v* stink
воображать *v* imagine
воображение *n* imagination
воодушевлять *v* hearten
вооружать *v* arm
вооружённый *adj* armed
вопить *v* yell
воплощать *v* embody
вопль *n* crying, wail
вопреки *c* despite
вор *n* prowler, thief
вор-карманник *n* pickpocket
воробей *n* sparrow
воровать *v* pilfer, steal
воровство *n* theft, heist
ворон *n* raven
ворона *n* crow
ворота *n* gate

ворота шлюза *n* floodgate
воротничок *n* collar
ворчать *v* grumble
ворчливый *adj* grouchy
восемнадцать *adj* eighteen
восемь *adj* eight
восемьдесят *adj* eighty
воск *n* wax
восклицать *v* exclaim
воскресенье *n* Sunday
воскрешать *v* resuscitate
воспитание *n* upbringing
воспитанная *adj* ladylike
воспитывать *v* educate
воспламенять *v* ignite
воспоминание *n* recollection
восприимчивый *adj* docile
воспринимать *v* perceive
восприятие *n* perception
воспроизводить *v* replicate
воссоединение *n* reunion
воссоединяться *v* rejoin
воссоздавать *v* recreate
восставать *v* revolt
восстанавливать *v* restore
восстание *n* uprising
восток *n* east
восточный *adj* eastern
восхищать *v* fascinate
восхищаться *v* admire
восхищение *n* admiration
восход *n* sunrise

восходить *v* mount
восьмой *adj* eighth
вошь *n* lice, louse
воюющий *adj* belligerent
впадина *n* cavity
вперед *pre* ahead
вперед *adv* forward
впереди *adv* before
впечатляющий *adj* impressive
впитывать *v* absorb
впитываться *v* soak in
впихивать *v* cram
вполне *adv* quite
впоследствии *adv* afterwards
впрыскивать *v* inject
враг *n* foe, enemy
вражда *n* feud
враждебность *n* hostility
враждебный *adj* adverse
вражеский *adj* hostile
вратарь *n* goalkeeper
врач *n* doctor
вращаться *v* rotate
вращение *n* rotation
вред *n* damage, harm
вредитель *n* pest
вредный *adj* harmful
вредоносность *n* malignancy
врезаться *v* ram
времена *n* times
временный *adj* temporary
время *n* time

B

B

время года *n* season
врождённый *adj* innate
вряд ли *adj* unlikely
все *adj* all
всё *pro* everything
всегда *adv* always
вселенная *n* universe
всемирный *adj* worldwide
всемогущий *adj* almighty
всецело *adv* entirely
вскоре *adv* soon
вслепую *adv* blindly
вслух *adv* aloud
всплывать *v* float
вспоминать *v* recollect
вспыхивать *v* flare-up
вспыхнуть *v* burst into
вспышка *n* outbreak
вставать *v* rise
вставлять *v* insert, install
встретиться *v* encounter
встреча *n* meeting
встречать *v* meet
встроенный *adj* built-in
встряхивать *v* jolt, shake
вступать *v* go in
вступаться *v* intercede
вступление *n* introduction
вторгаться *v* raid, invade
вторичный *adj* derivative
вторник *n* Tuesday
втыкать *v* stick

втягивать *v* retract
вуаль *n* veil
вулкан *n* volcano
вульгарно *adv* vulgar
вульгарность *n* vulgarity
вульгарный *adj* vulgar
вход *n* entrance
входить *v* come in
входить в док *v* dock
входящий *adj* incoming
вчера *adv* yesterday
вчера вечером *adv* last night
вшивый *adj* lousy
вы *pro* you
выбивать *v* knock out
выбирать *v* select, choose
выбоина *n* pothole
выбор *n* choice, option
выборка *n* excerpt
выборы *n* election
выбывать *v* drop out
выведывать *v* get out
вывих *n* wrench
вывихнуть *v* sprain
вывод *n* conclusion
выводить *v* deduce
выворачивать *v* turn out
выглядеть *v* look
выговор *n* scolding
выгода *n* benefit, profit
выгодный *adj* profitable
выгонять *v* oust

выгружать *v* unload
выдавать *v* extradite
выдающийся *adj* prominent
выделение *n* emission
выделяться *v* stand out, exude
выдержать *v* survive, endure
выдерживать *v* hold out
выдра *n* otter
выдуманный *adj* fictitious
выдумка *n* fiction
выживание *n* survival
выжимать *v* squeeze
вызвать *v* summon, call
вызов *n* defiance
вызывающий *adj* defiant
выкапывать *v* unearth
выкидыш *n* miscarriage
выключатель *n* switch
выключать *v* turn off
выковывать *v* forge
выкуп *n* redemption
выкупать *v* redeem
выливание *n* outpouring
вымирать *v* die out
вымогать *v* extort
вынашивать *v* breed
вынимать *v* take out
выносить *v* tolerate
вынуждать *v* necessitate
вынужденный *adj* obliged
выпалить *v* shoot
выпекать *v* bake

выпечка *n* pastry
выпивка *n* booze
выполнение *n* fulfillment
выполнимый *adj* feasible
выполнять *v* fulfill
выпуклость *n* bump
выпускать *v* let go
выравнивание *n* alignment
выравнивать *v* flatten
выражение *n* expression
выращивать *v* bring up
вырезать *v* cut out
вырождаться *v* degenerate
вырождение *n* degeneration
выручка *n* revenue
вырываться *v* break out
высадка *n* drop-off
высаживать *v* disembark
выселять *v* evict
высказывание *n* saying
выслеживать *v* trace
высмеивать *v* ridicule
высовываться *v* stick out
высокий *adj* high, tall
высокомерный *adj* insolent
высота *n* height
высочество *n* Highness
выставка *n* exhibition
выставлять *v* hold up
выстраивать *v* line up
выстрел *n* shot
высший *adj* superior

высылать v deport, exile
высылка n exile
вытекать v flow out; incur
вытерпеть v endure
вытеснять v supersede
вытирать v wipe
выть v howl, wail
выход n exit, outlet
выходить v go out
выходные дни n weekend
вычёркивать v cross out
вычет n deduction
вычисление n calculation
вычислять v calculate
вычитание n subtraction
вычитать v deduct
вычурный adj pretentious
вышивание n embroidery
вышивать v embroider
выяснять v ascertain
вяз n elm
вязать v knit; bind
вялый adj slack, lax
вянуть v fade, wither

Г

гавань n harbor, port
гадюка n viper
газ n gas, gauze
газета n newspaper
газетный ларек n newsstand
газон n lawn
галактика n galaxy
галантный adj gallant
галерея n gallery
галлон n gallon
галстук n necktie
галька n pebbles
гамак n hammock
гамбургер n burger
гангрена n gangrene
гангстер n gangster
гараж n garage
гарантировать v guarantee
гарантия n warranty
гардероб n wardrobe
гармония n harmony
гарнизон n garrison
гарнир n garnish
гарнировать v garnish
гарпун n harpoon
гасить v extinguish
гашиш n hashish
гвоздика n carnation
где adv where

где бы ни *c* wherever
гейзер *n* geyser
ген *n* gene
генерал *n* general
генетический *adj* genetic
гений *n* genius
геноцид *n* genocide
география *n* geography
геология *n* geology
геометрия *n* geometry
Германия *n* Germany
герметичный *adj* airtight
героизм *n* heroism
героин *n* heroin
героический *adj* heroic
герой *n* hero
герундий *n* gerund
герцог *n* duke
герцогиня *n* duchess
гибкий *adj* flexible
гиблое место *n* death trap
гигантский *adj* gigantic
гигиена *n* hygiene
гиена *n* hyena
гильдия *n* guild
гильотина *n* guillotine
гимн *n* anthem
гимназия *n* gymnasium
гинекология *n* gynecology
гипноз *n* hypnosis
гипотеза *n* hypothesis
гирлянда *n* garland

гитара *n* guitar
глава *n* chapter
главный *adj* principal
глагол *n* verb
гладиатор *n* gladiator
гладить утюгом *v* iron
гладкий *adj* smooth
гладко *adv* smoothly
гладкость *n* smoothness
глаз *n* eye
гласный звук *n* vowel
глашатай *n* herald
глина *n* clay
глоссарий *n* glossary
глотание *n* swallowing
глотать *v* swallow
глубина *n* depth
глубокий *adj* deep
глупость *n* stupidity
глупый *adj* fool, silly
глухой *adj* deaf
глухой удар *n* flop
глухота *n* deafness
глыба *n* lump
глюкоза *n* glucose
глянцевитый *adj* glossy
гнать *v* drift, drive
гнев *n* anger, wrath
гнездо *n* nest
гниение *n* corruption
гнилой *adj* putrid, rotten
гнить *v* decay, rot

гноиться *v* fester
гной *n* pus
гнусный *adj* heinous, odious
гобелен *n* tapestry
говорить *v* say, speak
говядина *n* beef
год *n* year
годность *n* fitness
годовой *adv* yearly
годовщина *n* anniversary
гол *n* goal
Голландия *n* Holland
голландский *adj* Dutch
голова *n* head
головная боль *n* headache
головоломка *n* puzzle
голод *n* famine, hunger
голодание *n* starvation
голодать *v* starve
голодный *adj* hungry
голос *n* voice, vote
голосование *n* ballot, poll
голосовать *v* vote
голубь *n* dove, pigeon
голый *adj* bare, naked
гончая *n* trackhound
гора *n* mount, mountain
гораздо *adv* by far
горбун *n* hunchback
гордо *adv* proudly
гордость *n* pride
гордый *adj* proud

горестный *adj* sorrowful
гореть *v* burn
горечь *n* bitterness
горизонт *n* horizon
горилла *n* gorilla
гористый *adj* mountainous
горло *n* gorge, throat
гормон *n* hormone
горняк *n* miner
город *n* city, town
городок *n* borough
городской *adj* civic, urban
горох *n* pea
гортань *n* larynx
горчица *n* mustard
горшок *n* pot
горький *adj* bitter
горько *adv* bitterly
горючий *n* combustible
горячий *adj* fervent, hot
господин *n* lord, mister
господство *n* dominion
гостиная *n* living room
гостиница *n* inn, hotel
гость *n* guest, visitor
готовить *v* cook
готовность *n* readiness
готовый *adj* ready
грабеж *n* robbery
грабитель *n* robber
грабить *v* rob
грабли *n* rake

гравий *n* gravel

гравировать *v* engrave

гравировка *n* engraving

град *n* hail

гражданин *n* citizen

гражданский *adj* civil

гражданство *n* citizenship

грамм *n* gram

грамматика *n* grammar

грамотный *adj* literate

гранат *n* pomegranate

граната *n* grenade

гранит *n* granite

граница *n* boundary

граничащий *adj* adjoining

граничить *v* adjoin

граничить с *v* border on

грант *n* grant

гранула *n* pellet

грань *n* edge, facet

графиня *n* countess

графический *adj* graphic

графство *n* county

гребень *n* comb

гребень горы *n* ridge

гребешок *n* crest

грейпфрут *n* grapefruit

Гренландия *n* Greenland

грести вёслами *v* paddle

греться *v* bask

грех *n* sin

греховный *adj* sinful

Греция *n* Greece

грецкий орех *n* walnut

греческий *adj* Greek

грешить *v* sin

грешник *n* sinner

гриб *n* mushroom

грилль *n* grill

гримаса *n* grimace

гримасничать *v* mow

грипп *n* flu

гриф *n* vulture

гроб *n* coffin

гробница *n* tomb

гроза *n* thunderstorm

гроздь *n* cluster

грозный *adj* formidable

гром *n* thunder

громадный *adj* tremendous

громкий *adj* loud

громко *adv* loudly

громкость *n* volume

громоздкий *adj* bulky

громыхать *v* rumble

гроссбух *n* ledger

грот *n* grotto

гротеск *adj* grotesque

грохот *n* rumble

грохотанье *n* rumbling

грохотать *v* crash, rattle

грубость *n* rudeness

грубый *adj* rough, coarse

груда *n* bulk, heap

грудь *n* breast
гружёный *adj* laden
груз *n* cargo, shipment
грузить *v* load
грузиться *v* embark
грузовик *n* truck
группа *n* group
грустный *adj* bereaved, sad
груша *n* pear
грыжа *n* hernia
грызть *v* gnaw, nibble
грызун *n* rodent
грязный *adj* dirty, messy
грязь *n* dirt, filth, mud
губа *n* lip
губительный *adj* detrimental
губка *n* sponge
гудение *n* buzzing
гудеть *v* buzz
гул *n* hum, uproar
гулкий *adj* resounding
гулять *v* go for a walk
гусеница *n* caterpillar
гуси *n* geese
густой *adj* thick
гусь *n* goose

Д

да *adv* yes
давление *n* pressure
давнишний *adj* long-standing
даже если *c* even if
далеко *adv* away, far
дальнобойщик *n* trucker
дама *n* lady
дамба *n* dam
дамская сумочка *n* handbag
дамское бельё *n* lingerie
Дания *n* Denmark
данные *n* data
дань *n* tribute
дар *n* gift
даритель *n* donor
даровать *v* bestow
дата *n* date
датировать *v* date
дать *v* give
два *n* two
двадцатый *adj* twentieth
двадцать *adj* twenty
дважды *adv* twice
двенадцатый *adj* twelfth
двенадцать *adj* twelve
дверной звонок *n* doorbell
дверной проём *n* doorway
дверь *n* door
двигатель *n* engine

двигать _v_ move
движение _n_ motion, move
двоеточие _n_ colon
двойной _adj_ double, dual
двор _n_ court, yard
двор фермы _n_ farmyard
дворец _n_ palace
дворецкий _n_ butler
двуязычный _adj_ bilingual
дебаты _n_ controversy, debate
дебет _n_ debit
дебют _n_ debut
дева _n_ maiden, virgin
девиз _n_ motto
девочка _n_ girl
девственность _n_ virginity
девушка _n_ maid, girl
девчонка _n_ gal
девяносто _adj_ ninety
девятнадцать _adj_ nineteen
девятый _adj_ ninth
девять _adj_ nine
дедушка _n_ grandfather
дежурство _n_ duty
дезертир _n_ deserter
дезодорант _n_ deodorant
действие _n_ action, deed
действительно _adv_ actually
действовать _v_ act
декабрь _n_ December
декан _n_ dean
декларация _n_ proclamation

декодировать _v_ decipher
декоративный _adj_ decorative
декорация _n_ décor
декорум _n_ decorum
декрет _n_ decree
делать _v_ do, make
делать покупки _v_ shop
делегация _n_ delegation
деление _n_ division
делить _v_ divide, share
делить пополам _v_ halve
дело _n_ affair, business
деловито _adv_ busily
дельта _n_ delta
дельфин _n_ dolphin
демократия _n_ democracy
демон _n_ demon
день _n_ day
день рождения _n_ birthday
деньги _n_ cash, money
депозит _n_ deposit
депрессия _n_ depression
деревенский _adj_ rural
деревня _n_ village
дерево _n_ tree
деревушка _n_ hamlet
деревянный _adj_ wooden
держать _v_ hold, keep
держать пари _v_ bet
держаться _v_ behave
держаться за _v_ hold on to
дёрн _n_ sod, turf

Д

десерт *n* dessert
десна *n* gum
деспот *n* despot
десятичный *adj* decimal
десяток *n* decade
десятый *n* tenth
десять *adj* ten
детализировать *v* detail
детектив *n* detective
детеныш зверя *n* cub
дети *n* children
детонатор *n* detonator
детонация *n* detonation
детская комната *n* nursery
детский *adj* childish
детский самокат *n* scooter
детство *n* childhood
дефективный *adj* defective
дефис *n* hyphen
дефицит *n* deficit
дешёвый *adj* cheap
деятельный *adj* busy, live
джентльмен *n* gentleman
джинсы *n* jeans
джунгли *n* jungle
диабет *n* diabetes
диабетический *adj* diabetic
диагноз *n* diagnosis
диагональный *adj* diagonal
диаграмма *n* diagram
диалект *n* dialect
диалог *n* dialogue

диаметр *n* diameter
диван *n* couch, sofa
дивиденд *n* dividend
дикий *adj* savage, wild
дикобраз *n* porcupine
дикость *n* savagery
диктатор *n* dictator
диктаторский *adj* dictatorial
диктатура *n* dictatorship
диктовать *v* dictate
диктор *n* announcer
дилемма *n* dilemma
дилер *n* dealer
динамит *n* dynamite
динамичный *adj* dynamic
династия *n* dynasty
динозавр *n* dinosaur
диплом *n* diploma
дипломат *n* diplomat
дипломатия *n* diplomacy
директор *n* director
диск *n* disk
дискуссия *n* discussion
дискутировать *v* dispute
диспут *n* dispute
дистиллировать *v* distill
дисциплина *n* discipline
дифтонг *n* diphthong
длина *n* duration
длинный *adj* long
длинный гудок *n* dial tone
длительный *adj* lasting

длиться дольше _v_ outlast
для _pre_ for
дневник _n_ journal
дневное время _n_ afternoon
дно _n_ bottom
до _pre_ before
до сих пор _adv_ hitherto
добавление _n_ addition
добавочный _adj_ additional
добро _n_ well
доброволец _n_ volunteer
добродетель _n_ virtue
доброта _n_ kindness
добрый _adj_ benign, kind
добывать _v_ gain, procure
добыча _n_ loot, prey
доверенность _n_ power of attorney
доверие _n_ credit, trust
доверчивый _adj_ gullible
доверять _v_ confide, trust
довольный _adj_ content
догадка _n_ guess
догадываться _v_ guess
догматический _adj_ dogmatic
договор _n_ contract, treaty
договорённость _n_ arrangement
догонять _v_ chase
дождливый _adj_ rainy
дождь _n_ rain
дожидаться _v_ await
дозаправиться _v_ refuel

дозировка _n_ dosage
дозор _n_ patrol
док _n_ dock
доказанный _adj_ proven
доказательство _n_ proof
доказывать _v_ vindicate
докладчик _n_ reporter
доктрина _n_ doctrine
документ _n_ document
долг _n_ debt, duty
долгосрочный _adj_ long-term
долгота _n_ longitude
должен _v_ must, ought to
должник _n_ debtor
должный _adj_ due
долина _n_ valley
доллар _n_ dollar
долото _n_ chisel
доля _n_ share
дом _n_ home, house
домашний _adj_ domestic
домашний очаг _n_ hearth
домашний скот _n_ livestock
домашняя птица _n_ poultry
доминирование _n_ domination
доминировать _v_ dominate
домовладелица _n_ landlady
домогаться _v_ solicit
домохозяйка _n_ housewife
доносить _v_ inform
дополнение _n_ complement
дополнительно _adv_ extra

допускать v let in, admit
допущение n presupposition
дорога n road
дорогой adj dear, pricey
дородный adj corpulent
досада n nuisance
доска n chalkboard
дословно adv verbatim
доставлять v furnish
достаток n affluence
достаточно adv enough
достаточный adj sufficient
достигать v achieve
достижение n achievement
достижимый adj attainable
достоинство n dignity
достойный adj worthy
доступ n access
доступный adj accessible
досуг n leisure
досье n dossier
досягаемость n reach
доход n income
дочь n daughter
драгоценный adj precious
дразнить v tease
драка n scuffle
дракон n dragon
драматический adj dramatic
драпировка n drape
древесина n wood
древний adj ancient

дремать v doze, snooze
дренаж n drainage
дрифтер n drifter
дробить v crush
дробовик n shotgun
дробь n fraction
дрова n firewood
дрожать v tremble
дрожжи n yeast
дрожь n shudder, tremor
дротик n dart
друг n friend
друг друга adj each other
другой adj another, other
дружба n friendship
дружелюбный adj amiable
дружеский adj amicable
дружище n buddy
дрянной adj crappy
дряхлый adj decrepit
дуб n oak
дубинка n club
дубликат n counterpart
дуга n arc, curve
думать v think
дуновение n blow, puff
дурачить v fool
дурман n dope
дуть v blow
дух n spirit
духи n perfume
духовенство n clergy

Д

духовка *n* oven
духовный *adj* spiritual
душ *n* shower
душа *n* soul
душевный *adj* psychic
душить *v* stifle, smother
душный *adj* stifling, stuffy
дуэль *n* duel
дым *n* fumes, smoke
дымиться *v* smoke
дымчатый *adj* smoked
дыня *n* melon
дыра *n* hole
дыхание *n* respiration
дышать *v* breathe
дьявол *n* devil
дьявольский *adj* diabolical
дьякон *n* deacon
дюжина *n* dozen
дюйм *n* inch
дядя *n* uncle

е

Евангелие *n* gospel
еврей *n* Jew
еврейский *adj* Jewish
Европа *n* Europe
европейский *adj* European
его *adj* his
его *pro* his
еда *n* food, meal
едва *adv* hardly, barely
единица *n* unit
единичный *adj* single
единобрачие *n* monogamy
единодушие *n* unanimity
единообразие *n* uniformity
единственно *adv* solely
единственный *adj* alone
единство *n* unity
едкий *adj* poignant
её *adj* her
её *pro* hers
ежевика *n* blackberry
ежегодный *adj* annual
ежедневник *n* diary
ежедневно *adv* daily
ежемесячно *adv* monthly
еженедельно *adv* weekly
ежечасно *adv* hourly
езда *n* drive
енот *n* raccoon

E

епархия *n* diocese
епископ *n* bishop
ересь *n* heresy
еретический *adj* heretic
если *c* if
если бы *c* supposing
если не *c* unless
естественно *adv* naturally
ехать *v* drive
ехать верхом *v* ride
еще *c* yet
ещё раз *adv* anew

Ж

жаба *n* toad
жадно есть *v* devour
жадность *n* greed
жадный *adj* avid, greedy
жажда *v* thirst
жаждать *v* crave, thirst
жаждущий *adj* thirsty
жалить *v* sting
жалкий *adj* miserable
жало *n* sting
жалоба *n* complaint
жаловать *v* confer, grant
жаловаться *v* complain

жалость *n* pity
жар *n* fever
жара *n* heat
жареный *adj* fried
жарить *v* fry
жарить в печи *v* roast
жарить на огне *v* broil
жаркое *n* roast
жасмин *n* jasmine
жатва *n* harvest
жгучий *adj* burning
ждать *v* wait
жевать *v* chew
жезл *n* baton
желание *n* desire, wish
желанный *adj* desirable
желать *v* desire, wish
железа *n* gland
железо *n* iron
желобок *n* groove
желток *n* yolk
желтый *adj* yellow
желудок *n* stomach
желудочный *adj* gastric
желудь *n* acorn
желчь *n* bile
жемчуг *n* pearl
жена *n* wife
женатый *adj* married
жениться *v* wed, marry
жених *n* groom, fiancé
женский *adj* feminine

женщина *n* woman
женщины *n* women
жены *n* wives
жеребёнок *n* foal
жертва *n* victim
жертвователь *n* donator
жертвовать *v* donate
жертвы *n* death toll
жест *n* gesture
жесткий *adj* harsh, tough
жестко *adv* harshly
жесткость *n* stiffness
жестокий *adj* cruel, grim
жестокость *n* atrocity
жестянка *n* can
жетон *n* token
живая природа *n* wildlife
живой *adj* alive
живописный *adj* picturesque
живопись *n* painting
живот *n* abdomen
животик *n* tummy
животное *n* animal
животный *adj* animal
жидкость *n* fluid, liquid
жизненные соки *n* sap
жизненный *adj* vital
жизнь *n* life
жилет *n* vest
жилище *n* dwelling
жир *n* fat, grease
жираф *n* giraffe

жирный *adj* fat, fatty
житель *n* inhabitant
житель востока *n* easterner
житель запада *adj* westerner
жить *v* be, live
жить за счёт *v* live off
жрица *n* priestess
жужжать *v* hum
жук *n* beetle
жулик *n* cheater
журавль *n* crane
журнал *n* magazine
журналист *n* journalist
жуткий *adj* horrible

3

З

за *pre* behind, beyond
за борт *adv* overboard
за границей *adv* overseas
забавный *adj* amusing
забастовка *n* strike
забвение *n* oblivion
забивать *v* slaughter
забивать гвоздь *v* clinch
забирать *v* take, withdraw
заблудившийся *adj* stray
заблудиться *v* get lost

3

заблуждаться *v* err
заблуждение *n* aberration
заболевать *v* sicken
заболоченный *adj* swamped
забор *n* fence
забота *n* care
заботиться *v* look after
заботливый *adj* caring
заброшенный *adj* deserted
забывать *v* forget
заведование *n* supervision
заведовать *v* supervise
завершать *v* end, conclude
завершающий *adj* conclusive
завершение *n* completion
завершённый *adj* complete
завершиться *v* culminate
заверять *v* reassure
завет *n* covenant
завещание *n* will
завещать *v* bequeath
завидовать *v* envy
зависеть *v* lean on, depend
зависимость *n* dependence
завистливый *adj* envious
зависть *n* envy
зависящий *adj* dependent
завладевать *v* obsess
завод *n* factory
заводить *v* wind up
завоевание *n* conquest
завоеватель *n* conqueror

завоёвывать *v* defeat
заворачивать *v* wrap
завтра *adv* tomorrow
завтрак *n* breakfast
завязывать *v* tie
загадка *n* riddle
загар *n* sunburn
загибать *v* bend down
заглатывать *v* gulp
заглянуть *v* stop by
заговор *n* conspiracy
заговорщик *n* conspirator
заголовок *n* heading
заграждение *n* barrage
загромождение *n* obstruction
загрубелый *adj* callous
загрязнение *n* contamination
загрязнять *v* contaminate
задавать темп *v* pace
задача *n* task
задевать *v* touch
задержание *n* detention
задерживать *v* delay
задержка *n* delay
задиристый *adj* quarrelsome
задний *adj* rear
задний двор *n* backyard
задняя часть *n* rear
задолженность *n* backlog
задувать *v* blow out
задумчивый *adj* thoughtful
задушить *v* strangle

задыхаться *v* asphyxiate
зажженный *adv* alight
зажигать *v* kindle, fire
зажим *n* clamp
зажимать *v* clip, clench
зазубренный *adj* ragged
заиграть *v* strike up
заигрывать *v* molest, flirt
заикаться *v* stammer
заканчивать *v* finalize
заканчиваться *v* run out
закат *n* sundown
закладывать *v* pledge
заклинание *n* spell
заключать *v* infer
заключаться *v* consist
заключенный *n* prisoner
заколдовывать *v* bewitch
закон *n* law
законность *n* legality
законный *adj* lawful
законодатель *n* lawmaker
закончиться *v* expire
закрывать *v* close, shut
закрытие *n* conclusion
закрытый *adj* closed
закуска *n* appetizer
закутывать *v* muffle
зал *n* hall
залив *n* gulf
залитый водой *adv* afloat
залог *n* bail

заложник *n* hostage
заманивание *n* enticement
заманчивый *adj* enticing
замасливать *v* grease
замачивать *v* soak
замедленный *adj* retarded
замедлять *v* slow down
замена *n* replacement
заменять *v* substitute
заместитель *n* deputy
заметка *n* memo, note
замечание *n* remark
замечательный *adj* remarkable
замок *n* castle; lock
замолчать *v* shut up
замороженный *adj* frozen
замысел *n* project
занавеска *n* curtain
занимать *v* occupy
заново *adv* newly
занятие *n* occupation
занятый *adj* engaged
заострённый *adj* edgy, pointed
заострять *v* sharpen
запад *n* west
западный *adj* western
запас *n* stock
запасать *v* hoard, reserve
запасной *adj* spare
запасы *n* supplies
запах *n* odor
запачканный *adj* soiled, filthy

3

3

запеканка *n* casserole
запирать *v* impound
запираться *v* deny
записная книжка *n* notebook
записывать *v* write down
запись *n* record
запланировать *v* plan
заплатка *n* patch
заплесневелый *adj* moldy
заповедь *n* commandment
запоздалый *adj* belated
запор *n* constipation
запрет *n* prohibition
запрещать *v* ban, forbid
запрещение *n* ban
запрос *n* inquiry
запрягать *v* hitch up
запугивать *v* intimidate
запугивающий *adj* daunting
запуск *n* launch
запускать *v* launch
запутанный *adj* tangled
запутывать *v* entangle
запущенный *adj* squalid
запчасть *n* spare part
запястье *n* wrist
запятая *n* comma
зарабатывать *v* earn
заработок *n* earnings
заражать *v* infect
зараженный *adj* infested
заразный *adj* contagious

заранее *adv* beforehand
зародыш *n* embryo
зарплата *n* salary
заряд *n* charge
заряжать *v* charge
засаленный *adj* greasy
заседание *n* sitting
засиживаться *v* linger
заслонять *v* shield
заслуга *n* merit
заслуживать *v* deserve
засов *n* bolt
засохший *adj* dried
заставлять *v* compel, force
застаиваться *v* stagnate
застёжка-молния *n* zipper
застенчивость *n* shyness
застенчивый *adj* bashful, shy
застой *n* stagnation
застойный *adj* stagnant
застолье *n* feast
застраховать *v* insure
застрелить *v* gun down
заступничество *n* intercession
засуха *n* drought
засушливый *adj* arid
засыпающий *adj* drowsy
затаенный *adj* covert
затаптывать *v* stamp out
затворник *n* recluse
затемнение *n* blackout
затемнять *v* darken

затененный *adj* shady
затмение *n* eclipse
затмить *v* outshine
затонувший *adj* sunken
затопление *n* flooding
затоплять *v* inundate
затор *n* jam
затрагивать *v* touch on
затрата *n* expense
затруднение *n* predicament
затруднять *v* embarrass
затупление *n* bluntness
затыкать *v* gag, plug
затычка *n* gag
затягивать *v* tighten
затянувшийся *adj* protracted
захват *n* capture
захватчик *n* invader
захватывать *v* capture
захлопывать *v* slam
заходить *v* come over
зачинщик *n* ringleader
защита *n* protection
защитник *n* defender
защитные очки *n* goggles
защищать *v* protect, defend
заявка *n* application
заявление *n* statement
заявлять *v* allege, state
заяц *n* hare
звезда *n* star
звёздочка *n* asterisk

звено *n* link
звереть *v* brutalize
зверь *n* beast
звон *n* ring
звонить *v* call, dial
звонить в колокол *v* toll
звонок *n* call
звук *n* sound
звучать *v* sound
здание *n* building
здание суда *n* courthouse
здесь *adv* here
здоровый *adj* healthy
здоровье *n* health
здравомыслие *n* sanity
здравый *adj* sane
зебра *n* zebra
зевать *v* yawn
зевота *n* yawn
зеленый *adj* green
земля *n* land, ground
земляк *n* countryman
земноводный *adj* amphibious
земной *adj* terrestrial
зенит *n* zenith
зеркало *n* mirror
зерно *n* corn, grain
зима *n* winter
зло *n* evil
злоба *n* malice, rancor
злобный *adj* malignant
зловещий *adj* sinister, eerie

3

зловонный *adj* stinking
злодей *n* villain
злой *adj* evil, wicked
злословие *n* slander
злость *n* spite
змей *n* serpent
змея *n* snake
знак *n* sign
знакомить *v* acquaint
знакомство *n* acquaintance
знаменатель *n* denominator
знамение *n* omen
знаменитый *adj* famous
знамя *n* banner
знание *n* knowledge
знание дела *n* know-how
знаток *n* ace, expert
знать *v* know
значение *n* meaning
значительный *adj* major
значить *v* signify
значок *n* badge
знойный *adj* torrid
зола *n* ash
золото *n* gold
золотой *adj* golden
зона *n* zone
зондирование *n* probing
зонт *n* umbrella
зоология *n* zoology
зоопарк *n* zoo
зрелище *n* spectacle

зрелость *n* maturity
зрелый *adj* mature, ripe
зрение *n* vision, eyesight
зреть *v* ripen
зритель *n* onlooker
зрительный *adj* visual
зуб *n* tooth
зубная боль *n* toothache
зубной *adj* dental
зубной врач *n* dentist
зубной камень *n* tartar
зубной протез *n* dentures
зубочистка *n* toothpick
зубы *n* teeth
зуд *n* itchiness
зыбучий песок *n* quicksand
зыбь *n* ripple
зять *n* brother-in-law

И

и *c* and
ива *n* willow
игла *n* needle
игнорировать *v* ignore
игра *n* game, play
игральные кости *n* dice
играть *v* play

игривый *adj* playful
игрок *n* player
игрушка *n* toy
идеальный *adj* ideal
идентичность *n* identity
идентичный *adj* identical
идеология *n* ideology
идет снег *v* snow
идея *n* idea
идиома *n* idiom
идиот *n* idiot
идиотский *adj* idiotic
идол *n* idol
идти *v* walk, go
идти следом *v* tail
идущий вверх *adv* uphill
иерархия *n* hierarchy
из *pre* from, out of, of
избавляться *v* discard
избегать *v* avoid
избивать *v* beat
избиение *n* beating
избирать *v* elect
избыток *n* surplus
избыточный *adj* superfluous
извергать *v* erupt
извержение *n* eruption
известность *n* fame
известняк *n* limestone
известь *n* lime
извещать *v* notify
извещение *n* notice

извилистый *adj* winding
извинение *n* apology
извинять *v* pardon
извиняться *v* apologize
извлекать *v* extract
извращать *v* pervert
извращенный *adj* perverted
изгиб *n* twist, curve
изгибать *v* curve, flex
изгнание *n* banishment
изгнанник *n* castaway
изгонять *v* banish
издавать декрет *v* decree
издание *n* edition, issue
издатель *n* publisher
изжога *n* heartburn
из-за *pre* because of
из-за того *adv* owing to
излагать *v* set forth
излечивать *v* remedy
излечимый *adj* curable
излюбленный *adj* favorite
измельчать *v* crumble up
измена *n* treason
изменение *n* change
изменить *v* change
изменник *n* traitor
изменять *v* change; betray
измерение *n* measurement
измерять *v* measure
изнасилование *n* rape
изнасиловать *v* rape

И

изнашивать *v* wear out
изнашиваться *v* wear down
изнеможение *n* exhaustion
изношенный *adj* worn-out
изобилие *n* abundance
изобиловать *v* abound
изобилующий *adj* abundant
изобильный *adj* affluent
изображать *v* portray
изображение *n* image
изобретать *v* invent
изобретение *n* invention
изогнутый *adj* crooked
изолировать *v* insulate
изоляция *n* insulation
изумительный *adj* astonishing
изумление *n* amazement
изумлять *v* astonish
изумруд *n* emerald
изучать *v* study, look into
изучение *n* learning
изъятие *n* withdrawal
изысканный *adj* elegant
изюм *n* raisin
изящество *n* elegance
икона *n* icon
икота *n* hiccup
или *c* or
иллюзия *n* illusion
иллюстрация *n* illustration
имбирь *n* ginger
имение *n* estate

иметь *v* have
иметь в виду *v* mean
иммигрант *n* immigrant
иммиграция *n* immigration
иммунитет *n* immunity
император *n* emperor
императрица *n* empress
империализм *n* imperialism
империя *n* empire
имперский *adj* imperial
импорт *n* importation
импортировать *v* import
импульс *n* impulse
импульсивный *adj* impulsive
имущество *n* belongings
имя *n* name
инаугурация *n* inauguration
иначе *adv* otherwise
инвалид *n* invalid
инвестировать *v* invest
инвестор *n* investor
индекс *n* index
инженер *n* engineer
инжир *n* fig
инициалы *n* initials
инициатива *n* initiative
инквизиция *n* inquisition
иногда *adv* sometimes
иностранец *n* foreigner
иностранный *adj* foreign
инспектор *n* inspector
инстинкт *n* instinct

инструктор *n* instructor
инструмент *n* tool
инсценировать *v* dramatize
интенсивность *n* intensity
интенсивный *adj* intense
интервал *n* interval
интервью *n* interview
интерес *n* interest
интересный *adj* interesting
интернировать *v* intern
интрига *n* intrigue
интригующий *adj* intriguing
инфекция *n* infection
инфильтрация *n* infiltration
инфляция *n* inflation
информатор *n* informer
информация *n* information
инъекция *n* injection
ипотека *n* mortgage
Ирландия *n* Ireland
ирландский *adj* Irish
иронический *adj* ironic
ирония *n* irony
иск *n* lawsuit
искажать *v* distort
искажение *n* distortion
искать *v* look for, seek
исключать *v* eliminate
исключая *pre* barring
исключение *n* exception
исключительно *adv* notably
ископаемое *n* fossil

искоренять *v* exterminate
искра *n* spark
искренний *adj* sincere
искренность *n* sincerity
искриться *v* sparkle
искупать *v* atone
искупление *n* atonement
искусный *adj* skillful
искусственный *adj* artificial
искусство *n* art
искушать *v* tempt
искушение *n* temptation
исламский *adj* Islamic
испанец *n* Spaniard
Испания *n* Spain
испанский *adj* Spanish
испарять *v* evaporate
исповедальня *n* confessional
исповедание *n* confession
исповедник *n* confessor
исповедовать *v* confess
исполнять *v* comply
использование *n* use
использовать *v* use, utilize
испортить *v* mess up
испорченный *adj* damaged
исправить *v* straighten out
исправление *n* correction
исправлять *v* amend
испуг *n* scare, dismay
испуганный *adj* afraid
испугать *v* frighten

И

испускать *v* emit
испытание *n* trial
испытывать *v* undergo, test
исследование *n* research
исследователь *n* explorer
исследовать *v* explore
иссушать *v* sap, dry up
истерический *adj* hysterical
истерия *n* hysteria
истец *n* plaintiff
истина *n* truth
истинный *adj* truthful
история *n* story, history
источник *n* source
истощать *v* attenuate
истощённый *adj* emaciated
истребление *n* annihilation
истреблять *v* destroy
исход *n* exodus
исходить *v* emanate
исхудавший *adj* attenuating
исцелитель *n* healer
исцелять *v* cure, heal
исчезать *v* disappear
исчерпывать *v* exhaust
Италия *n* Italy
итальянский *adj* Italian
иудаизм *n* Judaism
июль *n* July
июнь *n* June
йод *n* iodine

К

к *pre* towards, to
к берегу *adv* ashore
к тому же *adv* furthermore
кабан *n* wild boar
кабель *n* cable
кабина *n* cab
кавалерия *n* cavalry
кадры *n* staff
каждый *adj* each, every
казармы *n* barracks
казаться *v* seem
казино *n* casino
казначей *n* treasurer
как *c* as
как *adv* as, how
какао *n* cocoa
как-нибудь *adv* somehow
какой-нибудь *adj* any
календарь *n* calendar
калечить *v* mutilate
калибр *n* caliber, gauge
калибровать *v* calibrate
калория *n* calorie
калькулятор *n* calculator
кальмар *n* squid
каменистый *adj* rocky
каменоломня *n* quarry
каменщик *n* mason
камень *n* rock, stone

камин n fireplace
кампания n campaign
камуфляж n camouflage
канава n ditch
канавка n gutter
канал n canal, channel
канарейка n canary
кандалы n shackle
кандидат n candidate
кандидатура n candidacy
каникулы n vacation
каннибал n cannibal
каноэ n canoe
канталупа n cantaloupe
канун n eve
канцлер n chancellor
каньон n canyon
капанье n drip
капать v drip, drop
капеллан n chaplain
капитал n capital
капитализм n capitalism
капитан n captain
капитуляция n surrender
капкан n trap
капля n drop
капрал n corporal
капсула n capsule
капуста n cabbage
капюшон n hood
караван n caravan
карандаш n pencil

карат n carat
каратэ n karate
караул n sentry
карбюратор n carburetor
кардиология n cardiology
карикатура n caricature
каркас n frame
карлик n dwarf
карман n pocket
карта n map, chart, card
картина n painting, picture
картон n cardboard
картофель n potato
карьера n career
касательная n tangent
касаться v touch
каска n helmet
каскад n cascade
кассир n cashier
каста n caste
кастрюля n saucepan
катаклизм n cataclysm
катакомба n catacomb
каталог n catalog
катаракта n cataract
катастрофа n catastrophe
катафалк n hearse
категория n category
катехизис n catechism
катить v roll
католический adj catholic
католичество n Catholicism

К

кафедра *n* department
кафель *n* tile
кафетерий *n* cafeteria
качать *v* rock, swing
качаться *v* wag
качество *n* quality
кашель *n* cough
кашлять *v* cough
каштан *n* chestnut
каяться *v* repent
квадрат *n* square
квадратный *adj* square
квартальный *adj* quarterly
кенгуру *n* kangaroo
кепка *n* cap
керамический *n* ceramic
киловатт *n* kilowatt
килограмм *n* kilogram
километр *n* kilometer
кинжал *n* dagger
кинофильм *n* movie
киоск *n* booth, kiosk
кипа *n* pile
кипарис *n* cypress
кипятить *v* boil
кирпич *n* brick
кислород *n* oxygen
кислота *n* acid
кислотность *n* acidity
кислый *adj* sour
кисточка *n* paintbrush
кит *n* whale

кишечник *n* intestine
кишка *n* gut
клавиатура *n* keyboard
клавиша *n* key
кладбище *n* cemetery
кладовая *n* stockroom
клан *n* clan
кланяться *v* bow
клапан *n* valve
кларнет *n* clarinet
класс *n* class
классический *adj* classic
классная доска *n* blackboard
класть *v* set
класть в мешок *v* sack
клевать *v* peck
клевета *n* calumny
клеветать *v* defame
клей *n* glue
клеймо в ухе *v* earmark
клерк *n* clerk
клетка *n* cage
клещи *n* pincers
клиент *n* client
клиентура *n* clientele
климат *n* climate
климатический *adj* climatic
клин *n* wedge
кличка *n* nickname
клок *n* flock
клонирование *n* cloning
клонировать *v* clone

клоп *n* bug
клоун *n* clown
клочок *n* scrap, shred
клуб *n* club
клубника *n* strawberry
клубок *n* clew
клумба *n* flowerbed
клык *n* fang, tusk
ключ *n* key
ключица *n* collarbone
клясться *v* vow, swear
клятва *n* oath, pledge
книга *n* book
кнопка *n* tack, pin
кнут *n* whip
кобыла *n* mare
коварный *adj* sly
коварство *n* guile
ковбой *n* cowboy
ковёр *n* rug, carpet
коврик *n* mat
ковчег *n* ark
когда *adv* when
когда-нибудь *adv* someday
кого *pro* whom
коготь *n* claw
код *n* code
кое-что *adv* somewhat
кожа *n* leather, skin
кожица *n* peel
козел *n* goat
козлёнок *n* kid

кокаин *n* cocaine
кокос *n* coconut
коктейль *n* cocktail
кол *n* stake
колбаса *n* sausage
колготки *n* pantyhose, tights
колдовство *n* sorcery
колдун *n* sorcerer
колдунья *n* witch
колебание *n* swing
колебаться *v* fluctuate
колени *n* lap
коленная чашка *n* kneecap
колено *n* knee
колесо *n* wheel
колика *n* colic
количество *n* quantity
коллега *n* colleague
колледж *n* college
коллекционер *n* collector
коллекция *n* collection
колокол *n* bell
колокольня *n* belfry
колониальный *adj* colonial
колонизация *n* colonization
колония *n* colony
колонна *n* column
колоссальный *adj* colossal
колоть *v* stab
колыбель *n* cradle
колыхаться *v* waver
кольцо *n* ring

К

колючий *adj* thorny
колючка *n* thorn
ком *n* cob, lump
кома *n* coma
команда *n* team
командир *n* commander
комар *n* mosquito
комедия *n* comedy
комета *n* comet
комик *n* comedian
комитет *n* committee
комментарий *n* comment
коммерция *n* commerce
коммерческий *adj* commercial
коммуникация *n* communication
комната *n* room
комната отдыха *n* rest room
комок *n* clot
компактный *adj* compact
компания *n* company
компенсация *n* compensation
компетентность *n* competence
компетентный *adj* competent
комплексный *adj* complex
комплект *n* gang, kit
комплимент *n* compliment
композитор *n* composer
компонент *n* ingredient
компоновать *v* arrange
компост *n* manure
компромисс *n* compromise
компьютер *n* computer

кому *pro* whom
конверт *n* envelope
конвой *n* escort
конгресс *n* congress
конденсация *n* condensation
кондиционер *n* conditioner
кондоминиум *n* condo
кондуктор *n* conductor
конек *n* skate
конец *n* demise, end
конечно *adv* surely
конечность *n* limb
конкурент *n* competitor
конкуренция *n* rivalry
консервировать can
конспект *n* outline
конституция *n* constitution
консул *n* consul
консульство *n* consulate
консультант *n* adviser
консультация *n* consultation
контакт *n* contact, liaison
контактный *adj* sociable
контейнер *n* container
контекст *n* context
континент *n* mainland
контрабанда *n* contraband
контрабандист *n* smuggler
контраст *n* contrast
контроль *n* control
контур *n* contour
конура *n* kennel

К

конус n cone
конференция n conference
конфета n candy
конфискация n confiscation
конфисковать v confiscate
конфитюр n marmalade
конфликт n conflict
концентрат v concentrate
концентрация n concentration
концерт n concert
кончать v finish
кончаться v run out
кончик n tip
кончик пальца n fingertip
конюшня n stable
кооперация n cooperation
координатор n coordinator
копать v dig, excavate
копилка n piggy bank
копировать v copy
копить v amass, save
копыто n hoof
копье n spear
кора n bark, crust
корабль n ship
кордон n cordon
коренной зуб n molar
корень n root
корзина n basket
коридор n corridor
корица n cinnamon
коричневый adj brown

корка n crust
корма n stern
кормить v feed
кормление n feeding
кормушка n manger
корнет n cornet
коробка n box
корова n cow
королева n queen
королевский adj royal
король n king
корона n crown
коронарный adj coronary
коронация n coronation
короновать v crown
короткий adj brief, short
короткий сон n nap
коротко adv briefly
корпорация n corporation
корь n measles
косметика n cosmetic
космический adj cosmic
космонавт n astronaut
костёр n bonfire
костный мозг n bone marrow
кость n bone
костюм n suit
костюмер n dresser
кот n cat
котёл n boiler
котенок n kitten
который adj which

К

кофе *n* coffee
кофеин *n* caffeine
кошмар *n* nightmare
кощунство *n* sacrilege
коэффициент *n* coefficient
краб *n* crab
край *n* brim, brink
крайне *adv* extremely
крайний *adj* utmost
крапинка *n* speck
красивый *adj* good-looking
красить *v* color
краснеть *v* blush, redden
красное дерево *n* mahogany
красноречие *n* eloquence
красный *adj* red
красоваться *v* show off
красота *n* beauty
красоты *n* amenities
красочный *adj* colorful
красться *v* prowl, shirk
кратер *n* crater
краткий *adj* concise
краткость *n* brevity
кратный *adj* divisible
крах *n* wreckage, ruin
крахмал *n* starch
крахмальный *adj* starchy
креветка *n* shrimp
кредитор *n* creditor
крем для обуви *n* shoepolish
крематорий *n* crematorium

кремировать *v* cremate
крепкий *adj* firm, robust
крепость *n* fortress
кресло *n* armchair
крест *n* cross
крестить *v* baptize
крестоносец *n* crusader
крестьянин *n* peasant
крещение *n* baptism
кривошип *n* crank
кризис *n* crisis
крик *n* call, cry, shout
крикет *n* cricket
крики *n* shouting
криминальный *adj* criminal
кристалл *n* crystal
критерий *n* criterion
критика *n* criticism
критиковать *v* criticize
критический *adj* critical
кричать *v* call, cry, shout
кровавый *adj* bloody
кровать *n* bed
кровожадный *adj* bloodthirsty
кровоизлияние *n* hemorrhage
кровотечение *n* bleeding
кровоточить *v* bleed
кровь *n* blood
крокодил *n* crocodile
кролик *n* rabbit
кроме *pre* except
кроме того *adv* moreover

К

кроссворд *n* crossword
крот *n* mole
кроткий *adj* meek
кротко *adv* humbly
кротость *n* meekness
крошечный *adj* tiny
крошить *v* crumble
крошка *n* crumb
круг *n* circle
круглолицый *adj* chubby
круглый *adj* circular, round
круговорот *n* circulation
кружка *n* mug
крупа *n* cereal
крутить *v* wring, twist
крутой *adj* steep
крушение *n* downfall
крушить *v* smash, wreck
крыло *n* wing
крыльцо *n* porch
крыса *n* rat
крыша *n* roof
крышка *n* cover, lid
крюк *n* hook
кто *pro* who
кто бы ни *pro* whoever
кто-нибудь *pro* anybody
куб *n* cube
кубический *adj* cubic
кувшин *n* jug
кудрявый *adj* curly
кузнец *n* blacksmith

кукарекать *v* crow
кукла *n* doll, puppet
кулак *n* fist
кулинария *n* cooking
кульминация *n* climax
культивация *n* cultivation
культура *n* culture
культурный *adj* cultural
купаться *v* bathe
купон *n* coupon
курильщик *n* smoker
курить *v* smoke
курица *n* chicken, hen
куропатка *n* partridge
курс *n* course, trend
курсив *adj* italics
куртка *n* jacket, coat
курьёзный *adj* ludicrous
курьер *n* courier
кусать *v* bite
кусок мяса *n* steak
кусочек *n* bit
кусочек льда *n* ice cube
куст *n* bush, shrub
кухня *n* cuisine
куча *n* pile
куш *n* large sum
кушать *v* eat

К

Л

лабиринт *n* labyrinth, maze
лаборатория *n* lab
лавина *n* avalanche
лагерь *n* camp
лагуна *n* lagoon
ладонь *n* palm
лазарет *n* infirmary
лазер *n* laser
лак *n* varnish
лакировать *v* varnish
лампа *n* lamp
ландшафт *n* landscape
лапа *n* paw
ласка *n* caress
ласкать *v* caress, fondle
латать *v* patch
лачуга *n* shack
лаять *v* bark
лгать *v* lie
лгун *adj* liar
лебедь *n* swan
лев *n* lion
легализовать *v* legalize
легенда *n* legend
легион *n* legion
легкий *adj* easy, light
легкий по весу *n* lightweight
легкий туман *n* haze
легко *adv* easily

лёгкое *n* lung
лёд *n* ice
ледник *n* glacier
ледяной *adj* icy
лежать *v* lie
лежать в основе *v* underlie
лезвие *n* blade
лейкемия *n* leukemia
лейтенант *n* lieutenant
лекарство *n* medicine
лекция *n* lecture
ленивый *adj* lazy
леность *n* laziness
лента *n* ribbon, tape
леопард *n* leopard
лепесток *n* petal
лепетать *v* babble
лес *n* forest
лестница *n* staircase
лесть *n* flattery
летать *v* fly
лето *n* summer
летучая мышь *n* bat
лётчик *n* pilot
летящий *adj* volatile
лечение *n* cure, medication
лживый *adj* deceitful
ли *c* whether
ливень *n* rainfall
лига *n* league
лизать *v* lick
ликвидация *n* liquidation

ликёр *n* liqueur
ликовать *v* exult
ликующий *adj* triumphant
лимон *n* lemon
лимонад *n* lemonade
линейка *n* ruler
линза *n* lense
линия *n* line
линкор *n* battleship
линчевать *v* lynch
липкий *adj* adhesive
лирика *n* lyrics
лиса *n* fox
лисий *adj* foxy
лист *n* leaf
листочек *n* leaflet
литания *n* litany
литейный цех *n* foundry
литература *n* literature
литр *n* liter, litre
литургия *n* liturgy
лить *v* pour
лихой *adj* dashing
лихорадочный *adj* feverish
лицемер *adj* hypocrite
лицемерие *n* hypocrisy
лицензия *n* licence
лицо *n* face
личность *n* personality
личный *adj* personal
лишение *n* deprivation
лишённый *adj* indigent

лишь *c* only
лоб *n* forehead
лобзик *n* jigsaw
ловить *v* catch
ловкий *adj* deft
ловкость *n* dexterity
ловушка *n* snare, pitfall
логика *n* logic
логичный *adj* logical
лодка *n* boat
лодыжка *n* ankle
ложка *n* spoon
ложь *n* lie
лозунг *n* slogan
локализовать *v* localize
локон *n* curl
локоть *n* elbow
лом *n* crowbar
ломать *v* break
ломкий *adj* fragile
ломоть *n* chunk
ломтик *n* slice
лопата *n* shovel
лопать *v* guzzle
лоск *n* gloss
лосось *n* salmon
лосьон *n* lotion
лотерея *n* lottery, raffle
лошадь *n* horse
луг *n* meadow
лужа *n* pool
лук *n* onion

Л

лукавый *adj* cunning, wily
луковица *n* bulb
луна *n* moon
лунатизм *n* lunacy
луч *n* ray
лучина *n* splinter
лучший *adj* best, better
лысый *adj* bald
львица *n* lioness
льгота *n* charter, discount
льстить *v* flatter
любезность *n* courtesy
любезный *adj* courteous
любимый *adj* darling
любительский *adj* amateur
любить *v* love, affect
любовник *n* lover
любовь *n* affection, love
любой *adj* either, whatever
любопытный *adj* curious
любопытство *n* curiosity
любящий *adj* affectionate
люди *n* folks, people
люстра *n* chandelier
лягушка *n* frog

М

маг *n* magician
магазин *n* shop, store
магистраль *n* highway
магнат *n* tycoon
магнетизм *n* magnetism
магнит *n* magnet
магнитный *adj* magnetic
магнитофон *n* recorder
мадам *n* madam
мазок *n* smear
мазохизм *n* masochism
мазь *n* ointment
май *n* May
майор *n* major
мак *n* poppy
макет *n* model
максима *n* maxim
максимум *adj* maximum
маленькая *adj* petite
маленький *adj* little, small
малина *n* raspberry
маловажный *adj* petty
малоимущий *adj* deprived
мало-помалу *adv* little by little
малый *n* guy
мальчик *n* boy
малярия *n* malaria
мама *n* mom
мамонт *n* mammoth

мандарин *n* tangerine
мандат *n* mandate
манёвр *n* maneuver
манерность *n* mannerism
манеры *n* manners
манжета *n* cuff
маниакальный *adj* maniac
манить *v* beckon
манускрипт *n* manuscript
марать *v* blur, stain
мариновать *v* marinate
маркер *n* marker
Марс *n* Mars
март *n* March
маршал *n* marshal
маршрут *n* route
маска *n* mask
маскировать *v* disguise
маскировка *n* disguise
масса *n* mass
массаж *n* massage
массажист *n* masseur
массажистка *n* masseuse
массивный *adj* massive
массировать *v* massage
мастер *n* craftsman
мастеровой *n* artisan
мастерская *n* workshop
мат *n* mate
математика *n* math
материал *n* stuff
материализм *n* materialism

материнский *adj* maternal
материнство *n* motherhood
матка *n* uterus, womb
матрац *n* mattress
матрос *n* sailor
мать *n* mother
мачеха *n* stepmother
мачта *n* mast
маяк *n* lighthouse
маятник *n* pendulum
мгла *n* mist
мгновение *n* instant
мебель *n* furniture
меблировка *n* furnishings
мед *n* honey
медаль *n* medal
медальон *n* medallion
медведь *n* bear
медицина *n* medicine
медленно *adv* slowly
медленный *adj* slow
медлительный *adj* tardy
медлить *v* loiter
медь *n* copper
между *pre* amid, between
между тем *adv* meanwhile
мексиканский *adj* Mexican
мел *n* chalk
меланхолия *n* melancholy
мелкий *adj* shallow
мелкий дождь *n* drizzle
мелкий шрифт *n* small print

M

мелодичный *adj* melodic
мелодия *n* melody, tune
мелочность *n* pettiness
мелочный *adj* meticulous
мелькнуть *v* glimpse
мельница *n* mill
мемуары *n* memoirs
менингит *n* meningitis
менопауза *n* menopause
менструация *n* menstruation
мент *n* cop
менталитет *n* mentality
меньше *adj* fewer
меньший *adj* less, lesser
меньшинство *n* minority
меню *n* menu
меня самого *pro* myself
менять *v* alter, vary
мероприятие *n* affair
мёртвый *adj* dead
мерцание *n* glimmer
мерцать *v* flicker, gleam
Мессия *n* Messiah
местность *n* terrain
местный *adj* local
место *n* lieu, place, site
местоимение *n* pronoun
месть *n* revenge
месяц *n* month
металл *n* metal
металлический *adj* metallic
метафора *n* metaphor

метеор *n* meteor
метка *n* mark
меткий стрелок *n* marksman
метла *n* broom
метод *n* method
метрический *adj* metric
метро *n* subway
мех *n* fur
механизм *n* gear, machine
механик *n* mechanic
меховой *adj* furry
меч *n* sword
мечеть *n* mosque
меч-рыба *n* swordfish
мечта *n* dream
мечтать *v* dream
мечтать наяву *v* daydream
мешать *v* prevent; stir
мешок *n* sack
мигрант *n* migrant
мигрень *n* migraine
мигрировать *v* migrate
микроб *n* microbe
микроскоп *n* microscope
микрофон *n* microphone
миллиард *n* billion
миллиардер *n* billionaire
миллиграмм *n* milligram
миллиметр *n* millimeter
миллион *n* million
миллионер *n* millionaire
милосердие *n* mercy

M

милосердный *adj* merciful
милостыня *n* alms
миля *n* mile
миндаль *n* almond
минерал *n* mineral
миниатюра *n* miniature
минимум *n* minimum
министр *n* minister
мини-юбка *n* miniskirt
минное поле *n* minefield
минута *n* minute
мир *n* world, peace
мираж *n* mirage
мирный *adj* peaceful
мирской *adj* worldly
мирянин *n* layman
миска *n* basin, bowl
миссионер *n* missionary
миссия *n* mission
мистификация *n* hoax
мистический *adj* mystic
миф *n* myth
мишень *n* target
младенец *n* infant, baby
младенчество *n* infancy
младший *adj* junior
млекопитающее *n* mammal
мнение *n* opinion
многие *adj* many
много *adv* lots
многолетний *adj* perennial
многообразие *n* variety

множество *n* multitude
мобилизовать *v* mobilize
мобильный *adj* mobile
могила *n* grave
могучий *adj* powerful
мода *n* fashion
модель *n* model
модный *adj* fashionable
модуль *n* module
может быть *adv* maybe
мозаика *n* mosaic
мозаичный *adj* inlaid
мозг *n* brain
мой *pro* mine
мой *adj* my
мокрый *adj* wet, sloppy
молва *n* rumour
молекула *n* molecule
молитва *n* prayer
молиться *v* pray
моллюск *n* shellfish, clam
молния *n* lightning
молодой *adj* youthful
молодость *n* youth
молоко *n* milk
молот *n* hammer
молоть *v* grind
молочный *adj* milky
момент *n* moment
моментально *adv* momentarily
монарх *n* monarch
монархия *n* monarchy

M

монастырский *adj* monastic
монастырь *n* monastery
монах *n* monk, friar
монахиня *n* nun
монета *n* coin
монета в 10 центов *n* dime
монолог *n* monologue
монополия *n* monopoly
монотонность *n* monotony
монотонный *adj* monotonous
мораль *n* ethics, moral
морг *n* mortuary
моргать *v* blink
морда *n* muzzle
море *n* sea
морж *n* walrus
морковь *n* carrot
мороженое *n* ice cream
мороз *n* frost
морозный *adj* frosty
моросить *v* drizzle
морская болезнь *n* nausea
морской *adj* marine
морской берег *n* seashore
морской курорт *adj* seaside
морфий *n* morphine
морщина *n* wrinkle
морщиться *v* wrinkle
мост *n* bridge
мотель *n* motel
мотив *n* motive
мотоцикл *n* motorcycle

мотылек *n* moth
мох *n* moss
моча *n* urine
мочевой пузырь *n* bladder
мочиться *v* urinate
мочь *v* can, may
мошенник *n* con man, fraud
мошеннический *adj* fraudulent
мошенничество *n* fraud
моющийся *adj* washable
мрак *n* gloom
мрамор *n* marble
мрачный *adj* sullen, gloomy
мстительный *adj* vindictive
мудрость *n* wisdom
мудрый *adj* wise
муж *n* husband
мужественность *n* manliness
мужественный *adj* courageous
мужество *n* courage
мужской *adj* masculine
мужчина *n* male, man
мужчины *n* men
музей *n* museum
музыка *n* music
музыкант *n* musician
мука *n* flour
мул *n* mule
мумия *n* mummy
муравей *n* ant
мусор *n* garbage
мусорное ведро *n* trash can

мусульманский *adj* Muslim
муха *n* fly
мучение *n* torment
мученик *n* martyr
мученичество *n* martyrdom
мучительный *adj* agonizing
мучить *v* torment, tear
муштровать *n* drill
мчаться *v* rush, speed
мы *pro* we
мыслить *v* deem, think
мысль *n* thought
мыть *v* wash, mop
мыши *n* mice
мышца *n* muscle
мышь *n* mouse
мышьяк *n* arsenic
мэр *n* mayor
мягкий *adj* soft
мягко *adv* softly
мягкость *n* softness
мякоть *n* pulp
мясник *n* butcher
мясо *n* meat
мята *n* mint
мятеж *n* insurgency
мятежник *n* rebel

Н

на *pre* on, upon, at, by
на борту *adv* aboard
на одной линии *adv* abreast
на улице *adv* outdoors
на части *adv* asunder
набивать *v* pad, stuff
набивка *n* padding
наблюдатель *n* spectator
наблюдать *v* observe
наблюдение *n* observation
набожный *adj* pious
набор *n* set
наброситься *v* lash out
набросок *n* sketch
наверстать *v* catch up
наверх *adv* upstairs
наверху *pre* above
навес *n* awning
навещать *v* haunt, visit
навигация *n* navigation
нависающий *adj* impending
наволочка *n* pillowcase
навсегда *adv* forever
наглость *n* impertinence
наглый *adj* impertinent
наговаривать *v* denigrate
нагота *n* nudity
награда *n* reward
награждать *v* reward

нагревание *n* heating
нагреваться *v* heat
нагромождать *v* heap
нагружать *v* burden
нагруженный *adj* loaded
над *pre* over, above
надгробие *n* tombstone
надежда *n* hope
надежный *adj* reliable
надеющийся *adj* hopeful
надеяться *v* rely on
надзор *n* surveillance
надлежать *v* have to
надменность *n* arrogance
надменный *adj* arrogant
надоедать *v* bother
надоедливый *adj* bothersome
надпись *n* inscription
надрезание *n* incision
надувательство *n* swindle
наживка *n* bait
нажимать *v* press
назад *adv* backwards
название *n* title
назначать *v* appoint
назначать время *v* time
назначение *n* appointment
назойливый *adj* pushy
наибольший *adj* most
наивный *adj* naive
наизнанку *adv* inside out
наименьший *adj* least

наихудший *adj* worst
наказание *n* punishment
наказуемый *adj* punishable
наказывать *v* punish
накапливать *v* accumulate
накачивать *v* inflate, pump
накидка *n* cape
наклейка *n* sticker
наклон *n* bias, slope
наклонный *adj* slanted, oblique
наклонять *v* tilt, lean
наклоняться *v* incline
наковальня *n* anvil
наконец *adv* lastly
наконечник *v* spearhead
накопление *n* buildup
накрывать *v* cover
налагать вето *v* veto
налёт *n* raid
налётчик *n* hijacker
наличие *n* availability
наличный *adj* available
налог *n* tax
нам *pro* us
наматывать *v* wind
намёк *n* hint, inkling
намекать *v* hint
намекающий *adj* suggestive
намереваться *v* intend
намерение *n* intention
намеренно *adv* knowingly
нанимать *v* employ, hire

наносить *v* inflict
нападать *v* assail, strike
нападать на *v* hit back
нападение *n* assault
наперсник *n* confidant
напиваться *v* mug
напившийся *adj* drunk
написание *n* writing
написанный *adj* written
напиток *n* beverage
наполнение *n* filling
наполненный *adj* replete
наполнять *v* fill, flush
наполнять снова *v* refill
напоминание *n* reminder
напоминать *v* remind
направление *n* direction
направлять *v* direct
направляться *v* head for
напротив *adv* opposite
напряжение *n* voltage
напряженный *adj* tense, intensive
напугать *v* scare
нарезать *v* slice
наречие *n* adverb
наркотик *n* drug, narcotic
народный *adj* folksy
наружность *n* appearance
наружный *adj* outward
наручники *n* handcuffs
нарушать *v* violate

нарушение *n* infraction
нас *pre* us
насадка *n* nozzle
насекомое *n* insect
население *n* population
населять *v* populate
насильник *n* rapist
наслаждаться *v* enjoy, relish
наслаждение *n* enjoyment
наследие *n* heritage
наследник *n* heir
наследница *n* heiress
наследование *n* inheritance
наследовать *v* inherit
наследство *n* legacy
насмехаться *v* mock, scoff
насмешка *n* mockery
насос *n* pump
настаивать *v* insist
настойчивость *n* insistence
настойчивый *adj* persistent
настраивать *v* tune
настроение *n* mood
настройка *n* tuning
насупиться *v* frown
натягивать *v* strain
натяжение *n* strain
наука *n* science
научный *adj* scientific
наушники *n* headphones
нахальный *adj* cheeky
нахлынуть *v* flood

Н

находить *v* find
национальный *adj* national
нация *n* nation
начало *n* start, outset
начальный *adj* initial
начинать *v* begin, start
начинка *n* stuffing
начищать *v* polish
наш *adj* our
наш *pro* ours
не доверять *v* mistrust
не замечающий *adj* oblivious
не одобрять *v* disapprove
не подчиняться *v* disobey
не унывать *v* cheer up

неадекватный *adj* inadequate
небезопасность *n* insecurity
небеса *n* heaven
небесный *adj* heavenly
небо *n* sky
нёбо *n* palate
небоскреб *n* skyscraper
небрежность *n* negligence
небрежный *adj* careless
неброский *adj* unpretentious
неведающий *adj* unaware
невежливый *adj* impolite
неверие *n* disbelief
неверный *adj* untrue
невероятный *adj* unthinkable
невеста *n* bride
невестка *n* daughter-in-law

невзгода *n* misery
невидимый *adj* invisible
невинность *n* innocence
невинный *adj* innocent
невозможность *n* impossibility
невозможный *adj* impossible
невозмутимый *adj* composed
невредимый *adj* unharmed
невротический *adj* neurotic
невыгодный *adj* unprofitable
невыносимый *adj* unbearable
невысокий *adj* lowly
негибкий *adj* inflexible
негодный *adj* unfit
негодование *n* resentment
негодовать *v* resent
негодяй *n* scoundrel
неграмотный *adj* illiterate
недавний *adj* recent
недавно *adv* lately
недвижимость *n* property
недвижимый *adj* immobile
неделимый *adj* indivisible
неделя *n* week
недоверие *n* distrust
недоверчивый *adj* distrustful
недовольный *adj* discontent
недоедание *n* malnutrition
недомогание *n* distress
недорогой *adj* inexpensive
недосмотр *n* oversight
недоставать *v* fail, lack

недостаток *n* scarcity, lack
недостающий *adj* deficient
недоступный *adj* inaccessible
неженатый *adj* unmarried
нежно *adv* dearly
нежность *n* tenderness
нежный *adj* tender
независимый *adj* independent
незаконный *adj* illegal
незаметный *adj* unnoticeable
незамеченный *adj* unnoticed
нездоровый *adj* unhealthy
нездоровье *n* poor health
незнакомец *n* stranger
незнакомый *adj* unfamiliar
незрелость *n* immaturity
незрелый *adj* immature
неизбежный *adj* inevitable
неизвестность *n* suspense
неизлечимый *adj* incurable
неизменный *adj* unfailing
неизменяемый *adj* irreversible
неискренний *adj* insincere
неискренность *n* insincerity
неисправимый *adj* irreparable
неисправность *n* disrepair
неисправный *adj* faulty
неистовство *n* fury
неистовый *adj* violent, stark
неистовый крик *n* outcry
нейтрализовать *v* neutralize
нейтральный *adj* neutral

некоторый *adj* some, several
некурящий *n* nonsmoker
нелепый *adj* ridiculous
неловкий *adj* awkward
нелогичный *adj* irrational, illogical
нелояльность *n* disloyalty
нелояльный *adj* disloyal
немедленно *adv* instantly
немецкий *adj* German
немногие *adj* few
немного *adv* slightly
немой *adj* dumb, mute
немощный *adj* feeble
ненавидеть *v* hate, detest
ненавистный *adj* hateful
ненависть *n* hatred
ненадежный *adj* unreliable
ненастоящий *adj* unreal
ненасытный *adj* insatiable
ненормальность *n* abnormality
ненормальный *adj* abnormal
ненужный *adj* needless
необдуманный *adj* thoughtless
необходимость *n* necessity
необходимый *adj* necessary
необъяснимый *adj* inexplicable
необычный *adj* uncommon
неодобрение *n* disapproval
неодолимый *adj* invincible
неожиданный *adj* unexpected
неопытный *adj* inexperienced

Н

неосознающий *adj* unconscious
неоспоримый *adj* undeniable
неотвратимый *adj* imminent
неотделимый *adj* inseparable
неотразимый *adj* irresistible
неотъемлемый *adj* essential
неохотно *adv* reluctantly
неохотный *adj* reluctant
непобедимый *adj* unbeatable
неповиновение *n* disobedience
неподвижный *adj* motionless
неподходящий *adj* unsuitable
непокорный *adj* disobedient
непомерный *adj* prodigious
непонятный *adj* obscure
непопулярный *adj* unpopular
непослушный *adj* naughty
непостоянный *adj* fickle
непохожий *adj* dissimilar
неправильный *adj* wrong
непреклонный *adj* adamant
непрерывный *adj* continuous
непривязанный *adj* unattached
неприличие *n* indecency
непринужденный *adj* lavish
непристойность *n* obscenity
непристойный *adj* obscene
неприязнь *n* dislike
неприятный *adj* displeasing
непрозрачный *adj* opaque
непрочный *adj* fragile
непрямой *adj* indirect

неработающий *adj* idle;
unemployed
неравный *adj* unequal
неразбериха *n* mix-up
неразбитый *adj* unbroken
неразборчивый *adj* illegible
неразрывность *n* continuity
неразумный *adj* unreasonable
нерастворимый *adj* insoluble
нерв *n* nerve
нервный *adj* nervous
нереалистичный *adj* unrealistic
нерегулярный *adj* irregular
нерешающий *adj* indecisive
нерешённый *adj* undecided
нержавеющий *adj* rust-proof
неровный *adj* uneven
неряха *n* slob
неслучайный *adj* deliberate
неслыханный *adj* unheard-of
несовершенство *n* imperfection
несомненно *adv* indeed
неспокойный *adj* jumpy, restless
неспособность *n* inability
неспособный *adj* unable
несправедливо *adv* unfairly
нестабильный *adj* unstable
нестандартный *adj* substandard
нести *v* carry, bear
несчастливый *adj* unhappy
несчастный *adj* wretched
несчастье *n* unhappiness

несчастья *n* woes, disaster
нет *adv* no
нетерпеливый *adj* impatient
нетерпение *n* impatience
нетерпимость *n* intolerance
неточный *adj* inaccurate
нетронутый *adj* intact
неуважение *n* disrespect
неудача *n* misfortune
неудачник *n* loser
неудачный *adj* unlucky
неудобный *adj* inconvenient
неудобство *n* discomfort
неудовольствие *n* displeasure
неуловимый *adj* elusive, subtle
неумело латать *v* botch
неуместный *adj* inappropriate
неумолимый *adj* implacable
неупотребление *n* disuse
неустойчивость *n* instability
неустойчивый *adj* unsteady
неутомимый *adj* tireless
неф *n* nave
неформальный *adj* informal
нефть *n* petroleum
нехватка *n* shortage
нечастый *adj* infrequent
нечестивый *adj* profane
нечестность *n* dishonesty
нечестный *adj* dishonest
нечётный *adj* odd
нечистый *adj* impure

неясность *n* vagueness
ни *c* nor
ни один *pro* no one
ни один из *pre* none
ни тот ни другой *adv* neither
нигде *adv* nowhere
Нидерланды *n* Netherlands
ниже *adv* below, hereafter
нижнее бельё *n* underwear
нижний *adj* lower
низвергать *v* precipitate
низводить *v* relegate
низкий *adj* low
низложить *v* depose
низость *n* meanness
никакой *adj* neither
никель *n* nickel
никогда *adv* never
никотин *n* nicotine
никто *pro* nobody
нисходящий *adj* descending
нить *n* thread
ничего *n* nothing
но *c* but
новизна *n* novelty
новичок *n* beginner
новобранец *n* novice
новобрачный *adj* newlywed
нововведение *n* innovation
новость *n* news
новый *adj* new
нога *n* leg

Н

ноготь *n* fingernail
нож *n* knife
ножницы *n* scissors
ноздря *n* nostril
нора *n* burrow
Норвегия *n* Norway
норвежский *adj* Norwegian
норма *n* norm
нормализовать *v* normalize
нормально *adv* normally
нормальный *adj* normal
нормировать *v* standardize
нос *n* prow; nose
носатый *adj* nosy
носилки *n* stretcher
носильщик *n* bearer
носить *v* wear
носовой платок *n* handkerchief
носок *n* sock
носорог *n* rhinoceros
ностальгия *n* nostalgia
нотариус *n* notary
нотация *n* notation
ночная рубашка *n* nightgown
ночной *adj* nocturnal
ночь *n* night
ноша *n* burden
ношение *n* wear
ноябрь *n* November
нрав *n* temper
нравиться *v* like
нравственность *n* morality

нравственный *adj* moral
нудизм *n* nudism
нудист *n* nudist
нудный *adj* tedious
нуждаться *v* need
нуждающийся *adj* needy
нуль *n* zero
ныряльщик *n* diver
ныряние *n* plunge, diving
нырять *v* plunge, dive
нюанс *n* nuance
нюхать *v* sniff
нянечка *n* nanny
няня *n* nurse

О

оазис *n* oasis
оба *adj* both
обаятельный *adj* glamorous
обваливаться *v* collapse
обвинение *n* accusation
обвиняемый *n* culprit
обвинять *v* accuse
обдумывание *n* deliberation
обдумывать *v* consider
обед *n* lunch, dinner
обедать *v* dine

обезвоживать *v* dehydrate
обезличенный *adj* impersonal
обезоруживать *v* disarm
обезьяна *n* monkey
обёртка *n* wrapping
обёртывать *v* envelop
обеспечение *n* provision
обеспеченный *adj* well-to-do
обеспечивать *v* provide
обессиленный *v* prostrate
обесценение *n* devaluation
обесценивание *n* depreciation
обесценивать *v* devalue
обещание *n* promise
обжигать *v* scald, scorch
обжора *n* glutton
обивка *n* upholstery
обида *n* offence
обижать *v* offend
обитаемый *adj* habitable
обитать *v* inhabit, dwell
облава *n* manhunt
обладать *v* possess
облако *n* cloud
облачный *adj* cloudy
облегчать *v* relieve, alleviate
облегчение *n* relief, ease
обледенеть *v* freeze
обложение *n* imposition
обломки *n* debris
обломок *n* fragment
обман *n* deceit, fallacy

обманчивый *adj* misleading
обманщик *n* twister
обманывать *v* deceive, trick
обмен *n* interchange
обменивать *v* swap
обмениваться *v* interchange
обморок *n* faint
обнаженный *adj* nude
обнаруживать *v* discover
обнаруживаться *v* show up
обнаружитель *n* detector
обнимать *v* cuddle, hug
обниматься *v* embrace
обновление *n* renewal
обновлять *v* renew
обобщать *v* sum up
обогащать *v* enrich
обод *n* rim
ободрять *v* cheer
обожаемый *adj* adorable
обожание *n* adoration
обожать *v* adore
обозревать *v* overlook
обозрение *n* revue
обольщение *n* seduction
образец *n* pattern
образование *n* formation
образцовый *adj* exemplary
обрамлять *v* frame
обратимый *adj* reversible
обратная связь *n* feedback
обратно *adv* back

обратный *adj* backward
обратный счет *n* countdown
обращаться *v* address, treat
обращение *n* treatment
обрезание *n* circumcision
обрезок *n* clipping
обречённый *adj* doomed
обручение *n* engagement
обрушение *n* collapse
обрыв *n* precipice
обряд *n* rite
обсерватория *n* observatory
обследование *n* inspection
обслуживать *v* service
обстановка *n* scene
обсуждать *v* debate
обсуждение *n* discussion
обувной магазин *n* shoestore
обувь *n* footwear
обуздание *n* curb
обуздывать *v* daunt
обучать *v* train
обучение *n* training
обход *n* detour
обходить *v* bypass
обширный *adj* spacious
общаться *v* socialize
общежитие *n* dormitory
общественный *adj* public
общество *n* society
общий *adj* general
общительный *adj* genial

общность *n* community
объединение *n* association
объединять *v* unify, unite
объединяться *v* incorporate
объем *n* volume
объявление *n* announcement
объявлять *v* announce
объятие *n* hug
обыденный *adj* homely
обыкновенно *adv* ordinarily
обыкновенный *adj* ordinary
обыскивать *v* ransack
обычай *n* custom
обычный *adj* customary
обязанный *adj* liable
обязательный *adj* compulsory
обязательство *n* obligation
обязывать *v* obligate
овальный *adj* oval
овация *n* ovation
овечья шерсть *n* fleece
овощ *n* vegetable
овраг *n* ravine
овсянка *n* oatmeal
овца *n* sheep
оглавление *n* contents
оглушать *v* deafen
оглушающий *adj* stunning
оглушить ударом *v* stun
огненный *adj* fiery
огнеопасный *adj* flammable
огонь *n* fire

О

огораживание *n* enclosure
огораживать *v* enclose
огорчать *v* grieve
ограбление *n* robbery
ограничение *n* confinement
ограничивать *v* restrict, limit
огромный *adj* huge
огурец *n* cucumber
одалживать *v* loan, lend
одевание *n* dressing
одевать *v* clothe
одеваться *v* dress
одежда *n* clothes
одеяло *n* blanket
одеяние *n* apparel
один *adj* one
одиннадцатый *adj* eleventh
одиннадцать *adj* eleven
одинокий *adj* single
одиноко *adv* lonely
одиночество *n* loneliness
одиночка *n* loner
одиночный *adj* solitary
одиссея *n* odyssey
одна сотая часть *adv* percent
однажды *adv* once
однако *c* however
одноклассник *n* classmate
одобрение *n* approval
одобрять *v* approve
одометр *n* odometer
одурачивать *v* dupe

ожерелье *n* necklace
оживать *v* revive
оживить *v* animate
оживленный *adj* brisk, vivacious
ожидаемый *adj* coming, expected
ожидание *n* expectation
ожидать *v* expect
ожог *n* burn
озабоченность *n* preoccupation
озеро *n* lake
озлоблять *v* embitter
озорной *adj* mischievous
окаменелый *adj* petrified
океан *n* ocean
оккультный *adj* occult
оккупант *n* occupant
окно *n* window
околдовывать *v* enchant
около *pre* alongside, by
окончательный *adj* definitive
окорок *n* ham
окоченелый *adj* numb
окраина *n* outskirts
окраска *n* dye
окрашивать *v* dye, stain
окрестности *n* surroundings
окровавленный *adj* gory
окружать *v* encircle
окружение *n* encirclement
окружность *n* circumference
октябрь *n* October

O

окунать *v* submerge
окуривать *v* fumigate
оленина *n* venison
олень *n* deer
оливка *n* olive
олово *n* tin
омар *n* lobster
омлет *n* omelette
он *pro* he
она *pro* she
они *pro* they
опасение *n* misgiving
опасность *n* danger
опасный *adj* dangerous
опекунство *n* custody
опера *n* opera
операция *n* operation
опечатка *n* misprint
описание *n* description
описательный *adj* descriptive
описывать *v* describe
опиум *n* opium
оплакивать *v* deplore
оплата *n* payment
оплачивать *v* defray
опорожнять *v* evacuate
оправа *n* rim
оправдание *n* acquittal
оправдывать *v* acquit
определение *n* definition
определенно *adv* expressly
определённый *adj* certain

определять *v* determine
опробовать *v* probe
опровергать *v* disprove
опрокидывать *v* capsize
опрос *n* survey
опрятно *adv* neatly
опрятный *adj* tidy, neat
оптик *n* optician
оптимизм *n* optimism
оптический *adj* optical
опустошать *v* devastate
опустошение *n* devastation
опухать *v* swell
опухоль *n* swelling
опухший *adj* swollen
опыт *n* experience
опытность *n* proficiency
опытный *adj* expert
опьяненный *adj* intoxicated
опять *adv* afresh
оракул *n* oracle
орангутанг *n* orangutan
оранжерея *n* greenhouse
оратор *n* speaker
орать *v* shriek
орбита *n* orbit
орган *n* organ
организация *n* organization
организм *n* organism
органист *n* organist
ордер *n* warrant
ординация *n* ordination

O

орёл *n* eagle

орех *n* nut

ориентация *n* orientation

оркестр *n* orchestra

орнамент *n* ornament

орошать *v* irrigate

орошение *n* irrigation

орудие *n* weapon; tool

орудовать *v* wield

оружие *n* gun

оса *n* wasp

осада *n* siege

осадки *n* precipitation

осадок *n* sediment

осаждать *v* besiege

осанка *n* posture

освежать *v* refresh

освежающий *adj* refreshing

осветитель *n* lighter

осветлять *v* clear

освещать *v* illuminate

освещение *n* lighting

освобождать *v* release, free

освобождение *n* exemption

освящать *v* sanctify

оседать *v* sink in

осёл *n* donkey

осень *n* autumn

оскорбление *n* offense

оскорблять *v* insult

ослабевать *v* weaken

ослабевший *adj* weakened

ослаблять *v* slacken, loosen

ослеплять *v* blind

ослепляющий *adj* dazzling

осматривать *v* examine

оснащение *n* equipment

основа *n* base

основатель *n* founder

основной *adj* basic, main

основы *n* basics

основывать *v* establish

особенно *adv* especially

особенность *n* feature, trait

особенный *adj* special

оспа *n* smallpox

оставаться *v* remain

оставление *n* abandonment

оставлять *v* abandon

останавливать *v* discontinue

останки *n* remains, spoils

остановка *n* stop

остатки *n* leavings

остаток *n* remnant

остающийся *adj* remaining

остерегаться *v* beware

осторожность *n* caution

осторожный *adj* cautious

остров *n* island

остроконечный *adj* pointed

остроумие *n* wit

остроумный *adj* witty

острый *adj* acute, sharp

осудить *v* convict

O

осуждать v condemn

осуждение n blame

осушать v drain

осуществлять v implement

ось n axis

осьминог n octopus

осязаемый adj palpable

от pre from

отбеливание n bleach

отбеливать v bleach

отбивать v repulse

отбирать v deprive

отбрасывать v repel

отвага n audacity

отваживаться v dare

отважный adj bold

отвар n broth

отвергать v turn down

отвертка n screwdriver

ответ n answer

ответчик n defendant

отвечать v reply

отвлекать v distract

отводить v divert

отворачиваться v avert

отвращение n disgust

отвязывать v untie

отговаривать v dissuade

отдаленно adv remotely

отдаленный adj remote, devious

отдаляться v drift apart

отдел n department

отделение n segregation

отдельно adv apart

отдельный adj separate

отделяемый adj detachable

отделять v detach

отделяться v secede

отдушина n vent

отдых n recreation, rest

отдыхать v rest

отец n father

отечество n homeland

отзывчивый adj open-minded

отказ n denial, refusal

отказаться v give up

отказывать v refuse

отказываться v disclaim

откинуться v lean back

откладывать v postpone

отклонение n diversion

отклонять v overrule

отключить v unplug

откровение n revelation

откровенно adv frankly

откровенность n frankness

откровенный adj candid

открывать v open

открытие n opening

открытка n postcard

открытый adj open

открыться v open up

откупаться от v buy off

отличаться v differ

отличие *n* difference
отличный *adj* excellent
отмена *n* cancellation
отменять *v* revoke
отмерять *v* measure out
отмечать *v* denote
относительно *pre* concerning
относительный *adj* relative
отношение *n* relationship
отодвигать *v* move aside
отомстить *v* avenge
отпирать *v* unlock
отплачивать *v* retaliate
отпор *n* rebuff
отправитель *n* sender
отправляться *v* get off
отпрыск *n* offspring
отпугивать *v* scare away
отпускать *v* dismiss
отравление *n* poisoning
отравлять *v* poison
отражать *v* fend, reflect
отражение *n* reflection
отрезать *v* cut off
отрекаться *v* recant
отречение *n* abdication
отрицать *v* deny, disown
отрочество *n* boyhood
отрыжка *n* belch, burp
отряд *n* troop
отскакивать *v* bounce
отскок *n* bounce

отслаивание *n* lift-off
отсрочка *n* postponement
отставать *v* fall behind
отстёгивать *v* unfasten
отступать *v* recede
отступление *n* backoff
отсутствующий *adj* absent
отсюда *adv* hence
оттенок *n* shade
оттепель *n* thaw
отходить *v* depart
отходы *n* refuse
отцовский *adj* fatherly
отцовство *n* fatherhood
отчасти *adv* partially
отчаяние *n* despair
отчаянный *adj* desperate
отчет *n* report, account
отчётливый *adj* clear-cut
отчим *n* stepfather
отчитываться *v* report
отчищать *v* scour
отшельник *n* hermit
отъезд *n* departure
отыграть *v* win back
отыскать *v* retrieve
офис *n* office
официально *adv* formally
официант *n* waiter
официантка *n* waitress
оформлять *v* formalize
охлаждать *v* chill, cool

О

охлаждение *adj* cooling
охота *n* hunting
охотиться *v* hunt
охотник *n* hunter
охотно *adv* willingly
охрана *n* guard
охранять *v* protect
охрипший *adj* hoarse
оценка *n* appraisal
оцепенение *n* consternation
оцеплять *v* cordon off
очаг *n* furnace; focus
очарование *n* charm
очаровательный *adj* charming
очаровывать *v* captivate
очевидно *adv* obviously
очевидность *n* evidence
очевидный *adj* obvious
очень *adv* much, very
очень высокий *adj* lofty
очередной взнос *n* installment
очередь *n* queue
очертание *n* outline
очертания *n* loom
очертить *v* outline
очиститель *n* cleanser
очистка *n* purification
очищать *v* cleanse
очищать шкурку *v* peel
очищение *n* purge
очки *n* eyeglasses
ошеломить *v* daze

О

ошеломлённый *adj* dazed
ошибаться *v* mistake
ошибка *n* error, mistake
ошибочный *adj* erroneous
ощущать *v* sense
ощущение *n* sensation

П

павлин *n* peacock
падать *v* fall
падать дождем *v* rain
падение *n* fall, descent
падчерица *n* stepdaughter
пазуха *n* bosom
пакет *n* package
пакт *n* pact
палатка *n* pavilion, tent
палач *n* hanger
палец *n* finger
палец ноги *n* toe
палка *n* stick
паломник *n* pilgrim
палуба *n* deck
пальто *n* overcoat
памятник *n* monument
память *n* memory
паника *n* panic

панорама *n* panorama
пантера *n* panther
папка *n* folder, file
папочка *n* dad
папство *n* papacy
пар *n* steam
пара *n* pair, couple
парад *n* parade
парадокс *n* paradox
паразит *n* parasite
парализовать *v* immobilize
паралич *n* paralysis
параллель *n* parallel
параметры *n* parameters
парашют *n* parachute
парашютист *n* paratrooper
парень *n* fellow, lad
пари *n* bet
парик *n* wig
парикмахер *n* barber
парить *v* soar
парк *n* park
парковать *v* park
парламент *n* parliament
пароль *n* password
партизан *n* partisan
партия товара *n* consignment
партнёр *n* partner
парус *n* sail
парусник *n* sailboat
паспорт *n* passport
пассажир *n* passenger

пассивный *adj* passive
паста *n* paste
пастбище *n* pasture
пастель *n* crayon
пастеризовать *v* pasteurize
пастернак *n* parsnip
пастор *n* pastor
пастух *n* shepherd
пастырский *adj* pastoral
Пасха *n* Easter
пасынок *n* stepson
пат *n* stalemate
патент *n* patent
патио *n* patio
патриарх *n* patriarch
патриот *n* patriot
патрон *n* patron
патруль *n* patrol
паук *n* spider
паутина *n* spiderweb
пах *n* groin
пахать *v* plow, till
пахнуть *v* smell
пахотный *adj* arable
пачкать *v* soil
певец *n* singer
педагогика *n* pedagogy
педаль *n* pedal
педантичный *adj* pedantic
пекарь *n* baker
пеликан *n* pelican
пена *n* foam, lather

П

пенальти *n* penalty
пенициллин *n* penicillin
пенни *n* penny
пенсия *n* pension
пень *n* stub
пепельница *n* ashtray
первый *adj* premier
первый этаж *n* ground floor
пергамент *n* parchment
перебрасывать *v* overthrow
перевешивать *v* outweigh
перевод *n* interpretation
переводить *v* translate
переводчик *n* translator
перевозить *v* transport
переговоры *n* negotiation
перегонять *v* outrun
передавать *v* transfer
передача *n* transfer
передвигать *v* move
переделывать *v* redo
передний *adj* front
передний план *n* foreground
передышка *n* repose
пережить *v* outlive
перезаряжать *v* recharge
переизбирать *v* reelect
переиздавать *v* reprint
переиздание *n* reprint
перекипать *v* boil over
переключать *v* switch
перекресток *n* junction

переливание *n* transfusion
перелом *n* fracture
перемешивать *v* mix, shuffle
перемещать *v* dislodge
перемещение *n* relocation
перемирие *n* truce
перенимать *v* take over
переоценивать *v* revalue
перепархивать *v* flutter
перепел *n* quail
переписывать *v* rewrite
перепись *n* census
переплетать *v* intertwine
переполненный *adj* crowded
переполнять *v* overwhelm
перепонка *n* membrane
переправа *n* ferry
перепроверить *v* double-check
перепутанный *adj* deranged
перерастать *v* outgrow
перерыв *n* recess, break
пересаживать *v* transplant
пересекать *v* intersect
переставать *v* desist
перестараться *v* overdo
перестраивать *v* reconstruct
перестрелка *n* skirmish
переступить *v* overstep
пересчет *n* recount
перехитрить *v* double-cross
переходить *v* cross, pass
перец *n* pepper

перечислять *v* enumerate
перила *n* handrail, rail
периметр *n* perimeter
период *n* period
перо *n* feather
персик *n* peach
персонал *n* personnel
перспектива *n* perspective
перспективы *n* outlook
перфорация *n* perforation
перхоть *n* dandruff
перчатка *n* glove
песнь *n* chant
песня *n* song
песок *n* sand
пессимизм *n* pessimism
пестицид *n* pesticide
петиция *n* petition
петля *n* loop
петрушка *n* parsley
петух *n* rooster, cock
петь *v* sing
пехота *n* infantry
печалить *v* sadden
печаль *n* sadness
печатание *n* printing
печатать *v* print, type
печать *v* seal, stamp
печень *n* liver
печенье *n* biscuit, cookie
печь *n* heater, stove
пешеход *n* pedestrian

пещера *n* cave
пианино *n* piano
пианист *n* pianist
пиво *n* beer
пижама *n* pajamas
пик *n* peak
пикантность *n* zest
пила *n* saw
пилить *v* saw
пиломатериалы *n* lumber
пилот *n* pilot
пинать *v* kick
пингвин *n* penguin
пинта *n* pint
пинцет *n* tweezers
пионер *n* pioneer
пир *n* feast
пирамида *n* pyramid
пират *n* pirate
пиратство *n* piracy
пировать *v* revel
пирог *n* pie, tart
писатель *n* writer
писать *v* write
писклявый *adj* squeaky
пистолет *n* handgun
письмо *n* letter
питание *n* nutrition, diet
питательный *adj* nutritious
питон *n* python
пить *v* drink
питье *n* drink

пищать v squeak
пищеварение n digestion
пищевод n esophagus
пиявка n leech
плавание n swimming
плавать v sail, swim
плавка n fuse
плавник n fin
плакат n poster
плакать v weep
пламя n flame
план n agenda, plan
планета n planet
планировать v schedule
пластмасса n plastic
пластырь n plaster
плата n fee, payment
платина n platinum
платить v disburse, pay
плато n plateau
платформа n platform
платье n dress, gown
плачевный adj pitiful
плачущий adj tearful
плащ n raincoat, cloak
плевать v spit
племя n tribe
племянник n nephew
племянница n niece
плен n captivity
пленник n captive
плесень n mildew, mold

плесневеть v mold
плетеный adj woven
плетень n hurdle
плеть n scourge, lash
плечо n shoulder
плита n slab
пловец n swimmer
плод n fruit
плодоносный adj fruitful
плодородие n fertility
плодородный adj fertile
плоский adj flat
плоскость n plane
плот n raft
плотник n carpenter
плотность n density
плотный adj dense
плотский adj carnal
плохо adv badly
плохой adj bad
площадь n area
плутоний n plutonium
плюс pre plus
плюш adj plush
пневмония n pneumonia
по pre per
по соседству adj next door
по частям adv piecemeal
победа n victory
победитель n winner
победить v win
победный adj victorious

победоносный *adj* triumphant
побеждать *v* overpower
побережье *n* coast
поборник *adj* bigot, advocate
побороть *v* overcome
побуждать *v* excite
побуждающий *adj* challenging
побуждение *n* incentive
повар *n* cook
поведение *n* behavior
повелительный *adj* bossy
поверхность *n* surface
повесить *v* hang up
повиноваться *v* obey
поводок *n* leash
поводья *n* rein
поворачивать *v* turn
поворачиваться *v* swivel
поворот *n* turn
повреждать *v* injure
повреждение *n* deterioration
поврежденный *adj* hurt
повседневный *adj* casual
повсеместно *adv* overall
повторение *n* repetition
повторять *v* repeat
повышать *v* heighten
повышение *n* boost
повязка на глаза *n* blindfold
погибать *v* perish
поглаживание *n* stroke
поглощать *v* engulf

поглощающий *adj* absorbent
поглощение *n* intake
поглощённый *adj* engrossed
погода *n* weather
погоня *n* chase
пограничный *adj* borderline
погружать *v* immerse
погружение *n* immersion
погрузка *n* loading
под *pre* under, below
подавление *n* repression
подавленный *adj* dejected
подавлять *v* repress, quell
подагра *n* gout
подаяние *n* handout
подбирать *v* pick up
подбить *v* get down
подбородок *n* chin
подбрасывать *v* toss
подвал *n* basement
подвеска *n* pendant
подвешивать *v* suspend
подвиг *n* exploit, feat
подводить итог *v* summarize
подвязка *n* garter
подглядывать *v* peep
подгонка *n* fit
подгонять *v* urge, goad
подготовка *n* preparation
поддаваться *v* succumb
подделка *n* forgery
подделывать *v* fake

П

поддельный *adj* phoney
поддержание *n* maintenance
поддерживать *v* support
поддержка *n* support
поджаривать *v* toast
поджигатель *n* arsonist
поджог *n* arson
подзаголовок *n* subtitle
подземный *adj* underground
подкладка *n* lining
подключиться к *v* tap into
подкреплять *v* beef up
подкуп *n* bribe
подкупать *v* bribe
подливка *n* gravy
подлинность *n* authenticity
подлинный *adj* authentic
подметать *v* sweep
подмигивание *n* wink
подмигивать *v* wink
подмышка *n* armpit
поднимать *v* pick up
подниматься *v* ascend
поднос *n* tray
поднятие *n* raise
подобие *n* semblance
подобно *pre* like
подобный *adj* similar
подозревать *v* suspect
подозрение *n* suspicion
подол *n* lap, hem
подошва *n* sole

подписка *n* subscription
подписывать *v* underwrite
подпись *n* signature
подправлять *v* touch up
подпрыгивать *v* hop
подражание *n* imitation
подражать *v* imitate
подрезать *v* prune, trim
подробность *n* detail
подросток *n* teenager
подружка *n* girlfriend
подрывать *v* undermine
подсвечник *n* candlestick
подслащивать *v* sweeten
подслушивать *v* eavesdrop
подставка *n* stand
подставной *adj* dummy
подстрекать *v* incite
подсчитывать *v* count up
подтверждать *v* corroborate
подтяжки *n* suspenders
подушка *n* pillow
подход *n* approach
подходить *v* approach
подходящий *adj* appropriate
подчёркивать *v* underline
подчиненный *adj* subdued
подчинять *v* subdue
подчиняться *v* submit
подшивать *v* turn up
подъём *n* upheaval
поезд *n* train

П

поездка *n* trip
пожарник *n* firefighter
пожарный *n* fireman
пожертвование *n* donation
пожилой *adj* elderly
пожимать *v* shrug
пожинать *v* reap
пожирать *v* gobble
поза *n* pose
позади *pre* behind
позволить себе *v* afford
позволять *v* allow, let
позвонок *n* vertebra
позвоночник *n* backbone
поздний завтрак *n* brunch
поздно *adv* late
поздравлять *v* congratulate
позже *adv* later
позировать *v* pose
позитивный *adj* positive
позиция *n* standpoint
позорить *v* slur
позорный *adj* disgraceful
поиск *n* quest, search
пока *e* bye
пока *pre* until
пока *c* while
показ *n* display
показной *adj* ostentatious
показывать *v* show, expose
покачивать *v* wiggle
покаяние *n* repentance

покидать *v* leave
покинутый *adj* derelict
покладистый *adj* compliant
поклон *n* bow
поклонение *n* worship
поклонник *n* admirer
покойный *adj* deceased
поколение *n* generation
покорный *adj* submissive
покорять *v* enthrall, conquer
покров *n* cover
покровитель *n* patron
покрывать *v* cover
покрытый корой *adj* crusty
покупатель *n* customer
покупать *v* purchase, buy
покупка *n* purchase
покупка товаров *n* shopping
пол *n* floor, sex
полагать *v* presuppose
полагаться *v* repose
полдень *n* noon
поле *n* margin, field
полезный *adj* worthwhile
полёт *n* flight
ползать *v* crawl, creep
поливать *v* water
полигамия *n* polygamy
полигамный *adj* polygamist
поликлиника *n* clinic
полировать *v* polish
политик *n* politician

политика *n* policy, politics
полицейский *n* policeman
полиция *n* police
полк *n* regiment
полка *n* shelf
полки *n* shelves
полковник *n* colonel
полная ложка *n* spoonful
полностью *adv* completely
полнота *n* totality
полночь *n* midnight
полный *adj* full
половая зрелость *n* virility
половина *n* half
половинный *adj* half
положение *n* standing, position
положить *v* lay
поломка *n* breakdown
полоса *n* stripe
полоскать *v* gargle, rinse
полотенце *n* towel
полотно *n* linen
полоть *v* weed
полуостров *n* peninsula
полуось *n* axle
получатель *n* addressee
получать *v* receive, get
получение *n* receipt
полушарие *n* hemisphere
пользоваться *v* exploit
польский *adj* Polish
Польша *n* Poland

полярный *adj* polar
помещать *v* place
помещение *n* quarters
помидор *n* tomato
помимо *adv* aside from
помнить *v* remember
помнящий *adj* mindful
помогать *v* assist, help
помощник *n* helper, aide
помощь *n* help, aid
помпезность *n* pomposity
понедельник *n* Monday
понижать *v* step down
понижаться *v* go down
понимание *n* understanding
понимать *v* understand
понос *n* diarrhea
поношенный *adj* shabby
понятие *n* concept, notion
понятный *adj* understandable
понять *v* fathom out
поперек *pre* across
попечитель *n* guardian
поплатиться *v* forfeit
пополняться *v* replenish
поправка *n* amendment
поправляться *v* recuperate
по-прежнему *adv* still
попрошайка *n* beggar
попугай *n* parrot
популярность *n* celebrity
популярный *adj* popular

попытка *n* attempt
пора *n* pore; time
поражать *v* astound
поражение *n* defeat
порез *n* gash, slash
пористый *adj* porous
порицать *v* censure
порка *n* spanking
поровну *adv* fifty-fifty
порог *n* threshold
порода *n* breed
порождать *v* generate
порок *n* vice
пороть *v* flog
порох *n* gunpowder
порочить *v* smear
порочность *n* wickedness
порочный *adj* vicious
порошок *n* powder
портативный *n* portable
портить *v* defile, spoil
портной *n* tailor
портрет *n* portrait
Португалия *n* Portugal
португальский *adj* Portuguese
портфель *n* briefcase
поручение *n* errand
поручитель *n* guarantor
поручительство *n* voucher
порхать *v* hover
порция *n* portion, batch
порыв *n* gust, urge

порывистый *adj* puffy
порядок *n* order
посвящать *v* dedicate
посвящение *n* dedication
поселенец *n* settler
поселение *n* settlement
посеребрённый *adj* silverplated
посещать *v* attend, visit
посещение *n* attendance, visit
поскольку *c* as far as
послание *n* message
посланник *n* envoy
после *pre* after, since
последний *adj* last, latter
последователь *n* follower
последствие *n* consequence
последующий *adj* subsequent
пословица *n* proverb
послушание *n* obedience
послушный *adj* obedient
посмеиваться *v* chuckle
посмешище *n* target
посмотреть на *v* look at
пособие *n* gratuity
посол *n* ambassador
посольство *n* embassy
поспешно *adv* hastily
поспешность *n* rash
посредник *n* intermediary
посредничать *v* mediate
поставлять *v* supply
поставщик *n* supplier

постепенный *adj* gradual
постигать *v* conceive
посторонний *adj* extraneous
постоянный *adj* constant
постоянство *n* consistency
поступок *n* action, deed
постыдный *adj* shameful
посуда *n* crockery, utensil
посылать *v* dispatch
посылка *n* parcel
посягать *v* trespass
пот *n* sweat
потворствовать *v* indulge
потение *n* perspiration
потенциальный *adj* potential
потерпеть крах *v* crash
потеря *n* loss, miss
потеть *v* sweat
поток *n* stream, current
потолок *n* ceiling
потолочное окно *n* skylight
потомок *n* descendant
потомство *n* posterity
потому что *c* because
потоп *n* deluge
потребитель *n* consumer
потребление *n* consumption
потрясающий *adj* awesome
потрясение *n* shock
потрясенный *adj* shaken,
  shoked
потухший *adj* extinct

похвальный *adj* praiseworthy
похититель *n* kidnapper
похищать *v* abduct
похищать людей *v* kidnap
похищение *n* abduction
похлопывание *n* pat
походить *v* resemble
похожий *adj* alike
похороны *n* burial, funeral
похотливый *adj* lewd
поцелуй *n* kiss
почва *n* soil
почему *adv* why
почерк *n* handwritting
почет *n* honor
почитать *v* honour
почка *n* bud, kidney
почта *n* mail
почтальон *n* mailman
почтение *n* homage
почти *adv* almost
почтовый ящик *n* mailbox
пошатываться *v* wobble
пошлина *n* toll
пошлины *n* dues
поштучно *adv* apiece
поэзия *n* poetry
поэма *n* poem
поэт *n* poet
поэтому *adv* therefore
появление *n* appearance
появляться *v* appear

поясница _n_ loin
правило _n_ rule
правильно _adv_ right
правильность _n_ accuracy
правильный _adj_ accurate
правитель _n_ governor
правительство _n_ government
править _v_ rule
право _n_ right
право голоса _n_ franchise
правописание _n_ spelling
правый _adj_ right
прагматический _adj_ pragmatic
праздник _n_ holiday
праздничный _adj_ festive
празднование _n_ celebration
праздновать _v_ celebrate
практика _n_ practice
практикующий _adj_ practising
практический _adj_ practical
практичный _adj_ down-to-earth
прародитель _n_ ancestor
прачечная _n_ laundry
преамбула _n_ preamble
пребывание _n_ stay
превалировать _v_ prevail
превзойти _v_ outdo, excel
превосходить _v_ surpass
превосходный _adj_ superb
превосходство _n_ primacy
превращение _n_ conversion
превышать _v_ exceed

преграждать _v_ obstruct
предавать _v_ betray
преданность _n_ allegiance
преданный _adj_ committed
предательство _n_ betrayal
предвещать _v_ foreshadow
предвидение _n_ foresight
предвидеть _v_ foresee
предвкушать _v_ anticipate
предвкушение _n_ foretaste
предел _n_ limit
пределы _n_ scope
предисловие _n_ preface
предки _n_ ancestry
предлагать _v_ suggest, offer
предлог _n_ preposition
предложение _n_ proposal
предмет _n_ object, subject
предмет одежды _n_ garment
предназначение _n_ destination
предостерегать _v_ warn
предотвращать _v_ prevent
предписывать _v_ prescribe
предполагать _v_ assume
предположение _n_ assumption
предпосылка _n_ premise
предпочитать _v_ prefer
предпочтение _n_ preference
предпринимать _v_ undertake
предприятие _n_ enterprise
председатель _n_ chairman
предсказание _n_ prediction

предсказывать _v_ predict
представитель _n_ delegate
представлять _v_ represent
предстоящий _adj_ upcoming
предтеча _n_ precursor
предубеждение _n_ prejudice
предупреждать _v_ warn
предшествовать _v_ precede
предыдущий _adj_ previous
преемник _n_ successor
прежний _adj_ former
презентация _n_ presentation
президент _n_ president
президентство _n_ presidency
презирать _v_ despise
презрение _n_ contempt
презренный _adj_ despicable
презрительный _n_ scornful
преимущество _n_ advantage
прекращать _v_ cease
прелестный _adj_ pretty
прелюбодеяние _n_ adultery
прелюдия _n_ prelude
премия _n_ bonus
пренебрегать _v_ disregard
пренебрежение _n_ neglect
преподносить _v_ present
препятствие _n_ obstacle, block
препятствовать _v_ counteract
прерия _n_ prairie
прерогатива _n_ prerogative
прерывать _v_ interrupt

пресекать _v_ suppress
преследование _n_ pursuit
преследовать _v_ persecute
пресс _n_ press
пресса _n_ press
престиж _n_ prestige
преступление _n_ crime
претензия _n_ pretension
преувеличивать _v_ exaggerate
преуспевание _n_ prosperity
преуспевать _v_ succeed
прецедент _n_ precedent
при _pre_ by
прибавлять _v_ add
прибегать к _v_ resort
прибрежный _adj_ coastal
прибывать _v_ arrive
прибыль _n_ profit
прибыльный _adj_ lucrative
прибытие _n_ arrival
приверженец _n_ supporter
привет _e_ hello
приветливый _adj_ affable
приветствие _n_ welcome
приветствовать _v_ hail, greet
прививать _v_ vaccinate
прививка _n_ vaccination
привидение _n_ ghost
привилегия _n_ privilege
привинчивать _v_ screw
привлекать _v_ attract
привыкший _adj_ used to

П

привычка n habit
привычный adj familiar
привязанность n attachment
приглашать v invite
приглашение n invitation
пригнуться v bend down
приговаривать v sentence
приговор n sentence
пригодность n usefulness
пригород n suburb
пригоршня n handful
приготовится к v brace for
приграничный adj marginal
приданое n dowry
придерживаться v stick to
придираться v nag
придирчивый adj nitpicking
придумывать v fabricate
прием n admission
приемлемый adj acceptable
приемный adj adoptive
приз n prize
призвание n calling
призма n prism
признавать v admit, profess
признание n acknowledgement
призрак n phantom
призыв n appeal
призывать v call on
призывник n recruit
прийти в себя v get over
приказывать v command

прикасаться v touch
приклеивать v glue, paste
приключение n adventure
приковывать v rivet
прикосновение n touch
прикреплённый adj attached
прикреплять v attach, fasten
прикрытие n screen
прилавок n counter
прилаживать v fit
прилежание n diligence
прилежный adj diligent
прилив и отлив n tide
прилипать v adhere
приложение n annex
приманивать v lure
применимый adj applicable
применять v apply
пример n example
примирить v reconcile
примитивный adj elementary
принадлежать v belong
принижать v belittle
принимать v accept
приниматься v begin
приносить v bring
приношения n offering
принтер n printer
принуждать v enforce
принуждение n constraint
принц n prince
принцесса n princess

принцип *n* principle
принятие *n* acceptance
приняться за *v* get down to
приобретать *v* acquire
приобретение *n* acquisition
приоритет *n* priority
приостановка *n* suspension
приоткрытый *adj* ajar
припаивать *v* solder
приправа *n* seasoning
приравнять *v* equate
природа *n* nature
природный *adj* natural
приручать *v* tame
прислонять *v* recline
присоединять *v* connect
присоединяться *v* join
приставка *n* prefix
пристанище *n* asylum
пристань *n* wharf
пристойный *adj* decent
пристрастие *n* predilection
приступ гнева *n* tantrum
пристыженный *adj* ashamed
присуждение *n* award
присутствие *n* presence
присущий *adj* intrinsic
присяжные *n* jury
притворство *n* pretense
притворяться *v* pretend
приток *n* influx, tributary
притуплять *v* deaden, blunt

притча *n* parable
приучать *v* accustom
прихлёбывать *v* sip
приходить *v* come
приходской *adj* parochial
прихожанин *n* parishioner
прихоть *n* whim
прихрамывать *v* limp
причаливать *v* moor
причастие *n* communion, participle
причёска *n* hairdo
причина *n* cause, reason
причинять вред *v* harm
причитание *n* lament
причудливый *adj* fancy
пришивать *v* stitch
пришпоривать *v* spur
приют *n* lodging, shelter
приютить *v* shelter
приятель *n* comrade, pal
приятно *adv* nicely
приятный *adj* pleasant
пробираться *v* scramble
пробка *n* cork, plug
проблема *n* problem
проблеск *n* glimpse
пробуждать *v* evoke
пробуждение *n* awakening
провал *n* downfall
проваливаться *v* slump
проверка *n* check, test

П

проверять v verify
проветривать v air
провидение n providence
провинция n province
проводить опрос v quiz
проводник n guide
провозглашать v proclaim
провокация n provocation
проволока n wire
проворный adj agile, prompt
провоцировать v provoke
прогноз v forecast
прогнозировать v foretell
проговориться v give away
программа n program
программист n programmer
прогресс n progress
прогрессивный adj progressive
прогуливаться v stroll
прогулка n hike, outing
продавать v sell
продавец n seller
продавец книг n bookseller
продажа n sale
продвигать v promote
продвигаться v move forward
продвижение n advance
продевать нитку v thread
проделка v dodge
продлевать v protract
продовольствие n foodstuff
продолговатый adj oblong

продолжать v continue
продолжаться v go ahead, last
продолжение n continuation
продукт n product
продукты n groceries
продукция n produce
проект n project
проектировать v project
проживать v reside
проза n prose
прозевать v miss
прозрачный adj transparent
производить v produce
производство n production
произвол n outrage
произвольный adj arbitrary
произносить v pronounce
происхождение n origin
происшествие n happening
прокаженный n leper
проказа n leprosy
прокалывание n puncture
прокалывать v pierce
проклинать v curse, damn
проклятие n damnation
прокол n piercing
проколоть v prick
прокормить v subsist
прокурор n prosecutor
пролив n strait
проливать v shed, spill
пролог n prologue

пролом *n* breach, gap
проматывать *v* embezzle
промах *n* blunder, trip
промокать *v* soak up
проникать *v* penetrate
пропаганда *n* propaganda
пропитывать *v* saturate
проповедник *n* preacher
проповедовать *v* preach
проповедь *n* sermon
пропорция *n* proportion
пропуск *n* omission
пропускать *v* omit
прорастать *v* germinate
пророк *n* prophet
пророчество *n* prophecy
просвещать *v* enlighten
просеивать *v* sift
просить *v* beg, ask
просить о *v* apply for
прославлять *v* glorify
прослеживать *v* trace
просматривать *v* look through
проснувшийся *adj* awake
просроченный *adj* overdue
простираться *v* extend
просто *adv* simply
простой *adj* simple
просторный *adj* roomy
простота *n* simplicity
пространство *n* space
простуда *n* chill

простыни *n* sheets
просьба *n* request
протаптывать *v* trail
протест *n* fuss, protest
протестовать *v* protest
протечка *n* leakage
против *pre* against, versus
противиться *v* oppose
противник *n* assailant
противный *adj* opposite
противоречие *n* contradiction
протокол *n* protocol
прототип *n* prototype
протыкать *v* prod
протянутый *adj* outstretched
профессия *n* profession
профессор *n* professor
профиль *n* profile
прохлада *n* coolness
прохладный *adj* chilly
проход *n* aisle, passage
проходить *v* pass
прохожий *n* passer-by
процветать *v* prosper
процедура *n* procedure
процесс *n* process
процессия *n* procession
прочищать *v* purge
прочный *adj* sturdy
прошлое *n* antecedent
прошлый *adj* past
прощание *n* farewell

прощать v forgive
прощение n forgiveness
проявлять v manifest
прояснять v clear
пруд n pond
пружина n spring
пружинистый adj resilient
прыгать v jump, leap
прыжок n leap, jump
прыщ n pimple
прыщик n spot
прядильщица n spinster
пряжа n yarn
пряжка n buckle
прямая кишка n rectum
прямой adj direct
прямота n integrity
прясть v spin
прятать v hide
прятаться v hide oneself
псевдоним n pseudonym
психиатр n psychiatrist
психиатрия n psychiatry
психология n psychology
психопат n psychopath
птица n bird
публика n audience
публикация n publication
публиковать v publish
публично adv publicly
публичность n publicity
пугать v frighten

пуговица n button
пудинг n pudding
пузырёк n bubble
пулемёт n machine gun
пульс n pulse
пульсировать v pulsate
пуля n bullet
пункт n clause, item
пунктуальный adj punctual
пуп n belly button
пупок n navel
пустой adj void, empty
пустота n emptiness
пустыня n wilderness
пустяковый adj paltry
путаница n confusion
путеводитель n guidebook
путешествие n journey
путешествовать v travel
путь n way
пухлый adj plump
пушистый adj fuzzy
пушок n fluff
пчела n bee
пшеница n wheat
пылать v blaze
пылающий adj ablaze
пыль n dust
пыльный adj dusty
пыльца n pollen
пытать v torture
пытаться v try, attempt

П

пытка *n* torture
пьяница *n* drinker
пьянство *n* drunkenness
пюре *n* puree
пядь *n* span
пятиугольник *n* pentagon
пятка *n* heel
пятнадцать *adj* fifteen
пятнать *v* spot, catch
пятница *n* Friday
пятно *n* blot, stain, spot
пятый *adj* fifth
пять *adj* five
пятьдесят *adj* fifty

П

р

раб *n* slave
работа *n* job, work
работа по дому *n* housework
работать *v* work
работодатель *n* employer
рабочая сила *n* manpower
рабочий *n* worker
рабочий стол *n* desk
рабство *n* slavery
раввин *n* rabbi
равенство *n* equality

равнина *n* plain
равновесие *n* balance
равнодушие *n* indifference
равнозначный *adj* equivalent
равный *adj* equal, even
равняться *v* align
радиатор *n* radiator
радиация *n* radiation
радикальный *adj* radical
радио *n* radio
радиовещание *n* broadcast
радиолокатор *n* radar
радиус *n* radius
радовать *v* delight
радостно *adv* joyfully
радостный *adj* glad
радость *n* joy
радуга *n* rainbow
разбавлять *v* dilute
разбивать *v* rip apart
разбирать *v* take apart
разбитый *adj* broken
разбойник *n* bandit
разборчивый *adj* legible
разбрасывать *v* throw about
разваливаться *v* come apart
разведка *n* espionage
разведчик *n* scout
развертывание *n* deployment
развертывать *v* unfold
разветвление *n* ramification
разветвляться *v* branch out

развешивать *v* hang
развеять *v* chase away
развивать *v* develop
развиваться *v* progress
развитие *n* development
развлекать *v* amuse
развлечение *n* entertainment
развлечения *n* amusement
развод *n* divorce
разводиться *v* divorce
разворачивать *v* unwrap
развращать *v* corrupt
развращенность *n* depravity
развращенный *adj* perverse
развязывать *v* untie
разглаживать *v* smooth out
разглашать *v* divulge
разглядеть *v* discern
разговаривать *v* converse
разговор *n* conversation
разгонять *v* dispel
разгружать *v* discharge, unload
разгрузка *n* discharge
раздавать *v* dispense
раздавливать *v* squash
раздача *n* distribution
раздевалка *n* locker room
раздевать *v* undress, strip
разделение *n* partition, parting
разделяться *v* split up
раздражать *v* annoy, irritate
раздражающий *adj* annoying

раздражённый *adj* disgruntled
раздробить *v* shatter
раздувать *v* blow up
раздуваться *v* bloat
раздумье *n* meditation
раздутый *adj* bloated
разжалование *n* degradation
разжигать *v* inflame
различать *v* discriminate
различение *n* distinction
различие *n* discrepancy
различить *v* distinguish
различный *adj* varied, various
разлом *n* break
разлучать *v* sever
размазывать *v* smear
разматывать *v* unwind
размах *n* swing
размер *n* size
размешивать *v* stir
размещать *v* dispose
размещение *n* disposal
разминать *v* mash
размножать *v* propagate
размножение *n* reproduction
размораживать *v* defrost
размышление *n* consideration
разница *n* inequality
разногласие *n* discord
разногласия *n* friction
разнообразие *n* diversity
разнообразить *v* diversify

Р

разнорабочий *n* laborer
разоблачать *v* debunk
разогревать *v* warm up
разоружение *n* disarmament
разорять *v* plunder
разочаровывать *v* disappoint
разрабатывать *v* devise
разрастаться *v* expand
разрез *n* cut, slit
разрезать *v* cut, slit
разрешать *v* permit
разрешение *n* authorization
разрешить *v* resolve
разруха *n* shambles
разрушать *v* destroy
разрушение *n* demolition
разрушитель *n* destroyer
разрыв *n* rupture
разрывать *v* disrupt, tear
разрываться *v* burst
разум *n* mind
разумный *adj* advisable
разъедать *v* corrode
разъединять *v* disconnect
разъярять *v* enrage
рай *n* paradise
район *n* district
рак *n* cancer
ракета *n* missile
ракетка *n* racket
раковый *adj* cancerous
рама *n* frame

рана *n* sore, wound
ранг *n* rank
ранить *v* wound, injure
рано *adv* early
ранчо *n* ranch
раньше *adv* formerly
раса *n* race
расизм *n* racism
расист *adj* racist
раскалывать *v* splinter, split
раскаяние *n* contrition
раскрошить *v* crumble
распаковывать *v* unpack
распинать *v* crucify
расписание *n* timetable
расплавление *n* fusion
расплачиваться *v* pay off
расположение *n* favor, lay
распределять *v* distribute
распродажа *n* sellout
распроданный *adj* sold-out
распутывать *v* unravel
распятие *n* crucifix
рассвет *n* dawn
рассеивание *n* dispersal
рассеивать *v* scatter
рассеиваться *v* disperse
расселина *n* cleft
рассказ *n* story
рассказчик *n* teller
рассказывать *v* narrate, tell
расслаблять *v* relax

Р

рассматривать v consider
расспрашивать v interrogate
расставаться v part
расставлять v arrange
расстёгивать v unbutton
расстилать v spread
расстояние n distance
расстраивать v frustrate
рассуждение n reasoning
рассчитывать v calculate
раствор n solution
растворимый adj soluble
растворять v dissolve
растворяющий adj solvent
растение n plant
расти v sprout, grow
растительность n vegetation
растоптанный adj downtrodden
расточать v squander
раструб n bell
растягивать v stretch out
растягиваться v expand
растяжение n stretch
растянутый adj strained
растянуться v sprawl
расходиться v disagree
расходование n expenditure
расходы n spending
расцветать v blossom
расценивать v regard
расческа n hairbrush
расчесывать v comb

расчистка n clearance
расширять v broaden
расщелина n chasm
расщепление n disintegration
расщеплять v disintegrate
ратификация n ratification
рафинировать v refine
рацион n ration
рвать v vomit, tear
рваться v rip
рвение n eagerness
рвота n vomit
реагировать v react
реакция n reaction
реализм n realism
реальность n reality
реальный adj real
ребенок n kid, child
ребро n rib
рев n roar
реветь v roar
ревизия n revision
ревматизм n rheumatism
ревнивый adj jealous
ревность n jealousy
револьвер v revolver
регент n regent
регион n region
региональный adj regional
регистратор n receptionist
регистрация n registration
регулировать v regulate

Р

регулярно *adv* regularly
редиска *n* radish
редкий *adj* rare, sparse
редко *adv* seldom, rarely
режим *n* regime, mode
резак *n* chopper
резать *v* slash, cut
резерв *n* stockpile
резервуар *n* reservoir
резина *n* rubber, gum
резкий *adj* sharp
резко толкать *adj* jerk
резня *n* massacre
резолюция *n* resolution
результат *n* outcome
резчик *n* cutter
резюме *n* summary
резюмировать *v* recap
рейка *n* lath
река *n* river
реклама *n* advertising
рекламировать *v* advertise
рекомендации *n* guidelines
рекомендовать *v* recommend
реконструкция *n* renovation
рекорд *n* record
ректификация *n* rectification
ректор *n* rector
религиозный *adj* religious
религия *n* religion
реликвия *n* relic
ремень *n* strap, belt

ремесло *n* craft
ремонтировать *v* repair
репарация *n* reparation
репетировать *v* rehearse
репетитор *n* tutor, coach
репетиция *n* rehearsal
реплика *n* replica
репрессалия *n* reprisal
рептилия *n* reptile
репутация *n* reputation
ресничка *n* eyelash
республика *n* republic
ресторан *n* restaurant
ресурс *n* resource
референдум *n* referendum
рефлексивный *adj* reflexive
реформа *n* reform
рецензировать *v* revise
рецензия *n* review
рецепт *n* prescription
рецидив *n* relapse
речь *n* speech
решать *v* sort out, solve
решение *n* decision
ржаветь *v* rust
ржавчина *n* rust
ржавый *adj* rusty
римский папа *n* Pope
рис *n* rice
риск *n* hazard, risk
рискованный *adj* risky
рисковать *v* gamble, risk

Р

рисование *n* drawing, paint
рисовать *v* paint, depict
рисунок *v* draw
ритм *n* rhythm
риф *n* reef
рифма *n* rhyme
робкий *adj* timid
робость *n* timidity
ров *n* dike, trench
ровня *n* peer
рог *n* horn
рогатый скот *n* oxen
род *n* gender
родившийся *adj* born
родинка *n* birthmark
родители *n* parents
родиться *v* be born
родной *adj* native
родной город *n* hometown
родовой *adj* generic
родственник *n* relative
родственный *adj* akin, allied
родство *n* kinship
роды *n* delivery
рождение *n* birth
Рождество *n* Christmas
рожь *n* rye
роза *n* rose
розарий *n* rosary
розетка *n* outlet
розовый *adj* pink, rosy
рой *n* swarm

рок *n* doom
роковой *adj* fateful
ром *n* rum
роман *n* novel
романс *n* romance
роса *n* dew
роскошный *adj* luxurious
роскошь *n* luxury
Россия *n* Russia
рост *n* growth
ростовщик *n* pawnbroker
росток *n* sprout
рот *n* mouth
ртуть *n* mercury
рубашка *n* shirt
рубеж *n* frontier
рубец *n* hem, scar
рубин *n* ruby
рубить *v* chop, hack
ругать *v* chide
руда *n* ore
рука *n* arm, hand
рукав *n* sleeve
руководитель *n* chief, leader
руководить *v* administer
руководство *n* leadership
руководящий *adj* leading
рукопожатие *n* handshake
рукоятка *n* hilt
рукоять *n* handle
руль *n* rudder
румянец *n* blush

русалка *n* mermaid
русский *adj* Russian
рутинная работа *n* chore
рухлядь *n* junk
ручаться *v* vouch for
ручей *n* stream
ручка *n* pen
ручной *adj* manual
ручной работы *adj* handmade
рыба *n* fish
рыбак *n* fisherman
рыбный *adj* fishy
рывок *n* hitch, jerk
рыгать *v* burp, belch
рыдание *n* sob
рыдать *v* sob
рынок *n* market
рысь *n* lynx
рыцарь *n* knight
рычаг *n* lever
рычать *v* growl
рьяный *adj* zealous
рюкзак *n* backpack
ряд *n* series, row
рядом с *pre* beside

С

с *pre* with
с надеждой *adv* hopefully
с тех пор *pre* since
с того времени *adv* since then
саботаж *n* sabotage
саботировать *v* sabotage
саван *n* shroud
сад *n* garden
садист *n* sadist
садовник *n* gardener
сажа *n* soot
сажать *v* plant
салат *n* lettuce, salad
салун *n* saloon
салфетка *n* napkin
сама *pro* herself
самец животного *n* buck
самка *n* female
самолет *n* airplane
самооценка *n* self-esteem
самоубийство *n* suicide
самоуважение *n* self-respect
самый поздний *adj* latest
сандалия *n* sandal
санки *n* sleigh
санкция *n* sanction
сантиметр *n* centimeter
сапфир *n* saphire
саранча *n* locust

Р

сардина *n* sardine

сарказм *n* sarcasm

сатанинский *adj* satanic

сатира *n* satire

сахар *n* sugar

сбежать от *v* break away

сбережения *n* savings

сбивать с толку *v* baffle

сбить *v* run over

сборище *n* mob

сборник *n* compendium

сбрасывать *v* pull down

свадебный *adj* bridal

свадьба *n* wedding

свалка *n* dump, landfill

сваривать *v* weld

сварщик *n* welder

сведения *n* information

свежесть *n* freshness

свежеть *v* freshen

свежий *adj* fresh

свёкла *n* beet

свёкор *c* father-in-law

свержение *n* overthrow

сверкание *n* splendor

сверлить *n* drill

сверло *v* drill

свёртывание *n* coagulation

свертываться *v* curdle

сверхдержава *n* superpower

сверхурочно *adv* overtime

сверчок *n* cricket

свет *n* light

светить *v* shine

светиться *v* glow

светлость *n* lordship

светящийся *adj* luminous

свеча *n* candle

свидетель *n* witness

свидетельство *n* testament

свинец *n* lead

свинина *n* pork

свинка *n* mumps

свиное сало *n* lard

свинья *n* pig

свирепый *adj* atrocious

свист *n* whistle

свистеть *v* whistle

свитер *n* sweater

свиток *n* scroll

свобода *n* freedom

свободный *adj* vacant, free

свод законов *n* code

сводить с ума *v* madden

сводиться *v* boil down to

сводная сестра *n* stepsister

сводничать *v* pander

сводный брат *n* stepbrother

своевременный *adj* timely

своекорыстие *n* self-interest

своеобразный *adj* peculiar

связанный *adj* bound

связка *n* bunch

связующий *adj* binding

С

связывать *v* link, bind
связывать в узел *v* bundle
связь *n* tie, bond
святилище *n* sanctuary
святой *adj* holy
святость *n* holiness
священник *n* clergyman
священный *adj* sacred
священство *n* priesthood
сгибать *v* bend
сгущать *v* coagulate, condense
сдавать *v* turn in
сдавать в аренду *v* lease
сдаваться *v* surrender
сдвиг *n* shift
сделка *n* bargain
сдержанность *n* restraint
сдерживаемый *adj* pent-up
сдерживать *v* restrain
себе *pro* yourself
себя *pre* oneself, ourselves
себя *pro* themselves
север *n* north
северный *adj* northern
северный олень *n* reindeer
северо-восток *n* northeast
северянин *adj* northerner
сегодня *adv* today
сегодня вечером *adv* tonight
седло *n* saddle
седьмой *adj* seventh
сезонный *adj* seasonal

сейчас *adv* now
секрет *n* secret
секретарь *n* secretary
секретность *n* secrecy
секретный *adj* undercover
секс *n* sex
сексуальность *n* sexuality
секта *n* sect
сектор *n* sector
секунда *n* second
секция *n* section
сельдерей *n* celery
сельский *adj* rural
семейство *n* household, family
семестр *n* semester
семинария *n* seminary
семнадцать *adj* seventeen
семь *adj* seven
семьдесят *adj* seventy
семья *n* family
семя *n* seed
сенат *n* senate
сенатор *n* senator
сено *n* hay
сентябрь *n* September
сера *n* sulphur
сердечный *adj* cordial
сердитый *adj* angry
сердить *v* anger
сердце *n* heart
серебро *n* silver
середина *n* middle

середина лета *n* midsummer
серенада *n* serenade
сержант *n* sergeant
сероватый *adj* grayish
серп *n* sickle
серый *adj* gray
серьга *n* earring
серьёзно *adv* gravely, seriously
серьёзность *n* seriousness
серьезный *adj* grave, serious
сессия *n* session
сестра *n* sister
сеть *n* net, network
сеять *v* sow
сжатие *n* compression
сжатый *adj* terse, compressed
сжимать *v* squeeze
сигара *n* cigar
сигарета *n* cigarette
сигнал *n* signal
сиделка *n* nurse
сиденье *n* seat
сидеть *v* sit
сидр *n* cider
сила *n* strength
силуэт *n* silhouette
сильно ударять *v* maul
сильный *adj* strong
сильный удар *n* chop
сим *adv* hereby
символ *n* emblem, symbol
симметрия *n* symmetry

симпатичный *adj* lovable
симпатия *n* liking
симптом *n* symptom
симфония *n* symphony
синагога *n* synagogue
синий *adj* blue
синод *n* synod
синоним *n* synonym
синтез *n* synthesis
синяк *n* bruise
сирена *n* buzzer, siren
сиреневый *adj* purple
сироп *n* syrup
сирота *n* orphan
система *n* system
сито *n* strainer
ситуация *n* situation
сифилис *n* syphilis
сказка *n* tale
сказочный *adj* fabulous
скакать *v* skip
скакать галопом *v* gallop
скалолазание *n* rock climbing
скальп *n* scalp
скамья *n* bench
скандал *n* scandal
скатерть *n* tablecloth
скачок *n* skip
скелет *n* skeleton
скептик *adj* sceptic
скептический *adj* skeptic
скидка *n* discount, rebate

C

склад *n* warehouse
складка *n* pleat, crease
складчатый *adj* pleated
складывать *v* fold
склеп *n* vault
склон холма *n* hillside
склонность *n* leaning, penchant
склонный *adj* prone, inclined
скобка *n* staple, bracket
скобки *n* parenthesis
скоблить *v* scrape
сковорода *n* frying pan
скольжение *n* slip
скользить *v* slip, slide, glide
скользкий *adj* slippery
скопление *n* congestion
скорая помощь *n* ambulance
скорбеть *v* mourn
скорбный *adj* sorrowful
скорбь *n* grief, sorrow
скорее *adv* rather
скорлупа *n* hull, shell
скорость *n* speed
скорпион *n* scorpion
скорый *adj* rapid
скотобойня *n* butchery
скотский *adj* bestial
скотство *n* bestiality
скрести *v* scrub
скрип *n* creak
скрипач *n* violinist
скрипеть *v* creak

скрипка *n* violin
скромность *n* modesty
скромный *adj* modest
скрупулёзный *adj* scrupulous
скрученный *adj* twisted
скручивать *v* writhe, twist
скрывать *v* conceal
скрытно *adv* secretly
скрытый *adj* shrouded
скряга *n* miser
скудный *adj* scant
скука *n* boredom
скула *n* cheekbone
скульптор *n* sculptor
скульптура *n* sculpture
скупиться *v* dole out
скупо *adv* sparingly
скупой *adj* stingy
скучающий *adj* bored
скучный *adj* boring
слабеть *v* weaken
слабительное *adj* laxative
слабость *n* weakness
слабый *adj* weak
слабый свет *n* gleam
слава *n* glory
сладкий *adj* sweet
сладость *n* sweetness
слаксы *n* slacks
сланец *n* slate
сласти *n* sweets
слегка *adv* lightly

C

след *n* footstep, step

следить *v* track

следовать *v* follow

следствие *n* inquest

следующий *adj* next

слеза *n* tear

слепить *v* dazzle

слепой *adj* blind

слепота *n* blindness

слесарь *n* locksmith

слива *n* plum

сливаться *v* merge

сливки *n* cream

сливочный *adj* creamy

слизь *n* mucus

слиток *n* ingot

словарь *n* vocabulary

слово *n* word

слог *n* syllable

сложность *n* complexity

слой *n* layer

сломить *v* break down

слон *n* elephant

слоновая кость *n* ivory

слоняться *v* hang around

слуга *n* servant

служащий *n* employee

служба *n* employment

служебный *adj* official

служить *v* serve

слух *n* hearing

случай *n* case, incident

случайно *adv* incidentally

случайность *n* contingency

случайный *adj* accidental

случаться *v* occur

слушатель *n* listener

слушать *v* listen

слышать *v* hear

слышимый *adj* audible

слюна *n* saliva

смазка *n* lubrication

смазывать *v* lubricate

смежный *adj* adjacent

смело *adv* bravely

смелость *n* bravery

смелый *adj* brave

смена *n* shift

сменять *v* replace

смертельность *n* mortality

смертельный *adj* deadly

смертный *adj* mortal

смерть *n* death

смеситель *n* mixer

смесь *n* blend, mixture

смех *n* laughter, laugh

смешивать *v* confuse

смешиваться *v* mingle

смешной *adj* laughable

смеяться *v* laugh

сминать *v* crease

смирение *n* humility

смола *n* tar

смотреть *v* watch, look

C

смотри *v* behold
смотритель *n* caretaker
смуглый *adj* tanned
смущать *v* bewilder
смущение *n* confusion
смывать *v* wipe out
смягчать *v* mitigate, soften
смягчающий *adj* extenuating
смягчение *n* moderation
смятенный *adj* distraught
снабжать *v* supply
снайпер *n* sniper
снаружи *adv* outdoor, outside
снаряд *n* projectile
снаряжать *v* equip
снаряжение *n* outfit
снег *n* snow
снегопад *n* snowfall
снежинка *n* snowflake
снижать *v* bring down
снижение *n* recession
снизить цену *v* mark down
снизойти *v* condescend
снимать *v* skim, take off
снимать копию *v* duplicate
снимок *n* snapshot
сниться *v* dream
сноска *n* footnote
сносный *adj* bearable
собака *n* dog
собирать *v* assemble, collect
собираться *v* gather

соблазнять *v* seduce
соблюдать *v* observe
собрание *n* gathering
собственник *n* owner
собственность *n* ownership
собственный *adj* own
событие *n* event
сова *n* owl
совершать *v* perpetrate
совершенно *adv* altogether
совершенный *adj* perfect
совершенство *n* perfection
совесть *n* conscience
совет *n* council
советник *n* counselor
советовать *v* advise
советоваться *v* consult
советский *adj* soviet
совместимый *adj* compatible
совместно *adv* jointly
совместный *adj* cooperative
совпадать *v* concur
совпадающий *adj* concurrent
совпадение *n* coincidence
современный *adj* modern
согласие *n* accord
согласно *pre* according to
согласный звук *n* consonant
согласовывать *v* conform
соглашаться *v* agree, assent
сода *n* soda
содействовать *v* befriend

содержание *v* content
содержать *v* contain
соединение *n* connection
соединять *v* tie, connect
соединяться *v* unite
сожаление *n* regret
сожалеть *v* regret
сожалеющий *adj* sorry
созвездие *n* constellation
создавать *v* create
создание *n* creature
создатель *n* creator
созерцать *v* contemplate
сознание *n* consciousness
сознательный *adj* conscious
созревать *v* mellow, mature
созывать *v* convene, invite
сок *n* juice
сокращать reduce
сокращаться *v* dwindle, shorten
сокращение *n* abbreviation
сокровище *n* treasure
солдат *n* soldier
соленый *adj* salty
солидарность *n* solidarity
солнечный *adj* sunny, solar
солнце *n* sun
соловей *n* nightingale
солома *n* straw
соль *n* salt
сомневаться *v* doubt, hesitate
сомнение *n* doubt, hesitation

сомнения *n* scruples
сон *n* sleep, dream
сонливость *n* doze
сообщать *v* communicate
сообщение *n* message
сообщник *n* accomplice
сооружать *v* construct, erect
соответствие *n* conformity
соперник *n* contender
сопеть *v* wheeze
сопоставимый *adj* comparable
сопоставлять *v* compare
сопровождать *v* accompany
сопровождение *n* convoy
сопротивление *n* resistance
сопротивляться *v* resist
сопутствовать *v* conduct
сопутствующий *adj* collateral
соревнование *n* competition
сорняк *n* weed
сорок *adj* forty
сорт *n* sort
сосать *v* suck
сосед *n* neighbor
сосна *n* pine
сосок *n* nipple
состав *n* makeup
составитель *n* compiler
составлять *v* constitute
составлять план *v* plot
составной *adj* multiple
состояние *n* state

C

сострадание *n* compassion
состряпать *v* concoct, cook
состязаться *v* compete
сосуд *n* vessel
сосун *n* sucker
сотворение *n* creation
сотрудничать *v* collaborate
сотрясение *n* concussion
сотый *adj* hundredth
соус *n* sauce
соучастие *n* complicity
сохранение *n* conservation
сохранять *v* preserve
социализм *n* socialism
сочетание *n* combination
сочетать *v* combine
сочинение *n* composition
сочинять *v* compose
сочный *adj* juicy, mellow
сочувствие *n* sympathy
сочувствовать *v* sympathize
союз *n* conjunction
союзник *n* ally
спад *v* wane
спазм *n* spasm, cramp
спальное место *n* berth
спальня *n* bedroom
спаржа *n* asparagus
спасать *v* rescue, save
спасение *n* salvation
спаситель *n* savior
спать *v* sleep

сперма *n* sperm
специя *n* spice
спешиваться *v* dismount
спешить *v* hasten, rash
спешка *n* haste
спина *n* back
список *n* list
списывать *v* scrap, copy
спичка *n* match
сплав *n* alloy
сплетничать *v* gossip
сплетня *n* gossip
сплочение *n* rally
сплочённость *n* cohesion
спокойный *adj* calm, restful
спокойствие *n* tranquility
спонсор *n* sponsor
спонтанность *n* spontaneity
спонтанный *adj* spontaneous
спорить *v* argue
спорный *adj* contentious
спорт *n* sport
спортивный *adj* sporty
спортсмен *n* sportman
способ *n* manner
способность *n* ability
способный *adj* capable, able
спотыкаться *v* falter, stumble
справедливо *adv* justly
справедливый *adj* just
справиться *v* cope
справка *n* reference

C

справочник *n* directory
спрашивать *v* ask
спринцовка *n* syringe
спрятанный *adj* hidden
спуск *n* descent
спускать курок *v* trigger
спускаться *v* descend
спутник *n* satellite
спутывать *v* implicate, mix up
спящий *adj* asleep
сравнение *n* comparison
сравнивать *v* compare
сражаться *v* fight, combat
сражение *n* battle
среда *n* Wednesday
среди *pre* among
средний *n* average
средства *n* funds, means
средство *n* means
срок *n* period, term
срочность *n* urgency
срочный *adj* urgent
ссора *n* quarrel
ссориться *v* quarrel
ссуда *n* loan
ссылаться на *v* refer to
стабильность *n* stability
ставить *v* put
ставить диагноз *v* diagnose
ставить знак *v* mark
ставить экран *v* screen
ставка *n* rate

стадия *n* grade, stage
стадный *adj* gregarious
сталкиваться *v* clash, collide
сталь *n* steel
стандарт *n* standard
становиться *v* become
станция *n* station
старец *n* elder
старина *n* antiquity
старить *v* make old
старомодный *adj* old-fashioned
старость *n* old age
стартовать *v* lift off, start
старший *adj* senior
старшинство *n* superiority
старый *adj* old
статистика *n* statistic
статус *n* status
статуя *n* statue
статья *n* article
ствол *n* stem, trunk
стежок *n* stitch
стекло *n* glass
стена *n* wall
стенать *v* lament
стенография *n* shorthand
степень *n* extent
стерилизовать *v* sterilize
стиль *n* style
стиль жизни *n* lifestyle
стимул *n* spur, stimulus
стимулировать *v* stimulate

C

стимулятор *n* stimulant
стирать *v* erase, wash
стих *n* verse
сто *adj* hundred
стог сена *n* haystack
стоить *v* cost
стоический *adj* stoic
стойка *n* crutch, counter
стойкий *adj* staunch
стойкость *n* firmness
стойло *n* stall
стол *n* table
столб *n* stake, pole
столетие *n* centenary
столица *n* capital
столкновение *n* confrontation
столовая *n* dining room
столовая ложка *n* tablespoon
стон *n* groan, moan
стонать *v* moan, groan
стопка *n* stack
стопориться *v* stall
сторона *n* side, party
сторонящийся *adj* aloof
сточная труба *n* sewer
сточные воды *n* sewage
стоять *v* stand
стоящий *adj* rewarding
страдание *n* anguish
страдать *v* suffer, agonize
страдать от *v* suffer from
страна *n* country

страница *n* page
странник *n* wanderer
странность *n* oddity
странный *adj* odd, weird
страстно желать *v* lust
страстный *adj* passionate
страсть *n* passion, ardor
стратегия *n* strategy
страус *n* ostrich
страх *n* fright, fear
страховать *v* insure
страховка *n* insurance
страческий *adj* senile
страшиться *v* dread
страшный *adj* scary, fearful
стрела *n* arrow
стрелять *v* shoot, fire
стремительно *adv* speedily
стремительный *adj* speedy
стремиться *v* aim
стремиться к *v* aspire
стремление *n* aspiration
стремнина *n* chute
стремянка *n* stepladder
стресс *n* stress
стрессовый *adj* stressful
стрижка *n* haircut
стричь *v* clip, shear
строгать *v* whittle, addice
строгий *adj* strict
строгость *n* severity
строитель *n* builder

С

строительный *adj* constructive
строительство *n* construction
строить *v* build
стройный *adj* slender
структура *n* framework
струсить *v* chicken out
студент *n* student
стук *v* knock
стул *n* chair
ступа *n* mortar
ступать *v* tread
ступени *n* stairs
ступенька *n* stair
ступица *n* hub
ступни *n* feet
ступня *n* foot
стучать *n* knock
стыд *n* shame
стыдить *v* shame
стюардесса *n* stewardess
суббота *n* Saturday
субсидия *n* subsidy
субъект *n* subject
сувенир *n* souvenir
суверенитет *n* sovereignty
суд *n* court, justice
судиться *v* litigate
судороги *n* convulsion
судьба *n* destiny, fate
судья *n* judge
суеверие *n* superstition
суета *n* vanity

суетливый *adj* bustling
суждение *n* judgment
сук *n* bough
сумасбродство *n* extravagance
сумасшедший *adj* crazy
сумасшествие *n* craziness
суматоха *n* turmoil
сумерки *n* dusk, nightfall
сумка *n* bag
сумма *n* sum
суп *n* soup
супермаркет *n* supermarket
супруг *n* spouse
супружеский *adj* conjugal
супружество *n* matrimony
сурово *adv* sternly
суровый *adj* stern
сустав *n* joint
сутана *n* cassock
сухарь *n* dried crust
сухой *adj* dry
сушилка *n* dryer
сушить *v* dry
существенный *adj* substantial
существование *n* existence
существовать *v* exist
сущность *n* essence
сфера *n* sphere
схватить *v* grip, seize
схема *n* scheme
схематичный *adj* sketchy
схизма *n* schism

C

сходиться *v* converge
сходный *adj* similar
сходство *n* similarity
сцена *n* scene, stage
сценарий *n* scenario
сценический *adj* scenic
счастливый *adj* fortunate
счастье *n* happiness
счет *n* score; bill
счёт-фактура *n* invoice
счётчик *n* meter
считать *v* count
съедать *v* eat up
съедобный *adj* edible
съезжать *v* move out
сыворотка *n* whey
сын *n* son
сыр *n* cheese
сырая нефть *adj* crude oil
сырой *adj* raw, soggy
сэр *n* sir

C

Т

табак *n* tobacco
таблетка *n* pill
табличка *n* tablet
табурет *n* stool
таверна *n* tavern
таинственный *adj* mysterious
таинство *n* sacrament
тайна *n* mystery
тайный *adj* clandestine
так *adv* thus
так как *c* since
так называемый *adj* so-called
также *adv* either
такой *adj* such
такси *n* cab
такт *n* tact
тактика *n* tactics
тактический *adj* tactical
тактичный *adj* tactful
талант *n* talent
талантливый *adj* gifted
талия *n* waist
там *adv* there
таможня *n* customs
танец *n* dance
танцевать *v* dance
танцы *n* dancing
тапочки *n* slipper
таракан *n* cockroach

тарантул *n* tarantula
тарелка *n* plate
тариф *n* fare, tariff
тачка *n* wheelbarrow
тащить *v* drag, pull
таяние снега *n* dissolution
таять *v* melt, thaw
твердеть *v* harden
твердость *n* hardness
твердый *adj* hard, solid
творческий *adj* creative
творчество *n* creativity
те *adj* those
театр *n* theater
тезис *n* thesis
текст *n* text
текстура *n* texture
текущий *adj* current
телевидение *n* television
телеграмма *n* telegram
телеграф *n* telegraph
тележка *n* cart, wagon
телёнок *n* calf
телепатия *n* telepathy
телескоп *n* telescope
телесный *adj* bodily
телефон *n* phone
тело *n* body, torso
телятина *n* veal
тем временем *adv* meantime
тем не менее *c* nonetheless
тема *n* theme, topic

темнеть *v* darken
темноволосый *adj* brunette
тёмно-синий *adj* navy blue
темнота *n* darkness
тёмный *adj* dark
темп *n* pace
температура *n* temperature
тенденция *n* tendency
тенистый *adj* shady
теннис *n* tennis
тень *n* shadow
теория *n* theory
тепло *n* warmth
тепловатый *adj* lukewarm
тепловая волна *n* heatwave
тепловой удар *n* heatstroke
теплый *adj* warm
тёплый шарф *n* muffler
терапия *n* therapy
тереть *v* rub
термит *n* termite
термометр *n* thermometer
термостат *n* thermostat
терпеливый *adj* patient
терпение *n* patience
терпеть неудачу *v* miscarry
терпимость *n* tolerance
терпимый *adj* tolerable
терраса *n* terrace
территория *n* territory
террор *n* terror
терроризм *n* terrorism

Т

террорист *n* terrorist
терять *v* lose
терять сознание *v* pass out
тесно *adv* narrowly
тесто *n* dough
тесть *c* father-in-law
тесьма *n* band
тётя *n* aunt
техник *n* technician
техника *n* technique
технический *adj* technical
технология *n* technology
течение *n* flow, stream
течь *v* flow, leak
теща *n* mother-in-law
тигр *n* tiger
тип *n* type
типичный *adj* typical
тиран *n* tyrant
тирания *n* tyranny
тихий *adj* quiet
тишина *n* quietness
ткань *n* cloth, fabric
ткать *v* weave
тленный *adj* perishable
товарищ *n* companion
товарищество *n* companionship
товарный чек *n* sale slip
товары *n* merchandise
тогда *adv* then
тогда как *c* whereas
тоже *adv* also, too

токсин *n* toxin
токсический *adj* toxic
толкать *v* shove
толкать вперёд *v* propel
толковать *v* interpret
толпа *n* crowd, throng
толпиться *v* cluster, crowd
толстый *adj* thick
толчок *n* impact
толщина *n* thickness
только *adv* merely, only
томиться *v* yearn
тон *n* tone
тонкий *adj* fine, thin
тонкий ломтик *n* chip
тонко *adv* fine, thinly
тонна *n* ton
тоннель *n* tunnel
тонуть *v* drown, sink
топливо *n* fuel
топор *n* ax, hatchet
топтать *v* trample
торг *n* bargaining
торговать *v* trade, sell
торговаться *v* bargain
торговая марка *n* trademark
торговец *n* merchant
торговля *n* trade
торговый центр *n* mall
тормоз *n* brake
тормозить *v* brake
торопить *v* hurry

T

торопиться *v* hurry up
торс *n* torso
торт *n* cake
тосковать *v* long for
тост *n* toast
тостер *n* toaster
тот *adj* that
тот же самый *adj* same
тоталитарный *adj* totalitarian
точилка *n* sharpener
точка *n* dot, period
точка зрения *n* viewpoint
точность *n* precision
точный *adj* exact, precise
тошнотворный *adj* sickening
тощий *adj* meager
трава *n* grass, herb
травмировать *v* traumatize
трагедия *n* tragedy
трагический *adj* tragic
традиционный *adj* orthodox
традиция *n* tradition
траектория *n* trajectory
трактор *n* tractor
трамвай *n* tram
трамплин *n* springboard
транс *n* trance
трата *n* waste
тратить *v* spend
тратить впустую *v* waste
требование *n* claim
требовать *v* demand

требующий *adj* demanding
тревога *n* alarm, unrest
тревожить *v* disturb
тревожный *adj* alarming
трезвый *adj* sober
трение *n* friction
тренировать *v* coach
тренировка *n* coaching
тренога *n* tripod
трепать *v* heckle
трепет *n* awe, shiver
трепетать *v* tremble
треск *n* crack
треска *n* cod
третий *adj* third
треугольник *n* triangle
трещать *v* crack
трещина *n* split, fissure
три *adj* three
трибуна *n* grandstand
трибунал *n* tribunal
тривиальный *adj* trivial
тридцать *adj* thirty
триместр *n* trimester
тринадцать *adj* thirteen
триумф *n* triumph
трогательный *adj* appealing, touching
тройной *adj* triple
тромбоз *n* thrombosis
трон *n* throne
тропик *n* tropic

T

тропинка *n* lane, path, trail
тропический *adj* tropical
тростник *n* cane
тротуар *n* pavement
трофеи *n* trophy
труба *n* chimney, pipe
трубопровод *n* pipeline
труд *n* labor
трудности *n* hardship
трудность *n* difficulty
трудный *adj* arduous
труп *n* corpse
трус *n* coward
трусливо *adv* cowardly
трусость *n* cowardice
трущобы *n* slum
тряпка *n* rag
трясина *n* quagmire
тряска *n* jolt
трясти *v* shake
трястись *v* quake, quiver
трясущийся *adj* shaky
туалет *n* toilet
туберкулёз *n* tuberculosis
тугой *adj* tight
туда *adv* there
туловище *n* trunk, body
туман *n* fog
туманный *adj* foggy, hazy
тунец *n* tuna
туника *n* tunic
тупик *n* dead end

тупиковый *adj* deadlock
тупица *n* goof
тупой *adj* dull, blunt
турбина *n* turbine
туризм *n* tourism
турист *n* tourist
турок *adj* Turk
Турция *n* Turkey
тусклый *adj* dim
тускнеть *v* dim, tarnish
туфля *n* shoe
тучный *adj* obese
туша *n* carcass
тушить *v* quench, stew
тщательно *adv* thoroughly
тщательный *adj* thorough
тщеславный *adj* vain
тщетно *adv* vainly
тщетность *n* futility
тщетный *adj* futile
ты *pro* you
тыква *n* pumpkin
тысяча *adj* thousand
тысячелетие *n* millennium
тюлень *n* seal
тюльпан *n* tulip
тюремщик *n* jailer
тюрьма *n* jail, prison
тяга *n* draw, traction
тягач *n* tow truck
тягостный *adj* pressing
тяготеть *v* gravitate

тяжба *n* litigation
тяжёлый *adj* heavy
тяжесть *n* gravity, heaviness
тянуть *v* drag, pull

У

у *pre* by, at, with, of
убегать *v* flee, run away
убедительно *adv* earnestly
убедительный *adj* convincing
убеждать *v* persuade
убеждение *n* persuasion
убежище *n* refuge
убивать *v* kill, murder
убийство *n* murder
убийца *n* assassin
убирать *v* take away
убогое жилище *n* cabin
убой *n* slaughter
уборная *n* lavatory
уважать *v* respect
уважение *n* respect
уважительный *adj* respectful
уведомлять *v* notice
увеличение *n* increase
увеличивать *v* increase
увеличиваться *v* enlarge

уверенность *n* confidence
уверенный *adj* confident
уверять *v* assure
увечье *n* handicap
увиливание *n* evasion
увлажнять *v* dampen
увольнение *n* expulsion
увядший *adj* faded
увязнуть *v* bog down
угловой камень *n* cornerstone
углублять *v* deepen
угнетать *v* oppress
угнетение *n* oppression
уговаривать *v* persuade
угождать *v* please
угол *n* angle, corner
уголь *n* coal
угольный мусор *n* cinder
угомониться *v* settle down
угощение *n* treat
угрожать *v* threaten
угроза *n* menace, threat
угрюмый *adj* sullen
удалять *v* remove
удар *n* strike, beat
удар кулаком *n* punch
удар молнии *n* thunderbolt
удар ножом *n* stab
ударение *n* emphasis
ударять *v* bang, hit
ударяться *v* strike
удача *n* good luck

удачный *adj* successful
удваивание *n* duplication
удваивать *v* double
уделять *v* spare, give
удерживание *n* retention
удерживать *v* deter, rein
удивительный *adj* marvelous
удивление *n* surprise
удивлять *v* surprise
удивляться *v* wonder
удлинение *n* extension
удлиняться *v* lengthen
удобный *adj* comfortable
удобрение *n* compost
удобрять *v* fertilize
удобство *n* convenience
удовлетворять *v* satisfy
удовольствие *n* pleasure
удостоверять *v* attest
удушение *n* asphyxiation
уединение *n* privacy
уединенный *adj* secluded
ужас *n* horror
ужасать *v* appall, horrify
ужасающий *adj* appalling
ужасный *adj* awful, terrible
уже *adv* already
ужесточать *v* toughen
уживаться *v* get along
ужин *n* supper
узда *n* bridle
узел *n* knot

узел *n* knot
узкий *adj* narrow
узнавание *n* recognition
узнавать *v* recognize
узнать *v* find out
узурпировать *v* usurp
указание *n* indication
указать точно *v* pinpoint
указывать *v* point, show
уклейка *n* bleak
уклон *n* ramp
уклонение *n* avoidance
уклончивый *adj* evasive
уклоняться *v* flunk
укор *n* reproach
укорачивать *v* shorten
укорять *v* reproach
украшать *v* beautify
укреплять *v* fortify
укрепляться *v* strengthen
укрытие *n* hideaway
уксус *n* vinegar
укус *n* bite, sting
улей *n* beehive
улитка *n* snail
улица *n* street
улучшать *v* improve
улучшение *n* improvement
улыбаться *v* smile
улыбка *n* smile
ультиматум *n* ultimatum
ультразвук *n* ultrasound

у

умаляющий *adj* derogatory
умение *n* skill
уменьшать *v* diminish
уменьшаться *v* lessen
уменьшение *n* decrease
умеренный *adj* moderate
уместный *adj* relevant
умирать *v* die
умирающий *adj* dying
умиротворять *v* placate
умножать *v* multiply
умножение *n* multiplication
умный *adj* clever, smart
умолять *v* plead, implore
умственно *adv* mentally
умственный *adj* mental
университет *n* university
унижать *v* humiliate
унижаться *v* demean
унижение *n* affront
унизительный *adj* demeaning
уникальный *adj* unique
унификация *n* unification
уничтожать *v* destroy
уничтожение *n* ravage
унция *n* ounce
унылый *adj* despondent
упадок *n* decadence
упаковывать *v* pack
уплотнять *v* condense
упоминание *n* mention
упоминать *v* mention

упорствовать *v* persist
употребление *n* usage
управление *n* management
управлять *v* manage
упражнение *n* exercise
упражняться *v* exercise
упрашивать *v* beseech
упрёк *n* rebuke
упрекать *v* rebuke
упрощать *v* simplify
упрямство *n* obstinacy
упрямый *adj* obstinate
упустить *v* miss
упущение *n* lapse
уравнение *n* equation
ураган *n* hurricane
урегулировать *v* settle
урна *n* urn
уровень *n* level
уродство *n* ugliness
урожай *n* crop, yield
урок *n* class, lesson
усваивать *v* assimilate
усиление *n* reinforcements
усиливать *v* reinforce
усилие *n* effort
усилитель *n* amplifier
ускользать *v* evade
ускоритель *n* accelerator
ускорять *v* accelerate
условия *n* terms
условный *adj* conditional

успех *n* success
успокаивать *v* pacify, soothe
успокаиваться *v* calm down
уставиться *v* stare
усталость *n* fatigue
усталый *adj* tired, weary
устанавливать *v* fix, set up
установка *n* installation
устарелый *adj* obsolete
устно *adv* orally
устойчивость *n* steadiness
устойчивый *adj* steady
устоять *v* withstand
устрашающий *adj* frightening
устрашение *n* intimidation
устрица *n* oyster
устройство *n* device
уступать *v* concede
уступка *n* concession
усы *n* mustache
усыновление *n* adoption
усыновлять *v* adopt
утверждать *v* assert
утверждение *n* assertion
утечка *n* leak
утешать *v* console
утешение *n* comfort
утешитель *n* comforter
утка *n* duck
утолщать *v* thicken
утомительный *adj* exhausting
утончённость *n* delicacy

утончённый *adj* delicate
утро *n* morning
ухабистый *adj* bumpy
ухаживание *n* nursing
ухаживать *v* look after
ухаживать за *v* care for
ухищрение *n* gimmick
ухо *n* ear
уходить *v* depart
ухудшать *v* worsen
ухудшаться *v* become worse
ухудшение *n* deterioration
участвовать *v* participate
участие *n* participation
учащийся *n* learner
учебник *n* textbook
учебное пособие *n* workbook
ученик *n* apprentice
учёность *n* scholarship
ученый *adj* learned
учёный *n* scientist
учитель *n* teacher
учитывать *v* heed
учить *v* teach
учиться *v* learn
учреждать *v* establish
ушибать *v* bruise
ушная сера *n* earwax
ущерб *n* detriment
ущербный *adj* defective
уютный *adj* cozy
уязвимый *adj* vulnerable

Ф

фаза *n* phase

фазан *n* pheasant

факт *n* fact

фактически *adv* virtually

фактический *adj* factual

фактор *n* factor

фальшь *n* falsehood

фальшивый *adj* counterfeit

фамилия *n* last name

фанатизм *n* bigotry

фанатический *adj* fanatic

фантазия *n* fantasy

фарс *n* farce

фартук *n* apron

фарфор *n* porcelain

фарш *n* mincemeat

фасоль *n* bean

фатальный *adj* fatal

февраль *n* February

федеральный *adj* federal

фейерверк *n* fireworks

фекалии *n* dung

ферма *n* farm

фермент *n* ferment

фермер *n* farmer

фея *n* fairy

фиалка *n* violet

фигура *n* figure

физика *n* physics

физически *adv* physically

филей *n* sirloin

филиал *n* branch office

философ *n* philosopher

философия *n* philosophy

фильм *n* film

фильтр *n* filter

фильтровать *v* filter

фимиам *n* incense

финансировать *v* fund

финансовый *adj* financial

финансы *v* finance

Финляндия *n* Finland

финский *adj* Finnish

фирма *n* firm

флаг *n* flag

флагшток *n* flagpole

флейта *n* flute

флиртовать *v* flirt

фобия *n* phobia

фокус *n* focus

фокусник *n* magician

фон *n* background

фонарик *n* lantern

фонарь *n* torch

фонд *n* fund

фонтан *n* fountain

форель *n* trout

форма *n* shape, form

формальность *n* formality

формальный *adj* formal

формат *n* format

Ф

формула n formula
формулировка n wording
форт n fort
фортуна n luck
фосфор n phosphorus
фотоаппарат n camera
фотограф n photographer
фотография n photo
фотокопия n photocopy
фраза n phrase
Франция n France
французский adj French
фрахт n freight
фрегат n frigate
фрикаделька n meatball
фронт n front
фруктовый adj fruity
фруктовый сад n orchard
фундамент n foundation
фундук n hazelnut
функция n function
фунт n pound
фургон n van
фурор n furor
футбол n football
фьорд n fjord

Ф

Х

халат n robe
хаос n chaos
характер n character
характерный adj characteristic
харизма n charisma
хата n hut
хвала n praise
хвалить v praise
хвастать v boast
хвастаться v brag
хватать v grab, grasp
хватка n grip, grasp
хвост n tail
херес n sherry
химик n chemist
химический adj chemical
химия n chemistry
хирург n surgeon
хирургический adv surgical
хитрость n cunning
хитроумный adj crafty
хитрый adj tricky
хихикать v giggle
хлам n trash
хлеб n bread
хлестать v thresh, lash
хлопать v clap
хлопок n cotton
хмурый adj gloomy

хобби *n* hobby
ходить на лыжах *v* ski
ходьба *n* walk
хозяин *n* owner
хозяйка *n* hostess
холера *n* cholera
холестерин *n* cholesterol
холм *n* hill
холмистый *adj* hilly
холод *n* coldness
холодильник *n* refrigerator
холодный *adj* cold, frigid
холокост *n* holocaust
холостяк *n* bachelor
холст *n* canvas
хор *n* chorus
хорал *n* carol
хоронить *v* bury
хороший *adj* good
хорошо *adv* alright, okay
хотеть *v* want
хотя *c* although
храбрый *adj* valiant
храм *n* temple
хранение *n* storage
хранитель *n* custodian
хранить *v* store
храп *n* snore
храпеть *v* snore
христианский *adj* christian
христианство *n* Christianity
хромой *adj* lame

хромота *n* limp
хроника *n* chronicle
хронический *adj* chronic
хронология *n* chronology
хрупкий *adj* frail, tender
хрупкость *n* fragility
хрусткий *adj* crunchy
хрустящий *adj* crisp
хряк *n* boar
художник *n* artist, painter
худой *adj* skinny
худший *adj* worse
хулиган *n* hoodlum
хулиганство *n* mugging

Ц

царапать *v* claw, scratch
царапина *n* scratch
царство *n* kingdom
царствование *n* reign
царствовать *v* reign
царь *n* czar
цвести *v* bloom, flourish
цвет *n* color
цвет лица *n* complexion
цветистый *adj* flowery
цветок *n* flower

цветоножка *n* stalk
целибат *n* celibacy
целовать *v* kiss
целомудрие *n* chastity
целый *adj* entire, whole
цель *n* objective
цемент *n* cement
цена *n* cost, price
цензура *n* censorship
ценить *v* appreciate
ценное качество *n* asset
ценность *n* value
ценный *adj* valuable
цент *n* cent
центр *n* center, core
централизовать *v* centralize
центральный *adj* central
цепкость *n* tenacity
цепляться *v* cling
цепь *n* chain
церемония *n* ceremony
церковная скамья *n* pew
церковный гимн *n* hymn
церковный хор *n* choir
церковь *n* church
цех *n* workshop
цианид *n* cyanide
цивилизация *n* civilization
цивилизовать *v* civilize
цикл *n* cycle
циклон *n* cyclone
цилиндр *n* cylinder, drum

цинизм *n* cynicism
циничный *adj* cynic
цинк *n* zinc
цирк *n* circus
циркулировать *v* circulate
цистерна *n* cistern
цитирование *n* quotation
цитировать *v* quote
цифра *n* digit
цыган *n* gypsy
цыплёнок *n* chick

Ч

чавкать *v* munch
чай *n* tea
чайка *n* seagull
чайная ложка *n* teaspoon
чайник *n* kettle, teapot
час *n* hour
часовня *n* chapel
часовщик *n* watchmaker
частица *n* particle
частично *adv* partly
частичный *adj* partial
частный *adj* private
часто *adv* often
часто посещать *v* frequent

частота _n_ frequency
частый _adj_ frequent
часть _n_ part, piece
часы _n_ watch, clock
чаша _n_ bowl, chalice
чаша весов _n_ scale
чашка _n_ cup
чек _n_ paycheck
чеканить _v_ mint
чековая книжка _n_ checkbook
человек _n_ human being
человеческий _adj_ human
человечество _n_ humankind
челюсть _n_ jaw
чемодан _n_ suitcase
чемпион _n_ champion
чепуха _n_ nonsense
червь _n_ worm
чердак _n_ attic
чередоваться _v_ alternate
чередующийся _adj_ alternate
через _pre_ through
черемша _n_ ramson
череп _n_ skull
черепаха _n_ turtle
черепица _n_ tile
черкнуть _v_ scribble
чернила _n_ ink
черновик _n_ draft
чернослив _n_ prune
чернота _n_ blackness
чёрный _adj_ black

чёрный как смоль _adj_ pitch-black
чёрный ход _n_ backdoor
черствый _adj_ stale
чертёжная кнопка _n_ thumbtack
чесаться _v_ itch
чеснок _n_ garlic
честность _n_ honesty
честный _adj_ honest
честолюбивый _adj_ ambitious
честолюбие _n_ ambition
четверг _n_ Thursday
четвертый _adj_ fourth
четверть _n_ quarter
четыре _adj_ four
четырнадцать _adj_ fourteen
чечевица _n_ lentil
чешуя _n_ scale
чинить _v_ repair
чиновник _n_ official
число _n_ number
чистилище _n_ purgatory
чистить _v_ clean
чистить щеткой _v_ brush
чистота _n_ cleanliness
чистый _adj_ clean, pure
читатель _n_ reader
читать _v_ read
чиханье _n_ sneeze
чихать _v_ sneeze
член _n_ member
членство _n_ membership
чмокать _v_ smack

Ч

чрезмерность *n* excess
чрезмерный *adj* excessive
чтение *n* reading
что *adj* what
что-нибудь *pro* anything
чувства *n* feelings
чувственный *adj* sensual
чувство *n* feeling, sense
чувствовать *v* feel
чудной *adj* queer
чудо *n* marvel
чудовище *n* monster
чудовищный *adj* monstrous
чудотворный *adj* miraculous
чуять *v* smell

Ш

шаг *n* step
шагать *v* stride, walk
шакал *n* jackal
шале *n* chalet
шанс *n* chance
шантаж *n* blackmail
шар *n* globe, sphere
шарада *n* charade
шарф *n* scarf
шататься *v* stagger

шафер *n* best man
шахматы *n* chess
шахта *n* mine
шведский *adj* Sweedish
швейцар *n* janitor, usher
Швейцария *n* Switzerland
швейцарский *adj* Swiss
Швеция *n* Sweden
швея *n* seamstress
швырять *v* hurl
шевелиться *v* budge
шедевр *n* masterpiece
шелестеть *v* rustle
шелк *n* silk
шепот *n* whisper
шептать *v* whisper
шерсть *n* wool
шерстяной *adj* woolen
шест *n* post
шестнадцать *adj* sixteen
шестой *adj* sixth
шесть *adj* six
шестьдесят *adj* sixty
шеф-повар *n* chef cook
шея *n* neck
шикарный *adj* posh
шимпанзе *n* chimpanzee
шина *n* splint
шинковать *v* shred
шиньон *n* hairpiece
шипеть *v* hiss
ширина *n* breadth, width

широкий *adj* broad, wide
широко *adv* widely, broadly
широта *n* latitude
шить *v* sew
шитьё *n* sewing
шишка *n* lump, cone
шкатулка *n* casket
шкаф *n* cabinet, closet
школа *n* school
шланг *n* hose
шлепок *n* slap
шлифовать *v* file, polish
шлифовка *n* polishing
шляпа *n* hat
шнур *n* cord
шнурок *n* lace
шов *n* seam
шокировать *v* scandalize
шоколад *n* chocolate
шорты *n* briefs, shorts
шофёр *n* chauffeur
шпион *n* spy
шпионить *v* spy
шпора *n* spur
шпулька *n* spool
шрам *n* scar
шрапнель *n* shrapnel
шрифт *n* font
штаб-квартира *n* headquarters
штамп *n* stamp
штамповать *v* press
штат *n* state

штопать *v* darn
шторм *n* gale, storm
штормовой *adj* stormy
штрафовать *v* fine
штурвал *n* helm
штык *n* bayonet
шум *n* noise
шуметь *v* clamor
шумно *adv* noisily
шумный *adj* noisy
шуруп *n* screw
шутить *v* joke
шутка *n* joke
шутливо *adv* jokingly

Щ

щеголять *v* flaunt
щедрость *n* generosity
щека *n* cheek
щеколда *n* latch
щекотать *v* tickle
щекотка *n* tickle
щекотливый *adj* ticklish
щёлкать *v* click
щель *n* airspace, gap
щенок *n* puppy
щётка *n* brush

щипать *v* nip, pinch
щипок *n* pinch, nip
щипцы *n* tongs
щипчики *n* pliers
щит *n* shield
щупальце *n* tentacle

Э

эволюция *n* evolution
эгоизм *n* selfishness
эгоист *n* egoist
эгоистичный *adj* selfish
эйфория *n* euphoria
экватор *n* equator
экземпляр *n* copy
экзорцист *n* exorcist
экзотический *adj* exotic
экипаж *n* crew
экология *n* ecology
экономика *n* economy
экономить *v* economize
экономичный *adj* economical
экран *n* monitor
экскурсия *n* excursion
экспансивный *adj* effusive
экспедиция *n* expedition
эксперимент *n* experiment

экспирация *n* expiration
эксплуатация *n* exploitation
экспресс *n* express
экспромтом *adv* impromptu
экстаз *n* ecstasy
экстатический *adj* ecstatic
экстрадиция *n* extradition
эксцентричный *adj* eccentric
эластичный *adj* elastic
электрик *n* electrician
электрический *adj* electric
электричество *n* electricity
электронный *adj* electronic
элемент *n* element
элементарный *adj* elementary
эмбрион *n* embryo
эмигрант *n* emigrant
эмигрировать *v* emigrate
эмоция *n* emotion
энергичный *adj* strenuous
энергия *n* energy
энтузиазм *n* enthusiasm
энциклопедия *n* encyclopedia
эпидемия *n* epidemic
эпизод *n* episode
эпилепсия *n* epilepsy
эпитафия *n* epitaph
эпоха *n* epoch
эра *n* era
эскалатор *n* escalator
эскапада *n* escapade
эскиз *n* sketch

Щ

эскимосский *adj* husky
эссе *n* essay
эстетический *adj* aesthetic
эти *adj* these
этикет *n* etiquette
этикетка *n* label
этический *adj* ethical
этот *adj* this
эффективный *adj* efficient
эхо *n* echo

Ю

юбка *n* skirt
ювелир *n* jeweler
юг *n* south
юго-восток *n* southeast
юго-запад *n* southwest
южанин *n* southerner
южный *adj* southern
юмор *n* humor
юность *n* adolescence
юноша *n* adolescent
юношеский *adj* juvenile
юридический *adj* legal
юрист *n* lawyer

Я

я *pro* I
яблоко *n* apple
явление *n* phenomenon
явная улика *n* smoking gun
ягнёнок *n* lamb
ягуар *n* jaguar
яд *n* poison, venom
ядерный *adj* nuclear
ядовитый *adj* poisonous
язва *n* ulcer
язык *n* language, tongue
языческий *adj* pagan
язычник *n* heathen
яичник *n* ovary
яйцо *n* egg
якорь *n* anchor
яма *n* pit
ямс *n* yam
январь *n* January
Япония *n* Japan
японский *adj* Japanese
ярд *n* yard
яркий *adj* bright, vivid
яркость *n* brightness
ярлык *n* tag
ярмарка *n* fair
ярмо *n* yoke
яростный *adv* berserk
ярость *n* rage

Я

ясень *n* ash tree
ясно *adv* clearly
ясность *n* clarity
ясный *adj* plain, clear
ястреб *n* hawk

яхта *n* yacht
ячмень *n* barley
ящерица *n* lizard
ящик *n* case, chest

Order & Contact Information

Word to Word® Dictionaries

Item	Language	ISBN13
Word to Word®		
500X	Albanian	9780933146495
820X	Amharic	9780933146594
650X	Arabic	9780933146419
700X	Bengali	9780933146303
705X	Burmese	9780933146501
710X	Cambodian	9780933146402
715X	Chinese	9780933146228
520X	Czech	9780933146624
857X	Dari	9781946986603
660X	Farsi	9780933146334
530X	French	9780933146365
535X	German	9780933146938
664X	Georgian	9781946986627
540X	Greek	9780933146600
720X	Gujarati	9780933146983
545X	Haitian Creole	9780933146235
665X	Hebrew	9780933146587
725X	Hindi	9780933146310
728X	Hmong	9780933146532
551X	Hungarian	9780933146679
555X	Italian	9780933146518

Item	Language	ISBN13
730X	Japanese	9780933146426
735X	Korean	9780933146976
740X	Laotian	9780933146549
753X	Malayalam	9781946986610
755X	Nepali	9780933146617
760X	Pashto	9780933146341
575X	Polish	9780933146648
580X	Portuguese	9780933146945
765X	Punjabi	9780933146327
585X	Romanian	9780933146914
590X	Russian	9780933146921
830X	Somali	9780933146525
600X	Spanish	9780933146990
835X	Swahili	9780933146556
770X	Tagalog	9780933146372
780X	Thai	9780933146358
615X	Turkish	9780933146952
620X	Ukrainian	9780933146259
790X	Urdu	9780933146396
848X	Uzbek	9781946986696
795X	Vietnamese	9780933146969
5-895X	Word to Word® Class Set	

WORD to WORD
State Approved • Testing Dictionaries

All editions are two-way: English>Language / Language>English.
More languages in planning and production.

Word to Word® Dictionaries

Item	Language	ISBN13
Word to Word® with Subject Vocab		
653X	Arabic	9780933146563
703X	Bengali	9781946986061
718X	Chinese	9780933146570
533X	French	9780933146693
548X	Haitian Creole	9780933146709
583X	Portuguese	9781946986092
593X	Russian	9781946986078
603X	Spanish	9780933146723
793X	Urdu	9781946986085
798X	Vietnamese	9780933146686
5-105X	Word to Word® Subject Class Set	

Subject Vocabulary dictionaries include additional math science and social studies vocabulary. Approximately 2400 math terms, 4400 science terms, and 1700 social studies terms.

Subject vocabulary terms are translated one-way, English>Language.

WordtoWord.com - Discounts + eBooks

Special Online Pricing: Special tiered discount pricing based on quantity for online orders. Simple and fast.

eBooks: eBook versions of the Word to Word® series are available via web app or mobile app on Android and IOS. eBooks can be downloaded for offline use within the App.

Bulk eBook orders for school districts are available. Simple, private student access to eBooks, no student information necessary. Email us to learn more and request sample ebook.

support@wordtoword.com

wordtoword.com

(951) 296-2445

*For **eBook** versions add "e" to Item number:*
*(Print Spanish) 600X → **600Xe** (eBook Spanish)*

Order & Contact Us

Bilingual Dictionaries, Inc. is committed to providing quality bilingual materials and great service. Contact us by phone or email for a quote today:

Phone: 951-296-2445

Fax: 951-296-9911

Mail: PO Box 1154, Murrieta, CA 92562

Email: support@bilingualdictionaries.com

Visit our website to download our current catalog-order form, view our products and shop online.

BilingualDictionaries.com

WordtoWord.com

Amazon.com/WordtoWord

Special Dedication & Thanks

Bilingual Dictionaries, Inc. would like to thank all the teachers from various districts across the country for their useful input and great suggestions in creating a Word to Word® standard. We encourage all students and teachers using our bilingual learning materials to give us feedback. Please send your questions or comments via email.
support@bilingualdictionaries.com